The Ultimate Lean and Green

Cookbook for Beginners 2022

1200 <u>Days Recipes</u>

Edith Rose

Table Of Contents

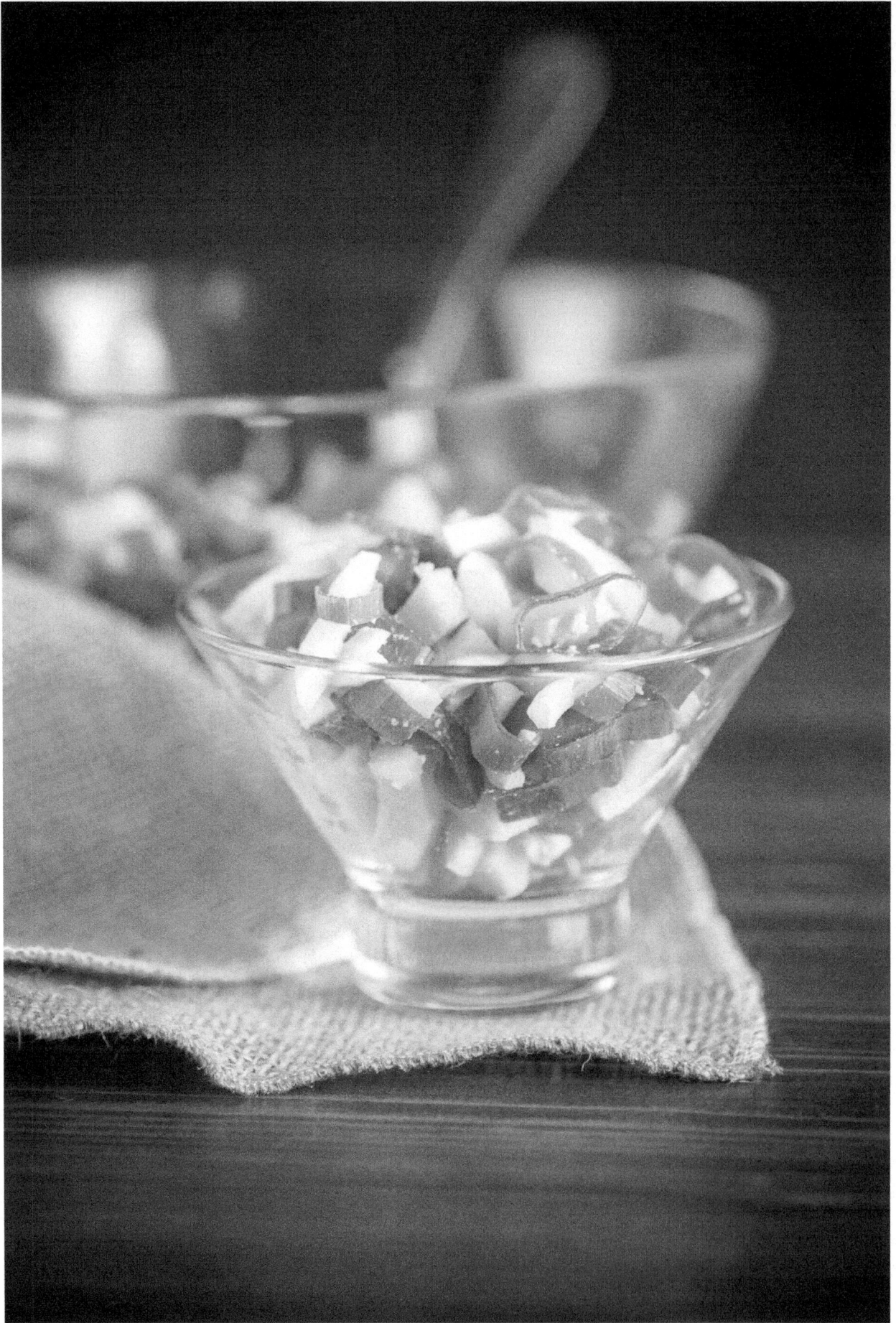

Introduction

A lot of people that are trying to figure out a way to prevent their weight from going up have been turning towards diets that have been called "lean and green." A lot of people have gotten this diet from celebrities such as Khloe Kardashian, Miranda Kerr, and even Michelle Obama. This diet is said to aid the body in losing weight and maintaining a healthy lifestyle free of hereditary inclinations. It incorporates foods such as kale, quinoa, brown rice salad, whole grains, plant-based proteins like beans and lentils, and vegetables like broccoli and asparagus. While a lot of the ingredients can be purchased at a grocery store near you, it does require a level of knowledge to know which foods are good sources for certain nutrients.

The belief that one can reduce their body fat percentage by eating foods that are healthy as opposed to those that are dietary poisons is not new. Back in the 1800s, before the dieting trend became popular, medical professionals were recommending a food plan which was low in fat and high in fruit and vegetables. This diet took place before famine was a daily reality for a large portion of the population. During this time, low-fat diets were offered as a way to prevent diseases such as heart disease and diabetes from reaching epidemic levels. This is actually the first time that "lean and green" diets were also known as "Heart Friendly Diets." Along with this, people who adhered to such a diet were believed to live longer than those who did not follow it. Only in the last several decades has there been a greater emphasis on calorie restriction and body fat reduction.

A lot of the lean and green diet is sometimes also referred to as healthy eating or a plant-based diet. Some think of it as a way of living that includes more than just food. People who adhere to this lifestyle try to get rid of toxic lifestyle habits such as smoking and heavy drinking while they do their best to exercise regularly. The foods which are part of the lean and green diet are rich in nutrients, but it can be challenging to know which meats, grains, and other foods are good for health. The main goal is not necessarily to control one's weight but to provide an overall healthy lifestyle.

When considering the advantages of a lean and green diet, it's vital to remember that no single diet fits all lifestyles. For instance, some people use a low-fat diet to cut back on calories without necessarily thinking about what they want their caloric intake to be. For someone who wants to have more calories while being able to fit into their clothes better, this type of meal plan will not work well for them. On the other hand, some people are able to live on a high-fat diet with no problems, but this does not mean that they are healthy.

The lean and green diet is not necessarily reserved for vegetarians, but it can also work well for those who choose to eat meat. For people who do not want to eat meat, there are many organic foods sold at health food stores that supply all of the nutrients needed for good health. The lean and green lifestyle can help someone achieve their weight-loss goals if done correctly. However, the most important thing is to make sure that one's diet is healthy overall rather than just one part of it.

HIGH-FIBER FRUITS

FATS & OILS

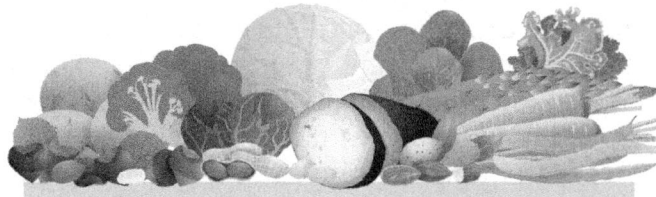

NUTS & HIGH-FIBER VEGETABLES

SKIM MILK, CHEESE & EGGS

PROTEINS

PROTEIN DIET

CHAPTER 1:

What Is Lean And Green Diet?

The lean and green diet is a weight-loss or weight-maintenance plan that combines a lean and green meal with "fueling," which is processed food. According to the diet, these nutritional Fuelings should be included in the diet while keeping overall calorie consumption under control. The fueling is really powdered food that is combined with a liquid such as water and then consumed as part of a regular diet. In addition to ingesting these fuels, dieters are advised to exercise for 30 minutes each day to lose weight. You may reduce your carb and sugar intake while still controlling your calorie intake by using fueling as a substitute for actual meals. The number of Fuelings you ingest, the amount of food you eat, and what you eat on this diet are all determined by the sort of weight-reduction plan you choose. However, on this diet, the overall calorie intake for adults is reduced to 800 to 1000 per day, which lets you lose about 12 lbs. of weight per 12 weeks on average.

What do you eat on the lean and green diet?
The following are the food items that you can opt for on this diet plan:
1. Meat:
The lean and green diet only allows 85% of lean meat on a diet; whether it is chicken, beef, turkey, lamb, pork, and ground meat, it all has to be lean. Lean meat has lower fat content, which makes it great to keep the caloric intake in control.

2. Seafood:
Seafood is best to have on any weight loss regime because it is free from saturated fats and brings a lot of nutritional value to the table. You can have all types of fish and seafood on this diet, including halibut, salmon, trout, lobster, tuna, shrimp, crab, scallops, etc.

3. Eggs:
Eggs are rich in protein and low in carbs; that's what makes eggs the right for this diet.

4. Soy products:
In soy products, tofu is the only product that is allowed on the lean and green diet because it is processed, and the caloric content is suitable for the lean diet.

5. Fats:
Not all fats are healthy, and there are a handful of options that you must try on this diet that includes most of the vegetable olive oil, walnut oil, canola oil, flaxseed oil. Other fats sources that can be incorporated into this diet include nuts and seeds, reduced-fat margarine, and olives.

6. Low carb vegetables:
All low-carb vegetables are a suitable fit for the Lean and green diet. So, except potatoes, yams, sweet potatoes, yellow squash, and beetroots, you can try every other vegetable on this diet, including spinach, cabbage, collard greens, cucumbers, mushrooms, celery, onion, tomatoes, garlic, ginger, eggplant, cauliflower, broccoli, bell peppers, zucchini, and spaghetti squash, etc.

7. Sugar-free snacks:
Snacks are usually loaded with carbs and sugar, so they must be avoided most of the time. But you have snacks in some amounts, then only try the sugar-free and low-carb snacks.

8. Sugar-free beverages:
In beverages, there are limited options as well. For most of this diet, water is the most recommended drink since it is zero caloric and comes with several health advantages. Besides that, you can have unsweetened almond milk, coconut milk, sugar-free tea, coffee

9. Condiments and seasonings:
In condiments and seasonings, there are no such restrictions; from dried herbs to salt, lemon juice, ground and whole spices, lime juice, yellow mustard, soy sauce, and salsa, you can use any. Whereas in syrups and sauces, stay from the sugar-rich varieties and try the sugar-free syrups, low-carb sweeteners, sugar-free ketchup and barbecue sauce, etc.

CHAPTER 2:

Benefits And Drawbacks

Weight Loss

Meal prepping is going to help you lose weight. Knowing what you are going to eat is very important if you want to lose weight.

Finish Cravings

Cravings are going to stop as you continue to meal prep. In just a few weeks, you will find that you no longer crave sugar or junk. Instead, you will be looking forward to the meals and snacks that you have prepared.

Stress Is a Killer

It can lead to a variety of health issues, including an increase in blood pressure. It can cause sleep issues, lower your immune system, and even cause digestive problems.

No More Indecision

You'll have a solution ready for you when you get home from work, weary and hungry. You open the cupboards, rummaging around while you wait for inspiration, but nothing springs to mind. With planning, this doesn´t happen.

No Worse Choices

Without a proper plan for your next meal, you may fall into the trap of going for the perceived 'easy option' of a takeaway or ready meal.

A More Balanced Diet

Take the time to think back on what exactly you have eaten the past week. You will probably realize that it was basically the same dish most of the time.

Much More Variety

Some individuals believe that planning your meals ahead of time is tedious because you already know what you're going to eat a few days ahead of time. This is far from the truth; planning actually encourages variety.

No Food Wastage While Saving Money

How often did you find wilted veggies in your refrigerator or have to throw away food that is past its expiry date? If you plan cleverly, making use of leftovers, using what is in your kitchen cupboards, freezing food in batches, very few food items will end up in your trashcan.

Less Arduous Arguing

You feel like a vegetarian dish; your partner wants hamburgers, but the kids plead for pizzas. Does this sound familiar? Your family may end up arguing unnecessarily over their next meal.

Go for Seasonal
Be clever and plan your meals according to the season. Not only will you have the freshest ingredients, but you will also look after your purse, as fresh items are cheaper when in season.

Saving Money
It is a huge misconception that healthy eating equals heavy spending. This is simply not true. There are many reasons why advance prepping can help you save money.

Potential Drawbacks of Lean and Green Diet
While the Lean and Green diet might be a successful weight reduction technique for a few, it has a few expected drawbacks.

Low in Calories
The Lean and Green 5&1 regimen is incredibly low in calories, with just 800–1,2000 calories per day, especially for those who are used to consuming at least 2,000 calories per day.
While this rapid calorie reduction may result in overall weight loss, studies have shown that it can result in significant muscle loss.
Moreover, low-calorie diets may diminish the number of calories your body consumes by as much as 23%. This slower digestion can last significantly after you quit confining calories.

May be Hard to Stay with
Every day, the 5&1 Plan includes 5 pre-packaged fuelings and 1 low-carb feast. As a result, it might be quite restrictive in terms of dietary choices and carbohydrate intake.
Because you may be tired of relying on pre-packaged foods for the bulk of your meals, it may be simple to sabotage your diet or develop cravings for alternative foods.
While the support plan is significantly less prohibitive, despite everything depends intensely on fuelings.

May Prompt Weight Regain
Weight recovery might be a worry after you stop the program.
Presently, no examination has inspected weight recapture after the Lean and Green diet. All things considered, in an investigation on a comparable, 16-week diet, members recovered a normal of 11 pounds (4.8 kg) within 24 weeks of completing the program.
One likely reason for weight recovery is your dependence on bundled food things. After the diet, it might be hard to change to looking for and preparing solid suppers.
Moreover, because of the sensational calorie limitation of the 5&1 Plan, some weight recovery may likewise be because of more slow digestion.

Lean and Green Fuelings Are Profoundly Handled
The Lean and Green diet depends intensely on pre-packaged food things. Indeed, you would eat 150 pre-packaged fuelings every month on the 5&1 Plan.
This is a reason for worry; the same number of these things are profoundly prepared.
They contain a lot of food-added substances, sugar substitutes, and prepared vegetable oils, which may hurt your gut well-being and add to constant aggravation.
Carrageenan, a typical thickener, and additive utilized in numerous fuelings, is gotten from red ocean growth. While research on its security is restricted, creature and test-tube contemplate proposing that it might contrarily influence stomach-related well-being and cause intestinal ulcers. Numerous fuelings likewise contain maltodextrin, a thickening specialist that has been appeared to spike glucose levels and harm your gut microbes.
While these added substances are likely sheltered in limited quantities, expending them much of the time on the Lean and Green diet may build your danger of symptoms.

The Program's Coach Is Not Well-Being Experts

Most Lean and Green coaches have effectively shed pounds on the program; however, they are not confirmed well-being experts.

Therefore, they are inadequate to give dietary or clinical exhortation. Hence, you should think about their direction while considering other factors and converse with your human services supplier if you have any worries. On the off chance that you have a current well-being condition, it's imperative to get the counsel of a clinical supplier or enlisted dietitian before beginning another diet program.

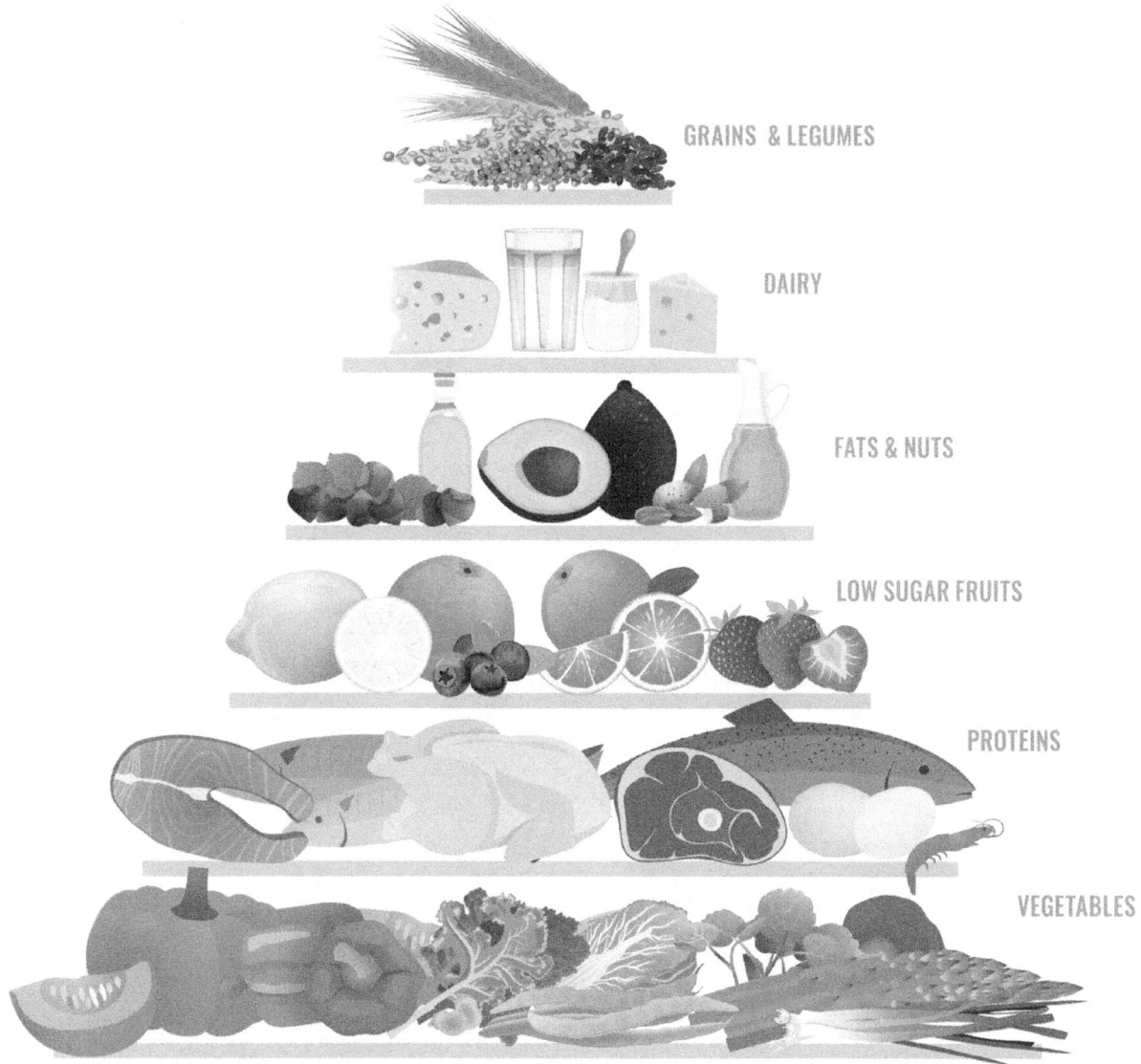

GRAINS & LEGUMES

DAIRY

FATS & NUTS

LOW SUGAR FRUITS

PROTEINS

VEGETABLES

LOW CARBOHYDRATE DIET

CHAPTER 3:

Foods To Avoid

There are a lot many foods that you can eat while following the Lean and Green Diet. However, you must know these foods by heart. This is true if you are new to this diet, and you have to strictly follow the 5&1 Lean and Green Diet Plan. Thus, this section is dedicated to the types of foods that are recommended and those to avoid while following this diet regimen.

Recommended foods

There are numerous categories of foods that can be eaten under this diet regimen. This section will break down the Lean and Green foods that you can eat while following this diet regime.

Lean Foods

Leanest Foods — These foods are considered to be the leanest as it has only up to 4 grams of total fat. Moreover, dieters should eat a 7-ounce cooked portion of these foods. Consume these foods with 1 healthy fat serving.

- Fish: Flounder, cod, haddock, grouper, Mahi, tilapia, tuna (yellowfin fresh or canned), and wild catfish.
- Shellfish: Scallops, lobster, crabs, shrimp
- Game meat: Elk, deer, buffalo
- Ground turkey or other meat: Should be 98% lean
- Meatless alternatives:14 egg whites, 2 cups egg substitute, 5 ounces seitan, 1 ½ cups 1% cottage cheese, and 12 ounces non-fat 0% Greek yogurt

Leaner Foods — These foods contain 5 to 9 grams of total fat. Consume these foods with 1 healthy fat serving. Make sure to consume only 6 ounces of a cooked portion of these foods daily:

- Fish: Halibut, trout, and swordfish
- Chicken: White meat such as breasts as long as the skin is removed
- Turkey: Ground turkey as long as it is 95% to 97% lean.
- Meatless options:2 whole eggs plus 4 egg whites, 2 whole eggs plus one cup egg substitute, 1 ½ cups 2% cottage cheese, and 12 ounces low fat 2% plain Greek yogurt

Lean Foods — These are foods that contain 10 g to 20 g total fat. When consuming these foods, there should be no serving of healthy fat. These include the following:

- Fish: Tuna (Bluefin steak), salmon, herring, farmed catfish, and mackerel
- Lean beef: Ground, steak, and roast
- Lamb: All cuts
- Pork: Pork chops, pork tenderloin, and all parts. Make sure to remove the skin
- Ground turkey and other meats:85% to 94% lean

- Chicken: Any dark meat
- Meatless options:15 ounces extra-firm tofu, 3 whole eggs (up to two times per week), 4 ounces reduced-fat skim cheese, 8 ounces part-skim ricotta cheese, and 5 ounces tempeh

Healthy Fat Servings — Healthy fat servings are allowed under this diet. They should contain 5 grams of fat and less than grams of carbohydrates. Regardless of what type of Lean and Green Diet plan you follow, make sure that you add between 0 and 2 healthy fat servings daily. Below are the different healthy fat servings that you can eat:

- 1 teaspoon oil (any kind of oil)
- 1 tablespoon low carbohydrate salad dressing
- 2 tablespoons reduced-fat salad dressing
- 5 to 10 black or green olives
- 1 ½ ounce avocado
- 1/3-ounce plain nuts including peanuts, almonds, pistachios
- 1 tablespoon plain seeds such as chia, sesame, flax, and pumpkin seeds
- ½ tablespoon regular butter, mayonnaise, and margarine

Green Foods

This section will discuss the green servings you still need to consume while following the Lean and Green Diet Plan. These include all kinds of vegetables that have been categorized from lower, moderate, and high in terms of carbohydrate content. One serving of vegetables should be at ½ cup unless otherwise specified.

Lower Carbohydrate - These are vegetables that contain low amounts of carbohydrates. If you follow the 5&1 Lean and Green Diet plan, these vegetables are good for you.

- A cup of green leafy vegetables, such as collard greens (raw), lettuce (green leaf, iceberg, butterhead, and romaine), spinach (raw), mustard greens, spring mix, bok choy (raw), and watercress.
- ½ cup of vegetables including cucumbers, celery, radishes, white mushroom, sprouts (mung bean, alfalfa), arugula, turnip greens, escarole, nopales, Swiss chard (raw), jalapeno, and bok choy (cooked).
- Moderate Carbohydrate - These are vegetables that contain moderate amounts of carbohydrates. Below are the types of vegetables that can be consumed in moderation:
- ½ cup of any of the following vegetables such as asparagus, cauliflower, fennel bulb, eggplant, portabella mushrooms, kale, cooked spinach, summer squash (zucchini and scallop).
- Higher Carbohydrates - Foods that are under this category contain a high amount of starch. Make sure to consume limited amounts of these vegetables.
- ½ cup of the following vegetables like chayote squash, red cabbage, broccoli, cooked collard and mustard greens, green or wax beans, kohlrabi, kabocha squash, cooked leeks, any peppers, okra, raw scallion, summer squash such as straight neck and crookneck, tomatoes, spaghetti squash, turnips, jicama, cooked Swiss chard, and hearts of palm.

Foods to avoid

The following foods are to be avoided; except it's included in the fuelings — they include:

- Fried foods: meats, fish, shellfish, vegetables, desserts like baked goods
- Refined grains: white bread, pasta, scones, hotcakes, flour tortillas, wafers, white rice, treats, cakes, cakes

- Certain fats: margarine, coconut oil, strong shortening
- Whole fat dairy: milk, cheddar, yogurt
- Alcohol: all varieties, no exception
- Sugar-sweetened beverages: pop, natural product juice, sports drinks, caffeinated drinks, sweet tea

The accompanying nourishments are beyond reach while on the 5&1 plan; however, included back during the 6-week progress stage and permitted during the 3&3 plan:

- Fruit: all kinds of fresh fruits
- Low fat or without fat dairy: yogurt, milk, cheddar

CHAPTER 4:

Who Is The Lean And Green Diet For?

We will now talk about who is the lean and green diet for and how your body transitions from one way to another. Before, the Lean and Green diet was used mainly to lower the incidence of seizures in epileptic children. People wanted to check out how the Lean and Green diet would work with an entirely healthy person as things usually go. This diet's primary purpose is to make your body switch from how it used to function to an entirely new way of creating energy, keeping you healthy and alive.

How Lean and Green Works?

Once you start following the Lean and Green Diet, you will notice that things are changing, first and foremost, in your mind. Before, carbohydrates were your main body's fuel and were used to create glucose so that your brain could function. Now you no longer feed yourself with them.

In the beginning, most people feel odd because their usual food is off the table. When your menu consists of more fats and proteins, it is natural to think that something is missing.

Your brain alarms you that you haven't eaten enough and sends you signals that you are hungry. It is literally "panicking" and telling you that you are starving, which is not correct. You get to eat, and you get to eat plenty of good food, but not carbs.

This condition usually arises during the first day or two. Afterward, people get used to their new eating habits. Once the brain "realizes" that carbs are no longer an option, it will focus on "finding" another abundant energy source: in this case, Fats.

Not only is your food rich in fats, but your body contains stored fats in large amounts. As you consume more fats and fewer carbs, your body "runs" on the fats, both consumed and stored. The best thing is that, as the fats are used for energy, they are burned. It is how you get a double gain from this diet. Usually, it will take a few days of consuming low-carb meals before you start seeing visible weight loss results. You will not even have to check your weight because the fat layers will be visibly reduced.

This diet requires you to lower your daily consumption of carbs to only 20 grams. For most people, this transition from a regular carb-rich diet can be quite a challenge. Most people are used to eating bread, pasta, rice, dairy products, sweets, soda, alcohol, and fruits, so quitting all these foods might be challenging.

However, this is all in your head. If you manage to win the "battle" with your mind and endure the diet for a few days, you will see that as time goes by, you no longer have cravings at all. Plus, the weight loss and the fat burn will be a great motivation to continue with this diet.

The Lean and Green diet practically makes the body burn fats much faster than carbohydrates; the foods you consume with this diet are exceptionally rich in fats. Carbs will be there, too but at far lower levels than before. Foods rich in carbohydrates are the body's primary fuel or the brain's food. (Our bodies turn carbs into glucose.) Because there are hardly any carbohydrates in this diet, the body will have to find a substitute source of energy to keep itself alive.

Many people who don't truly need to lose weight and are completely healthy still choose to follow the Lean and Green diet because it is a great way to keep their meals balanced. This lifestyle is also an excellent way to cleanse the body of toxins, processed foods, sugars, and unnecessary carbs.

The combination of these things is usually the main reason for heart failure, some cancers, diabetes, cholesterol, or obesity.

If you consult a nutritionist about this diet, they will unquestionably suggest it. If you want to cleanse your body and begin a diet that will keep you healthy, well-fed, and slim, the Lean and Green diet should be your first choice.

And what is the best thing about it besides the fact that you will balance your weight and lower the risk of many diseases? There is no yo-yo effect. The Lean and Green diet can be followed forever and has no side effects. It does not restrict you from pursuing it for a few weeks or a month. Once you get your body used to Lean and Green foods, you will not think about going back to the old ways of eating your meals.

CHAPTER 5:

How Can I Follow The Diet?

Practicing the Lean and Green diet gives you an option of about 60 Fuelings, but that is not to say you will still not have yearnings for other food options, especially those you are used to before taking up the diet plan.

All the recipes are readily available, and you can also take the option of dining out by following your guide. However, alcohol consumption is prohibited. You can order your meals easily or prepare them in your kitchen in a few minutes. You can easily get the needed tools to make your meals from your coach or request help from the online community.

You can get various ideas for your lean and green meals by visiting the brand Pinterest page. You will also get a recipe conversion guide that you can use whenever you have trouble with your recipe measurement.

You might face many challenges whenever you decide to eat out. However, it is not impossible to eat out. The brand advised you to let your lean and green meals be the only option when considering eating out to be on the safe side. By going through the dining out guide, you will know how to navigate buffets, order beverages, and select condiments and toppings for your meals.

It is straightforward to choose a plan and make your order that will be delivered instantly. Food preparation is swift, and the only area where you can face difficulty is adding water and nuking in the microwave. Anyone with no knowledge of cooking can easily tackle and get over the preparation of preparing the meals without breaking a sweat.

The Lean and Green coaches aim to help you adopt healthy habits. You will get weekly and monthly support calls from the Lean and Green coaches. Once you are a community member, you will also be able to partake in community events and have access to the nutrition support team, mainly composed of dietitians. Informational guides and FAQs can also be accessed online easily and for free.

The company says the recommended meals have a high "fullness index," which means that the high protein and fiber contents should help you to get satisfied for an extended period.

The meals you will be taking are tailored for the weight and fat loss purpose and may not win a cuisine competition. It is pertinent to note that the Lean and Green fuelings you will feed on will not contain flavors, artificial colors, or sweeteners.

No matter the plan you pick out, you start by using having a smartphone communique with a coach to help you determine which Lean and Green plan to follow, set weight loss desires, and make yourself familiar with the application.

Eating out can be challenging but still possible. If you love eating out, you can download Lean and Green's dining out guide. The guide comes with tips on how to navigate buffets, order beverages, and choose condiments. Aside from following the guide, you can also ask the chef to make substitutions for the ingredients used in cooking your food. For instance, you can ask the chef to serve no more than 7 ounces of steak and serve it with steamed broccoli instead of baked potatoes.

Opt for lean and green foods that have high fullness index. Eat foods that contain high protein and fiber content as they can keep you full for longer periods. Many nutrition experts highlight the importance of satiety when it comes to weight loss.

You have access to knowledgeable coaches. If you follow the Lean and Green diet plan, you can access knowledgeable coaches and become a part of a community that will give you access to support calls and community events. You also have a standby nutrition support team that can answer your questions.

No matter what diet plan you pick, begin by having a teleconference with a certain coach to determine which Lean and Green diet plan to follow, establish weight loss objectives, and acquaint yourself with the platform.

CHAPTER 6:

Breakfast Recipes

1. Alkaline Blueberry Spelt Pancakes

Preparation Time: 6 minutes
Cooking Time: 20 minutes
Servings: 3
Ingredients:

- 2 cups spelt flour
- 1 cup of coconut milk
- 1/2 cup alkaline water
- 2 tablespoons grapeseed oil
- 1/2 cup agave
- 1/2 cup blueberries
- 1/4 teaspoons sea moss

Directions:

1. Mix the spelt flour, agave, grapeseed oil, hemp seeds, and sea moss in a bowl. Add in 1 cup of hemp milk and alkaline water to the mixture until you get the consistent mixture you like.
2. Crimp the blueberries into the batter. Heat the skillet to moderate heat, then lightly coat it with the grapeseed oil.
3. Pour the batter into the skillet, then let them cook for approximately 5 minutes on every side. Serve and enjoy.

Nutrition: Calories: 203, Fat: 1.4 g, Carbs: 41.6 g, Proteins: 4.8 g

2. Alkaline Blueberry Muffins

Preparation Time: 5 minutes
Cooking Time: 20 minutes
Servings: 3
Ingredients:

- 1 cup of coconut milk
- 3/4 cup spelt flour
- 3/4 teff flour
- 1/2 cup blueberries
- 1/3 cup agave
- 1/4 cup sea moss gel
- 1/2 teaspoons sea salt
- grapeseed oil

Directions:

1. Adjust the temperature of the oven to 365°F. Grease 6 regular-size muffin cups with muffin liners.
2. In a bowl, mix sea salt, sea moss, agave, coconut milk, and flour gel until they are properly blended. You then crimp in blueberries.
3. Coat the muffin pan lightly with the grapeseed oil. Pour in the muffin batter. Bake for at least 30 minutes until it turns golden brown. Serve.

Nutrition: Calories: 160, Fat: 5 g, Carbs: 25 g, Proteins: 2 g

3. Crunchy Quinoa Meal

Preparation Time: 5 minutes
Cooking Time: 25 minutes
Servings: 2
Ingredients:
- 3 cups of coconut milk
- 1 cup rinsed quinoa
- 1/8 teaspoons ground cinnamon
- 1 cup raspberry
- 1/2 cup chopped coconuts

Directions:
1. In a saucepan, pour milk and bring to a boil over moderate heat. Add the quinoa to the milk, and then bring it to a boil once more.
2. You then let it simmer for at least 15 minutes on medium heat until the milk is reduced. Stir in the cinnamon, then mix properly.
3. Cover it, then cook for 8 minutes until the milk is completely absorbed. Add the raspberry and cook the meal for 30 seconds. Serve and enjoy.

Nutrition: Calories: 271, Fat: 3.7 g, Carbs: 54 g, Proteins: 6.5 g

4. Coconut Pancakes

Preparation Time: 5 minutes
Cooking Time: 15 minutes
Servings: 4

Ingredients:
- 1 cup coconut flour
- 2 tablespoons arrowroot powder
- 1 teaspoon baking powder
- 1 cup of coconut milk
- 3 tablespoons coconut oil

Directions:
1. In a medium container, mix in all the dry ingredients. Add the coconut milk and 2 tablespoons of coconut oil, then mix properly.
2. In a skillet, dissolve 1 teaspoon of coconut oil. Put the batter into the skillet, then swirl the pan to spread the batter evenly into a smooth pancake.
3. Cook it for like 3 minutes on medium heat until it becomes firm. Turn the pancake to the other side, then cook it for another 2 minutes until it turns golden brown.
4. Cook the remaining pancakes in the same process. Serve.

Nutrition: Calories: 377, Fat: 14.9 g, Carbs: 60.7 g, Protein: 6.4 g

5. Quinoa Porridge

Preparation Time: 5 minutes
Cooking Time: 25 minutes
Servings: 2
Ingredients:
- 2 cups of coconut milk
- 1 cup rinsed quinoa
- 1/8 teaspoons ground cinnamon
- 1 cup fresh blueberries

Directions:
1. In a saucepan, boil the coconut milk over high heat. Add the quinoa to the milk, then bring the mixture to a boil.
2. You then let it simmer for 15 minutes on medium heat until the milk is reducing. Add the cinnamon, then mix it properly in the saucepan.
3. Cover the saucepan and cook for at least 8 minutes until the milk is completely absorbed. Add in the blueberries, then cook for 30 more seconds. Serve.

Nutrition: Calories: 271, Fat: 3.7 g, Carbs: 54 g, Protein:6.5 g

6. Amaranth Porridge

Preparation Time: 5 minutes
Cooking Time: 30 minutes
Servings: 2
Ingredients:
- 2 cups of coconut milk
- 2 cups alkaline water
- 1 cup amaranth
- 2 tablespoons coconut oil
- 1 tablespoon ground cinnamon

Directions:
1. In a saucepan, mix the milk with water, then boil the mixture. You stir in the amaranth, then reduce the heat to medium.
2. Cook on medium heat, then simmers for at least 30 minutes as you stir it occasionally. Turn off the heat. Add in cinnamon and coconut oil, then stir. Serve.

Nutrition: Calories: 434, Fat: 35 g, Carbs: 27 g, Protein: 6.7 g

7. Banana Barley Porridge

Preparation Time: 15 minutes
Cooking Time: 5 minutes
Servings: 2
Ingredients:
- 1 cup divided unsweetened coconut milk
- 1 small peeled and sliced banana
- 1/2 cup barley
- 3 drops liquid stevia
- 1/4 cup chopped coconuts

Directions:
1. In a bowl, properly mix barley with half of the coconut milk and stevia. Cover the mixing bowl, then refrigerate for about 6 hours.

2. In a saucepan, mix the barley mixture with coconut milk—Cook for about 5 minutes on moderate heat. Then top it with the chopped coconuts and the banana slices. Serve.

Nutrition: Calories: 159, Fat: 8.4 g, Carbs: 19.8 g, Proteins: 4.6 g

8. Zucchini Muffins

Preparation Time: 10 minutes
Cooking Time: 25 minutes
Servings: 16
Ingredients:
- 1 tablespoon ground flaxseed
- 3 tablespoons alkaline water
- 1/4 cup walnut butter
- 3 medium over-ripe bananas
- 2 small grated zucchinis
- 1/2 cup coconut milk
- 1 teaspoon vanilla extract
- 2 cups coconut flour
- 1 tablespoon baking powder
- 1 teaspoon cinnamon
- 1/4 teaspoons sea salt

Directions:
1. Tune the temperature of your oven to 375°F. Grease the muffin tray with the cooking spray.
2. In a bowl, mix the flaxseed with water. In a glass bowl, mash the bananas, then stir in the remaining ingredients.
3. Properly mix and then divide the mixture into the muffin tray. Bake it for 25 minutes. Serve.

Nutrition: Calories: 127, Fat: 6.6 g, Carbs: 13 g, Protein: 0.7 g

9. Millet Porridge

Preparation Time: 10 minutes
Cooking Time: 20 minutes
Servings: 2
Ingredients:
- Sea salt
- 1 tablespoon finely chopped coconuts
- 1/2 cup unsweetened coconut milk
- 1/2 cup rinsed and drained millet
- 1-1/2 cups alkaline water
- 3 drops liquid stevia

Directions:

1. Sauté the millet in a non-stick skillet for about 3 minutes. Add salt and water, then stir. Let the meal boil, then reduce the amount of heat.
2. Cook for 15 minutes, then add the remaining ingredients. Stir—Cook the meal for 4 extra minutes. Serve the meal with a topping of the chopped nuts.

Nutrition: Calories: 219, Fat: 4.5 g, Carbs: 38.2 g, Protein: 6.4 g

10. Jackfruit Vegetable Fry

Preparation Time: 5 minutes
Cooking Time: 5 minutes
Servings: 6
Ingredients:

- 2 finely chopped small onions
- 2 cups finely chopped cherry tomatoes
- 1/8 teaspoons ground turmeric
- 1 tablespoon olive oil
- 2 seeded and chopped red bell peppers
- 3 cups seeded and chopped firm jackfruit - 1/8 teaspoons cayenne pepper - 2 tablespoons chopped fresh basil leaves - Salt

Directions:

1. In a greased skillet, sauté the onions and bell peppers for about 5 minutes. Add the tomatoes, then stir. Cook for 2 minutes.
2. Then add the jackfruit, cayenne pepper, salt, and turmeric—Cook for about 8 minutes. Garnish the meal with basil leaves. Serve warm.

Nutrition: Calories: 236, Fat: 1.8 g, Carbs: 48.3 g, Protein: 7 g

11. Zucchini Pancakes

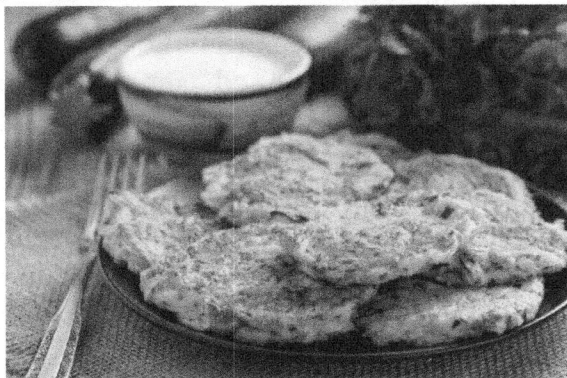

Preparation Time: 15 minutes
Cooking Time: 8 minutes
Servings: 8
Ingredients:

- 12 tablespoons alkaline water
- 6 large grated zucchinis
- Sea salt
- 4 tablespoons ground Flax Seeds
- 2 teaspoons olive oil
- 2 finely chopped jalapeño peppers
- 1/2 cup finely chopped scallions

Directions:

1. In a bowl, mix water, and the flax seeds, then set them aside. Pour oil into a large non-stick skillet, then heat it on medium heat. Then add the black pepper, salt, and zucchini.
2. Cook for 3 minutes, then transfer the zucchini into a large bowl. Add the flaxseed and the scallion mixture, then mix it.
3. Preheat a griddle, then grease it lightly with the cooking spray. Pour 1/4 of the zucchini mixture into the griddle, then cook for 3 minutes.
4. Flip the side carefully, then cook for 2 more minutes. Repeat the procedure with the remaining mixture in batches. Serve.

Nutrition: Calories: 71, Fat: 2.8 g, Carbs: 9.8 g, Protein: 3.7 g

12. Squash Hash

Preparation Time: 2 minutes
Cooking Time: 10 minutes
Servings: 2
Ingredients:

- 1 teaspoon onion powder
- 1/2 cup finely chopped onion
- 2 cups spaghetti squash
- 1/2 teaspoons sea salt

Directions:

1. Using paper towels, squeeze extra moisture from spaghetti squash. Place the squash into a bowl, then add the salt, onion, and onion powder.
2. Stir properly to mix them. Spray a non-stick cooking skillet with cooking spray, then place it over moderate

heat. Add the spaghetti squash to the pan.

3. Cook the squash for about 5 minutes. Flip the hash browns using a spatula. Cook for 5 minutes until the desired crispness is reached. Serve.

Nutrition: Calories: 44, Fat: 0.6 g, Carbs: 9.7 g, Protein: 0.9 g

13. Pumpkin Spice Quinoa
Preparation Time: 10 minutes
Cooking Time: 0 minutes
Servings: 2
Ingredients:
- 1 cup cooked quinoa
- 1 cup unsweetened coconut milk
- 1 large mashed banana
- 1/4 cup pumpkin puree
- 1 teaspoon pumpkin spice
- 2 teaspoons chia seeds

Directions:
1. In a container, mix all the ingredients. Seal the lid, then shake the container properly to mix. Refrigerate overnight. Serve.

Nutrition: Calories: 212, Fat: 11.9 g, Carbs: 31.7 g, Protein: 7.3 g

14. Chocolate Cherry Crunch Granola
Preparation Time: 10 minutes
Cooking Time: 20 minutes
Servings: 6
Ingredients:
- 3 cups rolled oats
- 2 cups assorted seeds, such as sesame, chia, sunflower, and pepitas (hulled pumpkin seeds)
- 1 cup sliced almonds
- 1 cup unsweetened coconut flakes
- 2 teaspoons vanilla extract
- 2 teaspoons ground cinnamon
- 1 teaspoon fine sea salt
- ½ cup of cocoa powder
- ½ cup pure maple syrup
- ¼ cup coconut oil or canola oil
- 1 cup dried cherries (unsweetened, if possible)
- 1 cup of chocolate chips

Directions:
1. Warm oven to 350°F. Spread 2 large baking sheets with parchment paper.
2. Stir the oats, seeds, almonds, and coconut in a large bowl. Add the vanilla, cinnamon, salt, and cocoa powder. Stir to combine.
3. In a frying pan on low, heat the maple syrup and coconut oil. Pour the warm syrup and oil over the oat mixture and stir to coat. On the prepared baking sheets, spread the granola in even layers.
4. Bake for 15 to 18 minutes, scraping and mixing occasionally, then remove from the oven.
5. Put in the dried cherries and chocolate chips, then return to the oven, now turned off but still warm, and let the granola cool and dry thoroughly.

Nutrition: Calories: 570, Fat: 31 g, Protein: 12 g

15. Mango Coconut Oatmeal

Preparation Time: 5 minutes
Cooking Time: 5 minutes
Servings: 2
Ingredients:
- 1½ cups water
- ½ cup 5-minute steel cut oats
- ¼ cup unsweetened canned coconut milk, plus more for serving (optional)
- 1 tablespoon pure maple syrup
- 1 teaspoon sesame seeds
- Dash ground cinnamon
- 1 mango, stripped, pitted, and divide into slices

- 1 tablespoon unsweetened coconut flakes

Directions:
1. In a frying pan over high heat, boil water. Put the oats and lower the heat. Cook, occasionally stirring, for 5 minutes.
2. Put in the coconut milk, maple syrup, and salt to combine. Get two bowls and sprinkle with the sesame seeds and cinnamon. Top with sliced mango and coconut flakes.

Nutrition: Calories: 373, Fat: 11 g, Carbs: 0 g, Protein: 12 g

16. Scrambled Eggs with Soy Sauce and Broccoli Slaw

Preparation Time: 5 minutes
Cooking Time: 10 minutes
Servings: 2
Ingredients:
- 1 tablespoon peanut oil, divided
- 4 large eggs
- ½ to 1 tablespoon soy sauce, tamari, or Bragg's liquid aminos
- 1 tablespoon water
- 1 cup shredded broccoli slaw or other shredded vegetables
- Kosher salt
- Chopped fresh cilantro for serving
- Hot sauce, for serving

Directions:
1. In a medium non-stick skillet or cast-iron skillet over medium heat, heat 2 teaspoons of peanut oil, swirling to coat the skillet.
2. In a small bowl, whip the eggs, soy sauce, and water until smooth. Pour the eggs into the pan and let the bottom set.
3. Using a wooden spoon, spread the eggs from one side to the other a couple of times so the uncooked portions on top pool into the bottom. Cook until the eggs are set.
4. In a medium container, stir together the broccoli slaw, the remaining 1 teaspoon of peanut oil, and a touch of salt. Divide the slaw between 2 plates.

5. Top with the eggs and scatter cilantro on each serving. Serve with hot sauce.

Nutrition: Calories: 222, Fat: 4 g, Carbs: 2 g, Protein: 12 g

17. Tasty Breakfast Donuts

Preparation Time: 5 minutes
Cooking Time: 5 minutes
Servings: 4
Ingredients:
- 43 grams' cream cheese
- 2 eggs
- 2 tablespoons almond flour
- 2 tablespoons erythritol
- 1 ½ tablespoons coconut flour
- ½ teaspoon baking powder
- ½ teaspoon vanilla extract
- 5 drops stevia (liquid form)
- 2 strips bacon, fried until crispy

Directions:
1. Rub coconut oil over the donut maker and turn it on. Pulse all ingredients except bacon in a blender or food processor until smooth (it should take around 1 minute).
2. Pour batter into donut maker, leaving 1/10 in each round for rising. Leave for 3 minutes before flipping each donut.
3. Leave for another 2 minutes or until the fork comes out clean when piercing them. Take donuts out and let cool. Crumble bacon into bits and use it to top donuts.

Nutrition: Calories: 60, Fat: 5 g, Carbs: 1 g, Protein: 3 g

18. Cheesy Spicy Bacon Bowls

Preparation Time: 10 minutes
Cooking Time: 22 minutes
Servings: 12
Ingredients:
- 6 strips bacon, pan-fried until cooked but still malleable
- 4 eggs
- 60 grams' cheddar cheese
- 40 grams' cream cheese, grated
- 2 Jalapenos, sliced and seeds removed
- 2 tablespoons coconut oil
- ¼ teaspoon onion powder

- ¼ teaspoon garlic powder
- Dash of salt and pepper

Directions:
1. Preheat oven to 375°F.
2. In a bowl, beat together eggs, cream cheese, jalapenos (minus 6 slices), coconut oil, onion powder, garlic powder, and salt and pepper.
3. Use the leftover bacon to grease on a muffin tray, rubbing it into each insert. Place bacon-wrapped inside the parameters of each insert.
4. Pour the beaten mixture halfway up each bacon bowl. Garnish each bacon bowl with cheese and leftover jalapeno slices (placing one on top of each).
5. Leave in the oven for about 22 minutes, or until the egg is thoroughly cooked and cheese is bubbly. Remove from oven and let cool until edible. Enjoy!

Nutrition: Calories: 259, Fat: 24 g, Carbs: 1 g, Protein: 10 g

19. Goat Cheese Zucchini Kale Quiche

Preparation Time: 35 minutes
Cooking Time: 1 hour 10 minutes
Servings: 4
Ingredients:
- 4 large eggs
- 8 ounces' fresh zucchini, sliced
- 10 ounces' kale
- 3 garlic cloves (minced)
- 1 cup of soy milk
- 1 ounce's goat cheese
- 1cup grated parmesan
- 1cup shredded cheddar cheese
- 2 teaspoons olive oil
- Salt and pepper, to taste

Directions:
1. Preheat oven to 350°F. Heat up 1 teaspoon of olive oil in a saucepan over medium-high heat. Sauté garlic for 1 minute until flavored.
2. Add the zucchini and cook for another 5-7 minutes until soft. Beat the eggs, and then add a little milk and Parmesan cheese.

3. Meanwhile, heat the remaining olive oil in another saucepan and add the cabbage. Cover and cook for 5 minutes until dry.
4. Slightly grease a baking dish with cooking spray and spread the kale leaves across the bottom. Add the zucchini and top with goat cheese.
5. Pour the egg, milk, and parmesan mixture evenly over the other ingredients. Top with cheddar cheese.
6. Bake for 50–60 minutes until golden brown. Check the center of the quiche; it should have a solid consistency. Let chill for a few minutes before serving.

Nutrition: Calories: 290, Carbohydrates: 15 g, Protein: 19 g, Fat: 18 g

20. Ricotta Ramekins

Preparation Time: 10 minutes
Cooking Time: 1 hour
Servings: 4
Ingredients:
- 6 eggs, whisked
- 1 and ½ pounds ricotta cheese, soft
- ½ pound stevia
- 1 teaspoon vanilla extract
- ½ teaspoon baking powder
- Cooking spray

Directions:
1. In a bowl, mix the eggs, ricotta, and the other ingredients except for the cooking spray and whisk well.
2. Grease 4 ramekins with the cooking spray, pour the ricotta cream in each and bake at 360°F for 1 hour. Serve cold.

Nutrition: Calories 180, Fat 5.3 g, Carbs 11.5 g, Protein 4 g

21. Chicken Lo Mein

Preparation Time: 15 minutes
Cooking Time: 30 minutes
Servings: 4
Ingredients:

- 2 tablespoons + 2 teaspoons sesame oil, divided - 790 g boneless. skinless chicken breasts, sliced
- ¼ teaspoon ground black pepper
- 2 tablespoons soy sauce
- 2 tablespoons oyster sauce
- 1 garlic clove, minced
- 2 teaspoons peeled and minced fresh ginger-root
- 2 spring onions, trimmed and sliced with white and green parts separated
- 110 g fresh mushrooms, divided
- 1 medium red bell pepper, membranes, and seeds removed
- 2 medium zucchinis (400 g), cut, sliced

Directions:

1. In a skillet, heat one teaspoon sesame oil over medium-high heat. Put the sliced chicken, season with black pepper, and cook until the chicken is done (internal temperature about 165°F). Dismiss from wok or skillet and set aside. While the chicken cooks, prepare the sauce by combining the oyster sauce, soy sauce, and 2 tablespoons of sesame oil in a bowl and whisking together. Set aside.
2. With the same skillet used to cook the chicken, heat 1 teaspoon sesame oil and put the garlic, ginger, and white spring onion pieces; cook until fragrant, about 1 minute.
3. Put the mushrooms and bell peppers and continue to cook until just tender, about 3 minutes. Add zucchini noodles and toss to combine.
4. Pour in the sauce and put the chicken; cook until zucchini is tender and the mixture is heated for 5 minutes. Garnish with green parts of spring onions.

Nutrition: Calories: 312, Protein: 9 g, Fat: 10 g, Carbs: 22 g

22. Pancakes with Berries

Preparation Time: 5 minutes
Cooking Time: 20 minutes
Servings: 2
Ingredients:
Pancake:

- 1 egg
- 50 g spelled flour
- 50 g almond flour
- 15 g coconut flour
- 150 ml of water
- Salt

Filling:

- 40 g mixed berries
- 10 g chocolate
- 5 g powdered sugar
- 4 tablespoons yogurt

Directions:

1. Put the flour, egg, and some salt in a blender jar. Add 150 ml of water. Mix everything with a whisk. Heat a coated pan.
2. Put in half of the batter. Once the pancake is firm, turn it over. Take out the pancake, add the second half of the batter to the pan, and repeat.
3. Melt chocolate over a water bath. Let the pancakes cool. Brush the pancakes with the yogurt. Wash the berry and let it drain. Put berries on the yogurt.
4. Roll up the pancakes, then sprinkle them with powdered sugar. Decorate the whole thing with the melted chocolate.

Nutrition: Calories: 298, Carbohydrates: 26 g, Protein: 21 g, Fat: 9 g

23. Omelet À La Margherita

Preparation Time: 10 minutes
Cooking Time: 20 minutes
Servings: 2
Ingredients:

- 3 eggs
- 50 g parmesan cheese
- 2 tablespoons heavy cream
- 1 tablespoon olive oil
- 1 teaspoon oregano
- Nutmeg
- Salt
- Pepper

For covering:

- 3 - 4 stalks of basil
- 1 tomato
- 100 g grated mozzarella

Directions:

1. Mix the cream plus eggs in a medium bowl. Add the grated parmesan, nutmeg, oregano, pepper, and salt, and stir everything. Heat the oil in a pan.
2. Add 1/2 of the egg and cream to the pan. Let the omelet set over medium heat, turn it, and then remove it.
3. Repeat with the second half of the egg mixture. Cut the tomatoes into slices and place them on top of the omelets. Scatter the mozzarella over the tomatoes.
4. Place the omelets on a baking sheet— Cook at 180 degrees for 5 to 10 minutes. Then take the omelets out and decorate them with the basil leaves.

Nutrition: Calories: 402, Carbohydrates: 7 g, Protein: 21 g, Fat: 34 g

24. Omelet with Tomatoes and Spring Onions

Preparation Time: 5 minutes
Cooking Time: 20 minutes
Servings: 3
Ingredients:

- 6 eggs
- 2 tomatoes
- 2 spring onions
- 1 shallot
- 2 tablespoons butter
- 1 tablespoon olive oil
- 1 pinch of nutmeg
- Salt and pepper

Directions:

1. Whisk the eggs in a bowl. Mix them and season them with salt and pepper. Peel the shallot and chop it up.
2. Clean the onions and cut them into rings. Wash the tomatoes and cut them into pieces—heat butter and oil in a pan.
3. Braise half of the shallots in it, then add half the egg mixture. Let everything set over medium heat. Scatter a few tomatoes and onion rings on top. Repeat with the second half of the egg mixture. In the end, spread the grated nutmeg over the whole thing.

Nutrition: Calories: 263, Carbohydrates: 8 g, Protein: 20.3 g, Fat: 24 g

25. Yogurt with Granola and Persimmon

Preparation Time: 5 minutes
Cooking Time: 5 minutes
Servings: 1
Ingredients:

- 150 g Greek-style yogurt
- 20 g oatmeal
- 60 g fresh persimmons
- 30 ml of tap water

Directions:

1. Put the oatmeal in the pan without any fat.
2. Toast them, stirring constantly, until golden brown.
3. Then put them on a plate and let them cool down briefly.
4. Peel the persimmon and put it in a bowl with the water. Mix the whole thing into a fine puree.
5. Put the yogurt, the toasted oatmeal, and the puree in layers in a glass and serve.

Nutrition: kcal: 286, Carbohydrates: 29 g, Protein: 1 g, Fat: 11 g

26. Smoothie Bowl with Spinach, Mango and Muesli
Preparation Time: 10 minutes
Cooking Time: 0 minutes
Servings: 1
Ingredients:
- 150 g yogurt
- 30 g apple
- 30 g mango
- 30 g low carb muesli
- 10 g spinach
- 10 g chia seeds

Directions:
1. Soak the spinach leaves and let them drain.
2. Peel the mango and cut it into strips.
3. Remove apple core and cut it into pieces.
4. Put everything except the mango together with the yogurt in a blender and make a fine puree out of it.
5. Put the spinach smoothie in a bowl.
6. Add the muesli, chia seeds, and mango.
7. Serve the whole thing

Nutrition: kcal: 362, Carbohydrates: 21 g, Protein: 12 g, Fat: 21 g

27. Fried Egg with Bacon

Preparation Time: 5 minutes
Cooking Time: 10 minutes
Servings: 1
Ingredients:
- 2 eggs
- 30 grams of bacon
- 2 tablespoons olive oil
- Salt
- Pepper

Directions:
1. Heat oil in the pan and fry the bacon.
2. Reduce the heat and beat the eggs in the pan.
3. Cook the eggs and season with salt and pepper.
4. Serve the fried eggs hot with the bacon.

Nutrition: kcal: 405, Carbohydrates: 1 g, Protein: 19 g, Fat: 38 g

28. Smoothie Bowl with Berries, Poppy Seeds, Nuts, and Seeds
Preparation Time: 15 minutes
Cooking Time: 0 minutes
Servings: 2
Ingredients:
- 5 chopped almonds
- 2 chopped walnuts
- 1 apple
- ¼ banana
- 300 g yogurt
- 60 g raspberries
- 20 g blueberries
- 20 g rolled oats, roasted in a pan
- 10 g poppy seeds
- 1 teaspoon pumpkin seeds
- Agave syrup

Directions:
1. Clean the fruit and let it drain.
2. Take some berries and set them aside.
3. Place the remaining berries in a tall mixing vessel.
4. Cut the banana into slices. Put a few aside.
5. Add the rest of the banana to the berries.
6. Remove the core of the apple and cut it into quarters.
7. Cut the quarters into thin wedges and set a few aside.
8. Add the remaining wedges to the berries.
9. Add the yogurt to the fruits and mix everything into a puree.
10. Sweeten the smoothie with the agave syrup.

11. Divide it into two bowls.
12. Serve it with the remaining fruit, poppy seeds, oatmeal, nuts, and seeds.

Nutrition: kcal: 284, Carbohydrates: 21 g, Protein: 11 g, Fat: 19 g

29. Whole Grain Bread and Avocado

Preparation Time: 5 minutes
Cooking Time: 0 minutes
Servings: 1
Ingredients:
- 2 slices of whole meal bread
- 60 g of cottage cheese
- 1 stick of thyme
- ½ avocado
- ½ lime
- Chili flakes
- Salt
- Pepper

Directions:
1. Cut the avocado in half.
2. Remove the pulp and cut it into slices.
3. Pour the lime juice over it.
4. Wash the thyme and shake it dry.
5. Remove the leaves from the stem.
6. Brush the whole wheat bread with the cottage cheese.
7. Place the avocado slices on top.
8. Top with the chili flakes and thyme.
9. Add salt and pepper and serve.

Nutrition: kcal: 490, Carbohydrates: 31 g, Protein: 19 g, Fat: 21 g

30. Porridge with Walnuts

Preparation Time: 5 minutes
Cooking Time: 10 minutes
Servings: 1
Ingredients:
- 50 g raspberries
- 50 g blueberries
- 25 g of ground walnuts
- 20 g of crushed flaxseed
- 10 g of oatmeal
- 200 ml nut drink
- Agave syrup
- ½ teaspoon cinnamon
- Salt

Directions:
1. Warm the nut drink in a small saucepan.
2. Add the walnuts, flaxseed, and oatmeal, stirring constantly.
3. Stir in the cinnamon and salt.
4. Simmer for 8 minutes.
5. Keep stirring everything.
6. Sweet the whole thing.
7. Put the porridge in a bowl.
8. Wash the berries and let them drain.
9. Add them to the porridge and serve everything.

Nutrition: kcal: 378, Carbohydrates: 11 g, Protein: 18 g, Fat: 27 g

31. Hemp Seed Porridge

Preparation Time: 5 minutes
Cooking Time: 5 minutes
Servings: 6
Ingredients:
- 3 cups cooked hemp seed
- 1 packet Stevia
- 1 cup coconut milk

Directions:
1. In a saucepan, mix the rice and the coconut milk over moderate heat for about 5 minutes as you stir it constantly.
2. Remove the pan from the burner then add the Stevia. Stir.
3. Serve in 6 bowls.
4. Enjoy.

Nutrition: Calories: 236, Fat: 1.8 g, Carbs: 48.3 g, Protein: 7 g

32. Mini Mac in a Bowl

Preparation Time: 5 minutes
Cooking Time: 15 minutes
Servings: 1
Ingredients:
- 5 ounces lean ground beef
- 2 tablespoons diced white or yellow onion.
- 1/8 teaspoon onion powder
- 1/8 teaspoon white vinegar
- 1 ounce dill pickle slices
- 1 teaspoon sesame seed
- 3 cups shredded Romaine lettuce
- Cooking spray

- 2 tablespoons reduced-fat shredded cheddar cheese
- 2 tablespoons Wish-Bone light thousand island as dressing

Directions:
1. Place a lightly greased small skillet on fire to heat.
2. Add your onion to cook for about 2-3 minutes. Next, add the beef and allow cooking until it's brown.
3. Next, mix your vinegar and onion powder with the dressing.
4. Finally, top the lettuce with the cooked meat and sprinkle cheese on it, add your pickle slices.
5. Drizzle the mixture with the sauce and sprinkle the sesame seeds.
6. Your mini mac in a bowl is ready for consumption.

Nutrition: Calories: 150, Protein: 21 g, Carbohydrates: 32 g, Fats: 19 g

33. Shake Cake Fueling

Preparation Time: 5 minutes
Cooking Time: 0 minutes
Servings: 1
Ingredients:
- 1 packet Optavia shakes.
- 1/4 teaspoon baking powder
- 2 tablespoons eggbeaters or egg whites
- 2 tablespoons water
- Other options that are not compulsory include sweetener, reduced-fat cream cheese, etc.

Directions:
1. Begin by preheating the oven.
2. Mix all the ingredients. Begin with the dry ingredients, and then add the wet ingredients.
3. After the mixture/batter is ready, pour gently into muffin cups.
4. Inside the oven, place, and bake for about 16-18 minutes or until it is baked and ready. Allow it to cool completely.
5. Add additional toppings of your choice and ensure your delicious shake cake is refreshing.

Nutrition: Calories: 896, Fat: 37 g, Carbohydrates: 115 g, Protein: 34 g

34. Optavia Biscuit Pizza

Preparation Time: 5 minutes
Cooking Time: 15-20 minutes
Servings: 1
Ingredients:
- 1/4 sachet Optavia buttermilk cheddar and herb biscuit
- 1/4 tablespoon tomato sauce
- 1/4 tablespoon low-fat shredded cheese
- ¼ bottle water
- Parchment paper

Directions:
1. Begin by preheating the oven to about 350°F
2. Mix the biscuit and water and stir properly.
3. In the parchment paper, pour the mixture and spread it into a thin circle. Allow cooking for 10 minutes.
4. Take it out and add the tomato sauce and shredded cheese.
5. Bake it for a few more minutes.

Nutrition: Calories: 478, Protein: 30 g, Carbohydrates: 22 g, Fats: 29 g

35. Lean and Green Smoothie

Preparation Time: 5 minutes
Cooking Time: 0 minutes
Servings: 1
Ingredients:
- 2 1/2 cups kale leaves
- 3/4 cup chilled apple juice
- 1 cup cubed pineapple
- 1/2 cup frozen green grapes
- 1/2 cup chopped apple

Directions:
1. Place the pineapple, apple juice, apple, frozen seedless grapes, and kale leaves in a blender.
2. Cover and blend until it's smooth.
3. Smoothie is ready and can be garnished with halved grapes if you wish.

Nutrition: Calories: 81, Protein: 2 g, Carbohydrates: 19 g, Fats: 1 g

36. Lean and Green Chicken Pesto Pasta

Preparation Time: 5 minutes
Cooking Time: 15 minutes
Servings: 1
Ingredients:

- 3 cups raw kale leaves
- 2 tablespoons olive oil
- 2 cups fresh basil - 1/4 teaspoon salt
- 3 tablespoons lemon juice
- 3 garlic cloves
- 2 cups cooked chicken breast
- 1 cup baby spinach
- 6 ounces uncooked chicken pasta
- 3 ounces diced fresh mozzarella
- Basil leaves red pepper flakes to garnish

Directions:

1. Start by making the pesto; add the kale, lemon juice, basil, garlic cloves, olive oil, and salt to a blender and blend until it's smooth.
2. Add salt and pepper to taste.
3. Cook the pasta and strain off the water. Reserve 1/4 cup of the liquid.
4. Get a bowl and mix everything, the cooked pasta, pesto, diced chicken, spinach, mozzarella, and the reserved pasta liquid.
5. Sprinkle the mixture with additional chopped basil or red paper flakes (optional). Now your salad is ready. You may serve it warm or chilled. Also, it can be taken as a salad mix-ins or as a side dish. Leftovers should be stored in the refrigerator inside an air-tight container for 3-5 days.

Nutrition: Calories: 244, Protein: 20.5 g, Carbohydrates: 22.5 g, Fats: 10 g

37. Open-Face Egg Sandwiches with Cilantro-Jalapeño Spread

Preparation Time: 20 minutes
Cooking Time: 10 minutes
Servings: 2
Ingredients:
For the cilantro and jalapeño spread

- 1 cup filled up fresh cilantro leaves and stems (about a bunch)
- 1 jalapeño pepper, seeded and roughly chopped
- ½ cup extra-virgin olive oil
- ¼ cup pepitas (hulled pumpkin seeds), raw or roasted
- 2 garlic cloves, thinly sliced
- 1 tablespoon freshly squeezed lime juice
- 1 teaspoon kosher salt

For the eggs

- 4 large eggs
- ¼ cup milk
- ¼ to ½ teaspoon kosher salt
- 2 tablespoons butter

For the sandwich

- 2 slices bread
- 1 tablespoon butter
- 1 avocado, halved, pitted, and divided into slices
- Microgreens or sprouts, for garnish

Directions:
To make the cilantro and jalapeño spread

1. In a food processor, combine the cilantro, jalapeño, oil, pepitas, garlic, lime juice, and salt. Whirl until smooth. Refrigerate if making in advance; otherwise set aside.
2. To make the eggs
3. In a medium bowl, whisk the eggs, milk, and salt.
4. Dissolve the butter in a skillet over low heat, swirling to coat the bottom of the pan. Pour in the whisked eggs.
5. Cook until they begin to set then, using a heatproof spatula, push them to the sides, allowing the uncooked portions to run into the bottom of the skillet.
6. Continue until the eggs are set.
7. To assemble the sandwiches
8. Toast the bed and spread with butter.
9. Spread a spoonful of the cilantro-jalapeño spread on each piece of toast. Top each with scrambled eggs.
10. Arrange avocado over each sandwich and garnish with microgreens.

Nutrition: Calories: 711, Total fat: 4 g, Cholesterol: 54 mg, Fiber: 12 g, Protein: 12 g, Sodium: 327 mg

38. Apple Kale Cucumber Smoothie

Preparation Time: 5 minutes
Cooking Time: 5 minutes
Servings: 1
Ingredients:
- ¾ cup water
- ½ green apple, diced
- ¾ cup kale
- ½ cucumber

Directions:
1. Toss all your ingredients into your blender then process till smooth and creamy.
2. Serve immediately and enjoy.

Nutrition: Calories: 86, Fat: 0.5 g, Carbs: 21.7 g, Protein: 1.9 g, Fiber: 0 g

39. Refreshing Cucumber Smoothie

Preparation Time: 5 minutes
Cooking Time: 5 minutes
Servings: 2
Ingredients:
- 1 cup ice cubes
- 20 drops liquid stevia
- 2 fresh limes, peeled and halved
- 1 teaspoon lime zest, grated
- 1 cucumber, chopped
- 1 avocado, pitted and peeled
- 2 cups kale

- 1 tablespoon creamed coconut
- ¾ cup coconut water

Directions:
1. Toss all your ingredients into your blender then process till smooth and creamy.
2. Serve immediately and enjoy.

Nutrition: Calories: 313, Fat: 25.1 g, Carbs: 24.7 g, Protein: 4.9 g, Fiber: 0 g

40. Cauliflower Veggie Smoothie

Preparation Time: 5 minutes
Cooking Time: 5 minutes
Servings: 4
Ingredients:
- 1 zucchini, peeled and chopped
- 1 Seville orange, peeled
- 1 apple, diced
- 1 banana
- 1 cup kale
- ½ cup cauliflower

Directions:
1. Toss all your ingredients into your blender then process till smooth and creamy.
2. Serve immediately and enjoy.

Nutrition: Calories: 71, Fat: 0.3 g, Carbs: 18.3 g, Protein: 1.3 g, Fiber: 0 g

CHAPTER 7:

Appetizers Recipes

41. Salmon Burger

Preparation Time: 15 minutes
Cooking Time: 15 minutes
Servings: 6
Ingredients:

- 16 ounces (450 g) pink salmon, minced
- 1 cup (250 g) prepared mashed potatoes
- 1 medium (110 g) onion, chopped
- 1 stalk celery (about 60 g), finely chopped
- 1 large egg (about 60 g), lightly beaten
- 2 tablespoons (7 g) fresh cilantro, chopped
- 1 cup (100 g) breadcrumbs
- Vegetable oil, for deep frying
- Salt and freshly ground black pepper

Directions:

1. Combine the salmon, mashed potatoes, onion, celery, egg, and cilantro in a mixing bowl. Season to taste and mix thoroughly. Spoon about 2 Tablespoon mixture, roll in breadcrumbs, and then form into small patties.
2. Heat oil in a non-stick frying pan. Cook your salmon patties for 5 minutes on each side or until golden brown and crispy.
3. Serve in burger buns and with coleslaw on the side if desired.

Nutrition: Calories 230, Fat 7, Carbs 20, Protein 18

42. Spinach and Cottage Cheese Sandwich

Preparation Time: 15 minutes
Cooking Time: 10 minutes
Servings: 4
Ingredients:

- 4 ounces (125 g) cottage cheese
- 1/4 cup (15 g) chives, chopped
- 1 teaspoon (5 g) capers
- 1/2 teaspoon (2.5 g) grated lemon rind
- 4 (2 oz. or 60 g) smoked salmon
- 2 cups (60 g) loose baby spinach
- 1 medium (110 g) red onion, sliced thinly
- 8 slices rye bread (about 30 g each)
- Kosher salt and freshly ground black pepper

Directions:

1. Preheat your griddle or Panini press.
2. Mix together cottage cheese, chives, capers, and lemon rind in a small bowl.
3. Spread and divide the cheese mixture on 4 bread slices. Top with spinach, onion slices, and smoked salmon.
4. Cover with remaining bread slices.
5. Grill the sandwiches until golden and grill marks form on both sides.
6. Transfer to a serving dish.
7. Serve and enjoy.

Nutrition: Calories 386, Fat 1, Carbs 18, Protein 1

43. Feta and Pesto Wrap

Preparation Time: 15 minutes
Cooking Time: 10 minutes
Servings: 4
Ingredients:

- 8 ounces (250 g) smoked salmon fillet, thinly sliced
- 1 cup (150 g) feta cheese
- 8 (15 g) Romaine lettuce leaves
- 4 (6-inch) pita bread
- 1/4 cup (60 g) basil pesto sauce

Directions:

1. Place 1 pita bread on a plate. Top with lettuce, salmon, feta cheese, and pesto sauce. Fold or roll to enclose filling. Repeat the procedure for the remaining ingredients.
2. Serve and enjoy.

Nutrition: Calories 408, Fat 2, Carbs 1, Protein 11

44. Cheese and Onion on Bagel

Preparation Time: 15 minutes
Cooking Time: 10 minutes
Servings: 4
Ingredients:

- 8 ounces (250 g) smoked salmon fillet, thinly sliced
- 1/2 cup (125 g) cream cheese
- 1 medium (110 g) onion, thinly sliced
- 4 bagels (about 80 g each), split
- 2 tablespoons (7 g) fresh parsley, chopped
- Freshly ground black pepper to taste

Directions:

1. Spread the cream cheese on each bottom's half of bagels. Top with salmon and onion, season with pepper, sprinkle with parsley, and cover with bagel tops.
2. Serve and enjoy.

Nutrition: Calories: 34, Carbs: 0 g, Fat: 1 g, Protein: 5 g

45. Bananas in Nut Cups

Preparation Time: 30 minutes
Cooking Time: 45 minutes
Servings: 6
Ingredients:

- 3/4 cup shelled pistachios
- 1/2 cup sugar
- 1 teaspoon ground cinnamon
- 4 sheets phyllo dough, (14 inches x 9 inches)
- 1/4 cup butter, melted

Sauce:

- 3/4 cup butter, cubed
- 3/4 cup packed brown sugar
- 3 medium firm bananas, sliced
- 1/4 teaspoon ground cinnamon
- 3 to 4 cups vanilla ice cream

Directions:

1. Finely chop sugar and pistachios in a food processor; move to a bowl, then mix in cinnamon. Slice each phyllo sheet into 6 four-inch squares, get rid of the trimmings. Pile the squares, then use plastic wrap to cover.
2. Pile 3 squares, flip each at an angle to misalign the corners. Force each stack on the sides and bottom of an oiled eight-oz. custard cup. Bake for 15-20 minutes in a 350 degrees F oven until golden; cool for 5 minutes. Move to a wire rack to cool completely.
3. Melt and boil brown sugar and butter in a saucepan to make the sauce; lower heat. Mix in cinnamon and bananas gently; heat completely. Put ice cream in the phyllo cups until full, then put banana sauce on top. Serve right away.

Nutrition: Calories 100, Fat 12, Carbs 2, Protein 4

46. Apple Salad Sandwich

Preparation Time: 15 minutes
Cooking Time: 10 minutes
Servings: 4
Ingredients:

- 4 ounces (125 g) canned pink salmon, drained and flaked
- 1 medium (180 g) red apple, cored and diced
- 1 celery stalk (about 60 g), chopped
- 1 shallot (about 40 g), finely chopped
- 1/3 cup (85 g) light mayonnaise
- 8 slices whole-grain bread (about 30 g each), toasted
- 8 (15 g) Romaine lettuce leaves
- Salt and freshly ground black pepper

Directions:

1. Combine the salmon, apple, celery, shallot, and mayonnaise in a mixing bowl. Season with salt and pepper.
2. Place 1 slice of bread on a plate, top with lettuce and salmon salad, and then covers with another slice of bread. Repeat the procedure for the remaining ingredients. Serve and enjoy.

Nutrition: Calories 121, Fat 1, Carbs 18, Protein 1

47. Buttermilk Ice Cream Shake

Preparation Time: 5 minutes
Cooking Time: 0 minutes
Servings: 4
Ingredients:

- 3 cups chilled buttermilk
- 1/2 cup cold lemon juice
- Pinch of salt
- 1/2 cup sugar

- 1/8 teaspoon grated lemon zest
- 1 cup vanilla ice cream
- Dash ginger

Directions

1. Blend or shake all of the ingredients. Serve the shake together with the ginger.

Nutrition: Calories 332, Fat 8, Carbs 1, Protein 14

48. Buttermilk Shake

Preparation Time: 5 minutes
Cooking Time: 0 minutes
Servings: 4
Ingredients:

- 1 pint vanilla ice cream
- 1 cup buttermilk
- 1 teaspoon grated lemon zest
- 1/2 teaspoon vanilla extract
- 1 drop lemon extract

Directions

1. In a blender container, combine all the ingredients and process them at high speed until smooth. Pour the drink into the glasses. Make sure to put all the leftovers inside the refrigerator.

Nutrition: Calories 309, Fat 26, Carbs 9, Protein 12

49. Cantaloupe Orange Milk Shakes

Preparation Time: 5 minutes
Cooking Time: 0 minutes
Servings: 4
Ingredients:

- 4-1/2 teaspoons orange juice concentrate
- 3/4 cup cubed cantaloupe
- 1 cup vanilla ice cream or frozen yogurt
- 3/4 cup milk
- 3 tablespoons sugar

Directions

1. Mix cantaloupe and orange juice concentrate in a blender. Cover the blender and process it until smooth. Add the sugar, milk, and ice cream.

2. Cover again and process until well-blended. Pour the mixture into the chilled glasses and serve.

Nutrition: Calories 252, Fat 9, Carbs 2, Protein 11

50. Cheese on Rye Bread

Preparation Time: 15 minutes
Cooking Time: 10 minutes
Servings: 4
Ingredients:
- 8 ounces (250 g) smoked salmon, thinly sliced
- 1/3 cup (85 g) mayonnaise
- 2 tablespoons (30 ml) lemon juice
- 1 tablespoon (15 g) Dijon mustard
- 1 teaspoon (3 g) garlic, minced
- 4 slices cheddar cheese (about 2 oz. or 30 g each)
- 8 slices rye bread (about 2 oz. or 30 g each)
- 8 (15 g) Romaine lettuce leaves
- Salt and freshly ground black pepper

Directions:
1. Mix together the mayonnaise, lemon juice, mustard, and garlic in a small bowl. Flavor with salt and pepper and set aside.
2. Spread dressing on 4 bread slices. Top with lettuce, salmon, and cheese. Cover with remaining rye bread slices.
3. Serve and enjoy.

Nutrition: Calories 321, Fat 1, Carbs 8, Protein 5

51. Bulgur Lamb Meatballs

Preparation Time: 10 minutes
Cooking Time: 15 minutes
Servings: 6
Ingredients:
- 1 and ½ cups Greek yogurt
- ½ teaspoon cumin, ground
- 1 cup cucumber, shredded
- ½ teaspoon garlic, minced
- A pinch of salt and black pepper
- 1 cup bulgur - 2 cups water
- 1 pound lamb, ground
- ¼ cup parsley, chopped
- ¼ cup shallots, chopped

- ½ teaspoon allspice, ground
- ½ teaspoon cinnamon powder
- 1 tablespoon olive oil

Directions:
1. In a bowl, combine the bulgur with the water, cover the bowl, leave aside for 10 minutes, drain and transfer to a bowl.
2. Add the meat, the yogurt, and the rest of the ingredients except the oil, stir well and shape medium meatballs out of this mix.
3. Heat up a pan with the oil over medium-high heat, add the meatballs, cook them for 7 minutes on each side, arrange them all on a platter and serve as an appetizer.

Nutrition: Calories 226, Fat 2, Carbs 1, Protein 3

52. Cucumber Bites

Preparation Time: 10 minutes
Cooking Time: 0 minutes
Servings: 12
Ingredients:
- 1 English cucumber, sliced into 32 rounds
- 10 ounces hummus
- 16 cherry tomatoes, halved
- 1 tablespoon parsley, chopped
- 1-ounce feta cheese, crumbled

Directions:
1. Spread the hummus on each cucumber round, divide the tomato halves on each, sprinkle the cheese and parsley on to, and serve as an appetizer.

Nutrition: Calories 209, Fat 2, Carbs 4, Protein 2

53. Hummus with Ground Lamb

Preparation Time: 10 minutes
Cooking Time: 15 minutes
Servings: 8
Ingredients:

- 10 ounces hummus
- 12 ounces lamb meat, ground
- ½ cup pomegranate seeds
- ¼ cup parsley, chopped
- 1 tablespoon olive oil
- Pita chips for serving

Directions:

1. Heat up a pan with the oil over medium-high heat, add the meat, and brown for 15 minutes stirring often.
2. Spread the hummus on a platter, spread the ground lamb all over, also spread the pomegranate seeds and the parsley, and serve with pita chips as a snack.

Nutrition: Calories 320, Fat 2, Carbs 1, Protein 11

54. Wrapped Plums

Preparation Time: 5 minutes
Cooking Time: 0 minutes
Servings: 8
Ingredients:

- 2 ounces prosciutto, cut into 16 pieces
- 4 plums, quartered
- 1 tablespoon chives, chopped
- A pinch of red pepper flakes, crushed

Directions:

1. Wrap each plum quarter

Nutrition: Calories 209, Fat 8, Carbs 4, Protein 4

55. Buckwheat Granola

Preparation Time: 15 minutes
Cooking Time: 30 minutes
Servings: 10
Ingredients:

- 2 cups raw buckwheat groats
- ¾ cup pumpkin seeds
- ¾ cup almonds, chopped
- 1 cup unsweetened coconut flakes
- 1 teaspoon ground cinnamon
- 1 teaspoon ground ginger
- 1 ripe banana, peeled

- 2 tablespoons maple syrup
- 2 tablespoons olive oil

Directions:

1. Preheat your oven to 350°F. In a bowl, place the buckwheat groats, coconut flakes, pumpkin seeds, almonds, and spices, and mix well.
2. In another bowl, add the banana, and with a fork, mash well.
3. Add to the buckwheat mixture maple syrup and oil, and mix until well combined.
4. Transfer the mixture onto the prepared baking sheet and spread it in an even layer. Bake for about 25–30 minutes, stirring once halfway through.
5. Remove the baking sheet from the oven and set it aside to cool.

Nutrition: Calories 342, Fat 7, Carbs 8, Protein 10

56. Apple Pancakes

Preparation Time: 15 minutes
Cooking Time: 24 minutes
Servings: 6
Ingredients:

- ½ cup buckwheat flour
- 2 tablespoons coconut sugar
- 1 teaspoon baking powder
- ½ teaspoon ground cinnamon
- 1/3 cup unsweetened almond milk
- 1 egg, beaten lightly
- 2 granny smith apples, peeled, cored, and grated

Directions:

1. In a bowl, place the flour, coconut sugar, and cinnamon, and mix well.

2. In another bowl, place the almond milk and egg and beat until well combined.
3. Now, place the flour mixture and mix until well combined.
4. Fold in the grated apples.
5. Cook for 1–2 minutes on each side.
6. Repeat with the remaining mixture.
7. Serve warm with the drizzling of honey.

Nutrition: Calories 588, Fat 3, Carbs 8, Protein 20

57. Matcha Pancakes

Preparation Time: 10 minutes
Cooking Time: 25 minutes
Servings: 6
Ingredients:

- 1 cup spelt flour
- 1 cup buckwheat flour
- 1 tablespoon matcha powder
- 1 tablespoon baking powder
- Pinch of salt
- ¾ cup unsweetened almond milk
- 1 tablespoon olive oil
- 1/3 cup raw honey

Directions:

1. In a bowl, add the flax meal and warm water and mix well. Set aside for about 5 minutes.
2. Now, place the flour mixture and mix until a smooth textured mixture is formed.
3. Cook for about 2–3 minutes.
4. Carefully flip the side and cook for about 1 minute.
5. Repeat with the remaining mixture.
6. Serve warm with the drizzling of honey.

Nutrition: Calories 345, Fat 12, Carbs 4, Protein 11

58. Smoked Salmon & Kale Scramble

Preparation Time: 10 minutes
Cooking Time: 9 minutes
Servings: 3
Ingredients:

- 2 cups fresh kale, tough ribs removed and chopped finely

- 1 tablespoon coconut oil
- Ground black pepper to taste
- ½ cup smoked salmon, crumbled
- 4 eggs, beaten

Directions:

1. In a wok, melt the coconut oil over high heat and cook the kale with black pepper for about 3–4 minutes.
2. Stir in the smoked salmon and reduce the heat to medium.
3. Add the eggs and cook for about 3–4 minutes, stirring frequently.
4. Serve immediately.

Nutrition: Calories 568, Fat 3, Carbs 5, Protein 10

59. Kale & Mushroom Frittata

Preparation Time: 15 minutes
Cooking Time: 30 minutes
Servings: 5
Ingredients:

- 8 eggs
- ½ cup unsweetened almond milk
- Salt and ground black pepper to taste
- 1 tablespoon olive oil
- 1 onion, chopped
- 1 garlic clove, minced
- 1 cup fresh mushrooms, chopped
- 1½ cups fresh kale, tough ribs removed and chopped

Directions:

1. Preheat oven to 350°F.
2. In a large bowl, place the eggs, coconut milk, salt, and black pepper, and beat well. Set aside.
3. In a large ovenproof wok, heat the oil over medium heat and sauté the onion and garlic for about 3–4 minutes.
4. Add the squash, kale, bell pepper, salt, and black pepper, and cook for about 8–10 minutes.
5. Stir in the mushrooms and cook for about 3–4 minutes.
6. Add the kale and cook for about 5 minutes.
7. Place the egg mixture on top evenly and cook for about 4 minutes, without stirring.

8. Transfer the wok to the oven and bake for about 12–15 minutes or until desired doneness.

9. Remove from the oven and place the frittata side for about 3–5 minutes before serving. Cut into desired-sized wedges and serve.

Nutrition: Calories 356, Fat 2, Carbs 4, Protein 8

60. Kale, Apple, & Cranberry Salad

Preparation Time: 15 minutes
Cooking Time: 15 minutes
Servings: 4
Ingredients:

- 6 cups fresh baby kale
- 3 large apples, cored and sliced
- ¼ cup unsweetened dried cranberries
- ¼ cup almonds, sliced
- 2 tablespoons extra-virgin olive oil
- 1 tablespoon raw honey
- Salt and ground black pepper to taste

Directions:

1. In a salad bowl, place all the ingredients and toss to coat well.
2. Serve immediately.

Nutrition: Calories 209, Fat 2, Carbs 5, Protein 8

61. Arugula, Strawberry, & Orange Salad

Preparation Time: 15 minutes
Cooking Time: 15 minutes
Servings: 4
Ingredients:
Salad

- 6 cups fresh baby arugula
- 1½ cups fresh strawberries, hulled and sliced
- 2 oranges, peeled and segmented

Dressing

- 2 tablespoons fresh lemon juice
- 1 tablespoon raw honey
- 2 teaspoons extra-virgin olive oil
- 1 teaspoon Dijon mustard
- Salt and ground black pepper to taste

Directions:

1. For the salad: In a salad bowl, place all ingredients and mix.
2. For the dressing: Place all ingredients in another bowl and beat until well combined.
3. Place dressing on top of the salad and toss to coat well.
4. Serve immediately.

Nutrition: Calories 389, Fat 8, Carbs 4, Protein 7

62. Lean and Green Crockpot Chili

Preparation Time: 3 minutes
Cooking Time: 45 minutes
Servings: 8
Ingredients:

- 1-pound boneless skinless chicken breasts, cut into strips
- ½ cup chopped onion
- 2 teaspoons ground cumin
- 1 teaspoon minced garlic
- ½ teaspoon chili powder
- Salt and pepper to taste
- 1 ½ cups water
- 1 can green enchilada sauce
- ½ cup dried beans, soaked overnight

Directions:

1. Place all ingredients in a pot.
2. Mix all ingredients until combined.
3. Close the lid and turn on the heat to medium.
4. Bring to a boil and allow to simmer for 45 minutes or until the beans are cooked.
5. Serve with chopped cilantro on top.

Nutrition: Calories: 84; Protein: 13.4 g; Carbs: 3.6 g, Fat: 1.7 g, Sugar: 0.8 g

63. Grilled Avocado Capers Crostini

Preparation Time: 10 minutes
Cooking Time: 20 minutes
Servings: 2
Ingredients:

- 1 avocado thinly sliced
- 9 ounces ripened cherry tomatoes
- 1 ½ ounces fresh bocconcini in water

- 2 teaspoons balsamic glaze
- 8 pieces Italian baguette
- ½ a cup basil leaves

Directions:

1. Preheat your oven to 375°F
2. Arrange your baking sheet properly before spraying them on top with olive oil.
3. Bake your item of choice until they are well done or golden brown. Rub your crostini with the cut side of garlic while they are still warm and you can season them with pepper and salt.
4. Divide the basil leaves on each side of bread and top up with tomato halves, avocado slices, and bocconcini. Season it with pepper and salt.
5. Broil it for 4 minutes and when the cheese starts to melt through, remove and drizzle balsamic glaze before serving.

Nutrition: Calories 278, Fat 10 g, Carbohydrates 37 g, Proteins 10 g, Sodium: 342 mg, Potassium: 277 mg

64. Caprese Stuffed Garlic Butter Portobellos

Preparation Time: 5 minutes
Cooking Time: 10 minutes
Servings: 6
Ingredients:

For Garlic butter

- 2 teaspoons butter
- 2 cloves garlic 1 teaspoon parsley finely chopped

For the mushrooms

- 6 large Portobello mushrooms, washed and dried well with a paper towel.
- 6 mozzarella cheese balls thinly sliced
- 1 cup grape tomatoes thinly sliced
- Fresh basil for garnishing

For balsamic glaze

- 2 teaspoons brown sugar
- ¼ cup balsamic vinegar

Directions:

1. Preheat the oven to broil, setting on high heat. Arrange the oven shelf and place it in the right direction.
2. Combine the garlic butter ingredients in a small pan and melt until the garlic

begins to be fragrant. Brush the bottoms of the mushroom and place them on the buttered section of the baking tray.

3. Flip and brush the remaining garlic over each cap. Fill each mushroom with tomatoes and mozzarella slices and grill until the cheese has melted. Drizzle the balsamic glaze and sprinkle some salt to taste.
4. If you are making the balsamic glaze from scratch, combine the sugar and vinegar in a small pan and reduce the heat to low. Allow it to simmer for 6 minutes or until the mixture has thickened well.

Nutrition: Calories 101, Fat 5 g, Carbohydrates 12 g, Proteins 2 g, Sodium: 58 mg, Potassium: 377 mg

65. Cheesy Mashed Sweet Potato Cakes

Preparation Time: 10 minutes
Cooking Time: 30 minutes
Servings: 4
Ingredients:

- ¾ cup bread crumbs
- 4 cups mashed potatoes
- ½ cup onions
- 2 cup grated mozzarella cheese
- ¼ cup fresh grated parmesan cheese
- 2 large cloves finely chopped
- 1 egg
- 2 teaspoons finely chopped parsley
- Salt and pepper to taste

Directions:

1. Line your baking sheet with foil. Wash, peel and cut the sweet potatoes into 6 pieces. Arrange them inside the baking sheet and drizzle a small amount of oil on top before seasoning with salt and pepper.
2. Cover with a baking sheet and bake it for 30 minutes. Once cooked, transfer them into a mixing bowl and mash them well with a potato masher.
3. To the sweet potatoes in a bowl, add green onions, parmesan, mozzarella, garlic, egg, parsley, and bread crumbs.

Mash and combine the mixture together using the masher.

4. Put the remaining ¼ cup of the breadcrumbs in a place. Scoop a teaspoon of mixture into your palm and form round patties around ½ inch thick. Dredge your patties in the breadcrumbs to cover both sides and set them aside.

5. Heat a tablespoon of oil in a medium nonstick pan. When the oil is hot, begin to cook the patties in batches 4 or 5 per session and cook each side for 6 minutes until they turn golden brown. Using a spoon or spatula, flip them. Add oil to prevent burning.

Nutrition: Calories 126, Fat 6 g, Carbs 15 g, Proteins 3 g, Sodium: 400 mg

66. Cheesy Garlic Sweet Potatoes

Preparation Time: 10 minutes
Cooking Time: 25 minutes
Servings: 4
Ingredients:
- Sea salt
- ¼ cup garlic butter melt
- ¾ cup shredded mozzarella cheese
- ½ cup parmesan cheese freshly grated
- 4 medium-sized sweet potatoes
- 2 teaspoons freshly chopped parsley

Directions:
1. Heat the oven to 400°F and brush the potatoes with garlic butter and season each with pepper and salt. Arrange the cut side down on a greased baking sheet until the flesh is tender or they turn golden brown.

2. Remove them from the oven, flip the cut side up and top up with parsley and parmesan cheese.

3. Change the settings of your instant fryer oven to broil and on medium heat, add the cheese and melt it. Sprinkle salt and pepper to taste. Serve them warm

Nutrition: Calories 356, Fat 9 g, Carbohydrates 13 g, Proteins 5 g, Potassium: 232 mg, Sodium: 252 mg

67. Crispy Garlic Baked Potato Wedges

Preparation Time: 5 minutes
Cooking Time: 10 minutes
Servings: 3
Ingredients:
- 3 teaspoons salt
- 1 teaspoon minced garlic
- 6 large russets
- ¼ cup olive oil
- 1 teaspoon paprika
- 2/3 finely grated parmesan cheese
- 2 teaspoons freshly chopped parsley

Directions:
1. Preheat the oven to 350°F and line the baking sheet with parchment pepper.

2. Cut the potatoes into half-length and cut each half in half lengthways again. Make 8 wedges.

3. In a small jug, combine garlic, oil, paprika, and salt and place your wedges in the baking sheets. Pour the oil mixture over the potatoes and toss them to ensure that they are evenly coated.

4. Arrange the potato wedges in a single layer on the baking tray and sprinkle salt and parmesan cheese if needed. Bake for 35 minutes turning the wedges once half side is cooked.

5. Flip the other side until they are both golden brown.
6. Sprinkle parsley and the remaining parmesan before serving.

Nutrition: Calories 324, Fat 6 g, Carbs 8 g, Proteins 2 g, Sodium: 51mg, Potassium: 120 mg

68. Sticky Chicken Thai Wings
Preparation Time: 10 minutes
Cooking Time: 30 minutes
Servings: 6
Ingredients:
- 3 pounds chicken wings removed
- 1 teaspoon sea salt to taste

For the glaze:
- ¾ cup Thai sweet chili sauce
- ¼ cup soy sauce
- 4 teaspoons brown sugar
- 4 teaspoons rice wine vinegar
- 3 teaspoons fish sauce
- 2 teaspoons lime juice
- 1 teaspoon lemon grass minced
- 2 teaspoons sesame oil
- 1 teaspoon garlic minced

Directions:
1. Preheat the oven to 350°F. Lightly spray your baking tray with a cooking tray and set it aside. To prepare the glaze, combine the ingredients in a small bowl and whisk them until they are well combined. Pour half of the mixture into a pan and reserve the rest.
2. Trim any excess skin off the wing edges and season it with pepper and salt. Add the wings to a baking tray and pour the sauce over the wings tossing them for the sauce to evenly coat. Arrange them in a single layer and bake them for 15 minutes.
3. While the wings are in the oven, bring your glaze to simmer in medium heat until there are visible bubbles.
4. Once the wings are cooled on one side, rotate each piece and bake for an extra 10 minutes. Baste them and return them into the oven to allow for more cooking until they are golden brown. Garnish with onion slices, cilantro,

chili flakes, and sprinkle the remaining salt. Serving with a glaze of your choice.

Nutrition: Calories: 256, Fat: 16 g, Carbohydrates 19 g, Proteins: 20 g, Potassium: 213 mg, Sodium: 561mg

69. Coconut Shrimp

Preparation Time: 15 minutes
Cooking Time: 15 minutes
Servings: 6
Ingredients:
- Salt and pepper
- 1-pound jumbo shrimp peeled and deveined
- ½ cup all-purpose flour

For batter:
- ½ cup beer
- 1 teaspoon baking powder
- ½ cup all-purpose flour
- 1 egg

For coating:
- 1 cup panko bread crumbs
- 1 cup shredded coconut

Directions:
1. Line the baking tray with parchment paper.
2. In a shallow bowl, add ½ cup flour for dredging, and in another bowl, whisk the batter ingredients. The batter should resemble a pancake consistency. If it is too thick, add a little mineral or beer whisking in between. In another bowl mix together the shredded coconut and bread crumbs.
3. Dredge the shrimp in flour, shaking off any excess before dipping in the batter, and coat it with bread crumb

mixture. Lightly press the coconut into the shrimp.

4. Place them into the baking sheet and repeat the process until you have several.
5. In a Dutch oven skillet, heat vegetable oil until it is nice and hot fry the frozen shrimp batches for 3 minutes per side. Drain them on a paper towel-lined plate.
6. Serve immediately with sweet chili sauce.

Nutrition: Calories: 409, Fat 11 g, Carbohydrates 46 g, Proteins 30 g, Sodium: 767 mg, Potassium: 345 mg

70. Spicy Korean Cauliflower Bites

Preparation Time: 15 minutes
Cooking Time: 30 minutes
Servings: 4
Ingredients:
- 2 eggs
- 1 lb. cauliflower
- 2/3 cups of corn starch
- 2 teaspoons smoked paprika
- 1 teaspoon garlic grated
- 1 teaspoon ginger grated
- 1 lb. panko
- 1 teaspoon sea salt

For the Korean barbecue sauce:
- 1 cup ketchup
- ½ cup Korea chili flakes
- ½ cup minced garlic
- ½ cup red pepper

Directions:
1. Cut the cauliflower into small sizes based on your taste and preference.
2. In a small bowl, add cornstarch and eggs and mix them until they are smooth.
3. Add onions, garlic, ginger, smoked paprika, and coat them with panko.
4. Apply some pressure so that the panko can stick and repeat this with all the cauliflower.

Nutrition: Calories: 141, Fat: 12 g, Carbs: 23 g, Protein: 27 g

71. Grilled Salmon Burger

Preparation Time: 15 minutes
Cooking Time: 10 minutes
Servings: 4
Ingredients:
- 16 ounces (450 g) pink salmon fillet, minced
- 1 cup (250 g) prepared mashed potatoes
- 1 shallot (about 40 g), chopped
- 1 large egg (about 60 g), lightly beaten
- 2 tablespoons (7 g) fresh coriander, chopped
- 4 Hamburger buns (about 60 g each), split
- 1 large tomato (about 150 g), sliced
- 8 (15 g) Romaine lettuce leaves
- 1/4 cup (60 g) mayonnaise
- Salt and freshly ground black pepper
- Cooking oil spray

Directions:
1. Combine the salmon, mashed potatoes, shallot, egg, and coriander in a mixing bowl. Season with salt and pepper.
2. Spoon about 2 tablespoons of mixture and form into patties.
3. Preheat your grill or griddle on high. Grease with cooking oil spray.
4. Grill the salmon patties for 4-5 minutes on each side or until cooked through. Transfer to a clean plate and cover to keep warm.
5. Spread some mayonnaise on the bottom half of the buns. Top with lettuce, salmon patty, and tomato. Cover with bun tops.
6. Serve and enjoy.

Nutrition: Calories: 395, Fat 18.0 g, Carbohydrates 38.8 g, Protein 21.8 g, Sodium 383 mg

72. Easy Salmon Burger

Preparation Time: 15 minutes
Cooking Time: 15 minutes
Servings: 6
Ingredients:
- 16 ounces (450 g) pink salmon, minced

- 1 cup (250 g) prepared mashed potatoes
- 1 medium (110 g) onion, chopped
- 1 stalk celery (about 60 g), finely chopped
- 1 large egg (about 60 g), lightly beaten
- 2 tablespoons (7 g) fresh cilantro, chopped
- 1 cup (100 g) breadcrumbs
- Vegetable oil, for deep frying
- Salt and freshly ground black pepper

Directions:

1. Combine the salmon, mashed potatoes, onion, celery, egg, and cilantro in a mixing bowl. Season to taste and mix thoroughly. Spoon about two tablespoon mixture, roll in breadcrumbs, and then form into small patties.
2. Heat oil in a non-stick frying pan. Cook your salmon patties for 5 minutes on each side or until golden brown and crispy.
3. Serve in burger buns and with coleslaw on the side if desired.
4. Enjoy.

Nutrition: Calories 230, Fat 7.9 g, Carbs 20.9 g, Protein 18.9 g, Sodium 298 mg

73. Salmon Sandwich with Avocado and Egg

Preparation Time: 15 minutes
Cooking Time: 10 minutes
Servings: 4
Ingredients:

- 8 ounces (250 g) smoked salmon, thinly sliced
- 1 medium (200 g) ripe avocado, thinly sliced
- 4 large poached eggs (about 60 g each)
- 4 slices whole-wheat bread (about 30 g each)
- 2 cups (60 g) arugula or baby rocket
- Salt and freshly ground black pepper

Directions:

1. Place 1 bread slice on a plate top with arugula, avocado, salmon, and poached egg.

2. Season with salt and pepper. Repeat the procedure for the remaining ingredients. Serve and enjoy.

Nutrition: Calories: 310, Fat: 18.2 g, Carbohydrates: 16.4 g, Protein: 21.3 g, Sodium: 383 mg

74. Salmon Spinach and Cottage Cheese Sandwich

Preparation Time: 15 minutes
Cooking Time: 10 minutes
Servings: 4
Ingredients:

- 4 ounces (125 g) cottage cheese
- 1/4 cup (15 g) chives, chopped
- 1 teaspoon (5 g) capers
- 1/2 teaspoon (2.5 g) grated lemon rind
- 4 (2 oz. or 60 g) smoked salmon
- 2 cups (60 g) loose baby spinach
- 1 medium (110 g) red onion, sliced thinly
- 8 slices rye bread (about 30 g each)
- Kosher salt and freshly ground black pepper

Directions:

1. Preheat your griddle or Panini press.
2. Mix together cottage cheese, chives, capers, and lemon rind in a small bowl. Spread and divide the cheese mixture on 4 bread slices. Top with spinach, onion slices, and smoked salmon.
3. Cover with remaining bread slices.
4. Grill the sandwiches until golden and grill marks form on both sides.
5. Transfer to a serving dish.
6. Serve and enjoy.

Nutrition: Calories: 261, Fat 9.9 g, Carbohydrates 22.9 g, Protein 19.9 g, Sodium - 1226 mg

75. Salmon Feta and Pesto Wrap

Preparation Time: 15 minutes
Cooking Time: 10 minutes
Servings: 4
Ingredients:

- 8 ounces (250 g) smoked salmon fillet, thinly sliced - 1 cup (150 g) feta cheese

- 8 (15 g) Romaine lettuce leaves
- 4 (6-inch) pita bread
- 1/4 cup (60 g) basil pesto sauce

Directions:

1. Place 1 pita bread on a plate. Top with lettuce, salmon, feta cheese, and pesto sauce. Fold or roll to enclose filling. Repeat procedure for the remaining ingredients.
2. Serve and enjoy.

Nutrition: Calories: 379, Fat 17.7 g, Carbohydrates: 36.6 g, Protein: 18.4 g, Sodium: 554 mg

76. Salmon Cream Cheese and Onion on Bagel

Preparation Time: 15 minutes
Cooking Time: 10 minutes
Servings: 4
Ingredients:

- 8 ounces (250 g) smoked salmon fillet, thinly sliced
- 1/2 cup (125 g) cream cheese
- 1 medium (110 g) onion, thinly sliced
- 4 bagels (about 80 g each), split
- 2 tablespoons (7 g) fresh parsley, chopped - Freshly ground black pepper, to taste

Directions:

1. Spread the cream cheese on each bottom's half of bagels. Top with salmon and onion, season with pepper, sprinkle with parsley, and then cover with bagel tops.
2. Serve and enjoy.

Nutrition: Calories: 309, Fat 14.1 g, Carbohydrates 32.0 g, Protein 14.7 g, Sodium 571 mg

77. Greek Baklava

Preparation Time: 20 minutes
Cooking Time: 20 minutes
Servings: 18
Ingredients:

- 1 (16 oz.) package phyllo dough
- 1 lb. chopped nuts
- 1 cup butter
- 1 teaspoon ground cinnamon
- 1 cup water
- 1 cup white sugar
- 1 teaspoon vanilla extract
- 1/2 cup honey

Directions:

1. Preheat the oven to 175°C or 350°F. Spread butter on the sides and bottom of a 9x13-in pan.
2. Chop the nuts, then mix with cinnamon; set it aside. Unfurl the phyllo dough, then halve the whole stack to fit the pan. Use a damp cloth to cover the phyllo to prevent drying as you proceed. Put two phyllo sheets in the pan, then butter well. Repeat to make eight layered phyllo sheets. Scatter 2-3 tablespoons Nut mixture over the sheets, place two more phyllo sheets on top, butter, and then sprinkle with nuts. Layer as you go. The final layer should be six to eight phyllo sheets deep.
3. Make square or diamond shapes with a sharp knife up to the bottom of the pan. You can slice into four long rows for diagonal shapes. Bake until crisp and golden for 40 minutes.
4. Meanwhile, boil water and sugar until the sugar melts to make the sauce; mix in honey and vanilla. Let it simmer for 20 minutes.
5. Take the baklava out of the oven, then drizzle with sauce right away; cool. Serve the baklava in cupcake papers. You can also freeze them without cover. The baklava will turn soggy when wrapped.

Nutrition: Calories: 393, Total Carbohydrates: 37.5 g, Cholesterol: 27 mg, Total Fat: 25.9 g, Protein: 6.1 g, Sodium: 196 mg

78. Glazed Bananas in Phyllo Nut Cups

Preparation Time: 30 minutes
Cooking Time: 40 minutes
Servings: 6
Ingredients:
- 3/4 cup shelled pistachios
- 1/2 cup sugar
- 1 teaspoon ground cinnamon
- 4 sheets phyllo dough, (14x9 inches)
- 1/4 cup butter, melted

Sauce:
- 3/4 cup butter, cubed
- 3/4 cup packed brown sugar
- 3 medium firm bananas, sliced
- 1/4 teaspoon ground cinnamon
- 3 to 4 cups vanilla ice cream

Directions:
1. Finely chop sugar and pistachios in a food processor; move to a bowl, then mix in cinnamon. Slice each phyllo sheet into 6 four-inch squares, get rid of the trimmings. Pile the squares, then use plastic wrap to cover.
2. Slather melted butter on each square one at a time, then scatter a heaping tablespoonful of pistachio mixture. Pile three squares; flip each at an angle to misalign the corners.
3. Force each stack on the sides and bottom of an oiled eight-oz. custard cup. Bake for 15-20 minutes in a 350°F oven until golden; cool for 5 minutes. Move to a wire rack to completely cool.
4. Melt and boil brown sugar and butter in a saucepan to make the sauce; lower heat.
5. Mix in cinnamon and bananas gently; heat completely. Put ice cream in the phyllo cups until full, then put banana sauce on top. Serve right away.

Nutrition: Calories: 735, Total Carbohydrates: 82 g, Cholesterol: 111 mg, Total Fat: 45 g, Fiber: 3 g, Protein: 7 g, Sodium: 468 mg

79. Salmon Apple Salad Sandwich

Preparation Time: 15 minutes
Cooking Time: 10 minutes
Servings: 4
Ingredients:
- 4 ounces (125 g) canned pink salmon, drained and flaked
- 1 medium (180 g) red apple, cored and diced
- 1 celery stalk (about 60 g), chopped
- 1 shallot (about 40 g), finely chopped
- 1/3 cup (85 g) light mayonnaise
- 8 slices whole-grain bread (about 30 g each), toasted
- 8 (15 g) Romaine lettuce leaves
- Salt and freshly ground black pepper

Directions:
1. Combine the salmon, apple, celery, shallot, and mayonnaise in a mixing bowl. Season with salt and pepper.
2. Place 1 slice of bread on a plate, top with lettuce and salmon salad, and then covers with another slice of bread. Repeat the procedure for the remaining ingredients.
3. Serve and enjoy.

Nutrition: Calories: 315, Fat 11.3 g, Carbohydrates 40.4 g, Protein 15.1 g, Sodium 469 mg

80. Smoked Salmon and Cheese on Rye Bread

Preparation Time: 15 minutes
Cooking Time: 10 minutes
Servings: 4
Ingredients:
- 8 ounces (250 g) smoked salmon, thinly sliced
- 1/3 cup (85 g) mayonnaise
- 2 tablespoons (30 ml) lemon juice
- 1 tablespoon (15 g) Dijon mustard
- 1 teaspoon (3 g) garlic, minced
- 4 slices cheddar cheese (about 2 oz. or 30 g each)
- 8 slices rye bread (about 2 oz. or 30 g each)

- 8 (15 g) Romaine lettuce leaves
- Salt and freshly ground black pepper

Directions:

1. Mix together the mayonnaise, lemon juice, mustard, and garlic in a small bowl. Flavor with salt and pepper and set aside.
2. Spread dressing on 4 bread slices. Top with lettuce, salmon, and cheese. Cover with remaining rye bread slices.
3. Serve and enjoy.

Nutrition: Calories: 365, Fat: 16.6 g, Carbohydrates: 31.6 g, Protein: 18.8 g, Sodium: 951 mg

CHAPTER 8:

Soups And Salads Recipes

81. Cream of Potato Soup

Preparation Time: 1 hour
Cooking Time: 5 hours
Servings: 6
Ingredients:

- ½ cup (120 ml) Carb Countdown dairy beverage
- ½ cup (120 ml) heavy cream
- ½ cup (50 g) Ketone's mix
- ½ cup (50 g) chopped onion
- ½ head cauliflower, chunked
- 1 quart (960 ml) chicken broth Guar or xanthan (optional)
- 5 scallions, sliced

Direction:

1. In your slow cooker, put cauliflower, broth, and onion. Close and set the slow cooker to low and run for about 4 to 5 hours.
2. We used a hand mixer to purée the soup right in the slow cooker; so alternatively, you should pass the cauliflower and onion into your blender or food processor, along with 1 cup (240 ml) of broth. Purée until entirely smooth, and then blend into the Ketatoes, either way. If the cauliflower has been withdrawn from the slow cooker for purée, add the purée back in and whisk it back into the remaining broth.
3. Stir in the Carb Countdown and cream. If you believe it needs it, thicken it a little more with guar or xanthan.

4. To taste, apply salt and pepper and mix in the sliced scallions. Serve instantly hot or chill and serve as Vichyssoise.

Nutrition: Calories 49 Protein 12 g, Carbohydrates 13 g, Dietary Fiber 6 g, Usable Carbs 7 g

82. Swiss Cheese and Broccoli Soup

Preparation Time: 10 minutes
Cooking Time: 1 hour
Servings: 6-8
Ingredients:

- Guar or xanthan
- 2 cups (360 g) shredded Swiss cheese
- 1 cup (240 ml) heavy cream
- 1 cup (500 ml) Carb Countdown dairy beverage
- 10 ounces (560 g) frozen chopped broccoli, thawed
- 28 ounces (400 ml) chicken broth
- 1 tablespoon (28 g) butter
- 1 tablespoon (420 g) minced onion

Direction:

1. Sauté the onion into the butter in a big, heavy-bottomed saucepan until it is transparent. Put the broccoli and the chicken broth in the pan and cook for 20 to 30 minutes until the broccoli is very soft.
2. Mix in the Countdown Carb and some cream. Brought it to a simmer again.

3. Now mix in the cheese, a little at a time, allowing each batch to melt before adding any more. Thicken a bit with guar or xanthan when all the cheese is melted if you think it needs it, and then serve.

Nutrition: Protein 20 g, Carbohydrates 7 g, Dietary Fiber 2 g, Usable Carbs 5 g Calories 365

83. Tavern Soup

Preparation Time: 8-10 hours
Cooking Time: 1 hour
Servings: 8
Ingredients:
- 1/2 teaspoon hot pepper sauce
- 1 teaspoon salt or Vega-Sal
- 24 ounces (500 ml) light beer
- 1 pound (900 g) sharp cheddar cheese, shredded
- 1 teaspoon pepper
- 1/2 cup (30.4 g) chopped fresh parsley
- 1/2 cup (60 g) shredded carrot
- 1/2 cup (60 g) finely diced green bell pepper
- 1/2 cup (60 g) finely diced celery
- Guar or xanthan
- quarts (3 L) chicken broth

Direction:
1. Mix in your slow cooker celery, broth, green pepper, onion, parsley, and pepper. Close the slow cooker, set it to low, and let it steam for 6 to 8 hours (it won't hurt for a little longer).
2. To purée the vegetables in the slow cooker right there until the time is up, use a handheld blender to scoop them out with a slotted spoon, and purée them in the blender, and add them to the slow cooker.
3. Now swirl a little at a time in the cheese until it's all melted. Add the hot pepper sauce, beer, salt, or Vega-Sal, and mix until the foaming ends.
4. To thicken the broth, use guar or xanthan until it is about sour cream thickness. Cover the pot again, turn it too heavy, and simmer for an additional 20 minutes before eating.

Nutrition: Protein 18 g, Carbohydrates 3 g, Usable Carbs 3 g Calories 385

84. Broccoli Blue Cheese Soup
Preparation Time: 1 hour
Cooking Time: 1 hour
Servings: 6-8
Ingredients:
- 1 cup (120 g) crumbled blue cheese
- ¼ cup (60 ml) heavy cream
- 1 pound (455 g) frozen broccoli, thawed
- 1½ quarts (1.4 L) chicken broth
- 1 cup (240 ml) Carb Countdown dairy beverage
- 1 turnip, peeled and diced
- 1 tablespoon (28 g) butter
- 1 cup (160 g) chopped onion

Direction:
1. Sauté the onion in the butter over medium-low heat in a broad saucepan — you don't want it to tan.
2. Until the onion is soft and transparent, add the chicken broth and the turnip to your pot. Brought the blend to a boil and let it cook for 20 to 30 minutes over medium to low heat.
3. Put in the thawed broccoli and cook for the next 20 minutes.
4. With a slotted spoon, scoop the vegetables out and put them in a Mixer. A ladleful broth is added to the

mix, and the blender runs until the vegetables are finely puréed. Shift the mixture back to your pot. Stir in the Countdown Carbohydrate, the heavy cream, and the blue cheese. Simmer for the next 5 to 10 minutes stirring periodically, and serve.

Nutrition: Protein 14 g, Carbohydrate 9 g, Dietary Fiber 3 g, Usable Carbs 6 g Calories 109

85. Cream of Mushroom Soup

Preparation Time: 6 hours
Cooking Time: 1 1/2 hour
Servings: 5-7
Ingredients:

- ½ cup (120 g) light sour cream
- ½ cup (120 ml) heavy cream
- 1 quart (960 ml) chicken broth
- tablespoons (28 g) butter
- ¼ cup (25 g) chopped onion
- 8 ounces (225 g) mushrooms, sliced
- Guar or xanthan (optional)

Direction:

1. Sauté the onion and mushrooms in the butter in a large, heavy skillet until the mushrooms soften and change color. Move them to a slow cooker. Put in the broth. Cover your slow cooker, set it low and let it cook for 5 to 6 hours.
2. Scrape out the vegetables with a slotted spoon when the time is up, and stick them in your blender or any food processor.
3. Add in enough broth to help them quickly process and finely purée them. Put the puréed vegetables back into the slow cooker, using a rubber scraper to clean out any last piece. Now whisk in the heavy cream and sour cream and apply to taste the salt and pepper. If you think it deserves it, thicken the sauce a little with guar or xanthan. Serve asp.

Nutrition: Protein 6 g, Carbohydrates 5 g, Dietary Fiber 1 g, Usable Carbs 4 g Calories 164

86. Olive Soup

Preparation Time: 20 minutes
Cooking Time: 1 hour
Servings: 6-8
Ingredients:

- Pepper
- Salt or Vega-Sal
- ¼ cup (60 ml) dry sherry
- ½ teaspoon guar or xanthan
- 1 cup (100 g) minced black olives (You can buy cans of minced black olives.)
- 1 cup (240 ml) heavy cream
- cups (0.9 L) chicken broth, divided

Direction:

1. Put 1/2 cup (120 ml) of the chicken broth with the guar gum in the blender and pulse for a few moments. Pour the remainder of the stock and the olives into a saucepan and add the blended mixture.
2. Heat and then whisk in the milk before simmering. Return to a boil, stir in the sherry, then apply salt and pepper to taste.

Nutrition: Carbohydrates 3,5 g, Fiber 1,1 g, Usable Carbs 2,5 g, Protein 2,5 g Calories 127

87. Salmon Soup

Preparation Time: 15 minutes
Cooking Time: 21 minutes
Servings: 4
Ingredients:

- 1 pound salmon fillets
- 1 tablespoon olive oil
- 1 cup carrots, peeled and chopped
- ½ cup celery stalk, chopped ¼ cup yellow onion, chopped 1 cup cauliflower, chopped 3 cups chicken broth

- Salt and ground black pepper, as required ¼ cup fresh parsley, chopped

Direction:

1. Arrange a steamer trivet in the lower part of the Instant Pot and pour 1 cup of water.
2. Place the salmon fillets on top of the trivet in a single layer.
3. Secure the lid and switch to the role of "Seal."
4. Cook on "Manual" with "High Pressure" for about 7-8 minutes.
5. Press "Cancel" and carefully do a "Quick" release.
6. Remove the lid and transfer the salmon onto a plate. Cut the salmon into bite-sized pieces.
7. Remove the water and trivet from Instant Pot.
8. Add the oil in Instant Pot and select "Sauté." Then add the carrot, celery and onion and cook for about 5 minutes or until browned completely.
9. Press "Cancel" and stir in the cauliflower and broth.
10. Secure the lid and switch to the role of "Seal."
11. Cook on "Manual" with "High Pressure" for about 8 minutes.
12. Press "Cancel" and do a "Natural" release.
13. Remove the lid and stir in salmon pieces and black pepper until well combined.
14. Serve immediately with the garnishing of parsley.

Nutrition: Calories: 233, Fat: 11.6 g, Protein: 26.7 g, Carbs: 6 g, Net Carbs: 4.2 g, Fiber: 1.8 g

88. Tomato Cucumber Avocado Salad

Preparation Time: 15 minutes
Cooking Time: 0 minutes
Servings: 4
Ingredients:

- 12 oz cherry tomatoes, cut in half
- 5 small cucumbers, chopped
- 3 small avocados, chopped
- ½ teaspoon ground black pepper
- 2 tablespoons olive oil
- 2 tablespoons fresh lemon juice
- ¼ cup fresh cilantro, chopped
- 1 teaspoon sea salt

Directions:

1. Add cherry tomatoes, cucumbers, avocados, and cilantro into the large mixing bowl and mix well.
2. Mix together olive oil, lemon juice, black pepper, and salt and pour over salad.
3. Toss well and serve immediately.

Nutrition: Calories 442, Fat 31 g, Carbs 30.3 g, Sugar 4 g, Protein 2 g, Cholesterol 0 mg

89. Creamy Cauliflower Soup

Preparation Time: 15 minutes
Cooking Time: 15 minutes
Servings: 6
Ingredients:

- 5 cups cauliflower rice
- 8 oz cheddar cheese, grated
- 2 cups unsweetened almond milk
- 2 cups vegetable stock
- 2 tablespoons water
- 1 small onion, chopped
- 2 garlic cloves, minced
- 1 tablespoon olive oil
- Pepper
- Salt

Directions:

1. Heat olive oil in a large stockpot over medium heat.
2. Add onion and garlic and cook for 1-2 minutes.
3. Add cauliflower rice and water. Cover and cook for 5-7 minutes.
4. Now add vegetable stock and almond milk and stir well. Bring to boil.
5. Turn heat to low and simmer for 5 minutes.
6. Turn off the heat. Slowly add cheddar cheese and stir until smooth.
7. Season soup with pepper and salt.
8. Stir well and serve hot.

Nutrition: Calories 214, Fat 15 g, Carbs 3 g, Sugar 3 g, Protein 16 g, Cholesterol 40 mg

90. Chicken Zucchini Noodles
Preparation Time: 20 minutes
Cooking Time: 5 minutes
Servings: 2
Ingredients:
- 1 large zucchini, spiralized
- 1 chicken breast, skinless & boneless
- ½ tbsp jalapeno, minced
- 2 garlic cloves, minced
- ½ teaspoon ginger, minced
- ½ tbsp fish sauce
- 2 tablespoons coconut cream
- ½ tbsp honey - ½ lime juice
- 1 tablespoon peanut butter
- 1 carrot, chopped
- 2 tablespoons cashews, chopped
- ¼ cup fresh cilantro, chopped
- 1 tablespoon olive oil
- Pepper - Salt

Directions:
1. Heat olive oil in a pan over medium-high heat.
2. Season chicken breast with pepper and salt. Once the oil is hot, add chicken breast into the pan and cook for 3-4 minutes per side or until cooked.
3. Remove chicken breast from pan. Shred chicken breast with a fork and set aside. In a small bowl, mix together peanut butter, jalapeno, garlic, ginger, fish sauce, coconut cream, honey, and lime juice. Set aside.
4. In a large mixing bowl, combine together spiralized zucchini, carrots, cashews, cilantro, and shredded chicken. Pour peanut butter mixture over zucchini noodles and toss to combine.
5. Serve immediately and enjoy.

Nutrition: Calories 353, Fat 21 g, Carbs 20.5 g, Sugar 8 g, Protein 25 g, Cholesterol 54 mg

91. Healthy Broccoli Salad
Preparation Time: 25 minutes
Cooking Time: 0 minutes
Servings: 6
Ingredients:
- 3 cups broccoli, chopped
- 1 tablespoon apple cider vinegar
- ½ cup Greek yogurt
- 2 tablespoons sunflower seeds
- 3 bacon slices, cooked and chopped
- 1/3 cup onion, sliced
- ¼ teaspoon stevia

Directions:
1. In a mixing bowl, mix together broccoli, onion, and bacon.
2. In a small bowl, mix together yogurt, vinegar, and stevia and pour over broccoli mixture. Stir to combine.
3. Sprinkle sunflower seeds on top of the salad.
4. Store salad in the refrigerator for 30 minutes.
5. Serve and enjoy.

Nutrition: Calories 90, Fat 9 g, Carbs 4 g, Sugar 5 g, Protein 2 g, Cholesterol 12 mg

92. Chicken Casserole
Preparation Time: 15 minutes
Cooking Time: 40 minutes
Servings: 4
Ingredients:
- 1 lb. cooked chicken, shredded
- ¼ cup Greek yogurt
- 1 cup cheddar cheese, shredded
- ½ cup salsa
- 4 oz cream cheese, softened
- 4 cups cauliflower florets
- 1/8 teaspoons black pepper
- ½ teaspoon kosher salt

Directions:
1. Add cauliflower florets into the microwave-safe dish and cook for 10 minutes or until tender.
2. Add cream cheese and microwave for 30 seconds more. Stir well.
3. Add chicken, yogurt, cheddar cheese, salsa, pepper, and salt, and stir everything well.
4. Preheat the oven to 375°F.
5. Bake in preheated oven for 20 minutes.
6. Serve hot and enjoy.

Nutrition: Calories 429, Fat 23 g, Carbs 6 g, Sugar 7 g, Protein 44 g, Cholesterol 149 mg

93. Instant Pot Chipotle Chicken & Cauliflower Rice Bowls
Preparation Time: 10 minutes
Cooking Time: 20 minutes
Servings: 4
Ingredients:
- 1/3 cup salsa
- 1 quantity of 14.5 oz. of can fire-roasted diced tomatoes
- 1 canned chipotle pepper + 1 teaspoon sauce
- ½ teaspoon dried oregano
- 1 teaspoon cumin
- 1 ½ lb. boneless, skinless chicken breast
- ¼ teaspoon salt
- 1 cup of reduced-fat shredded Mexican cheese blend
- 4 cups of frozen riced cauliflower
- ½ medium-sized avocado, sliced

Directions:
1. Combine the first ingredients in a blender and blend until they become smooth
2. Place the chicken in its pot and pour the sauce over it. Cover the lid and close the pressure valve. Put it on high heat for 20 minutes. Let the pressure release on its own before opening. Remove the piece and the chicken and then add it back to the sauce.
3. Microwave the riced cauliflower according to the directions on the package
4. Before you serve, divide the riced cauliflower, cheese, avocado, and chicken equally among the 4 bowls.

Nutrition: Calories: 287 Protein: 35 g, Carbohydrates: 19 g, Fat: 12 g

94. Baked Cod and Vegetables
Preparation Time: 15 minutes
Cooking Time: 15 minutes
Servings: 4
Ingredients:
- 1 lb. cod fillet
- 8 oz asparagus, chopped
- 3 cups broccoli, chopped

- ¼ cup parsley, minced
- ½ teaspoon lemon pepper seasoning
- ½ teaspoon paprika
- ¼ cup olive oil
- ¼ cup lemon juice
- 1 teaspoon salt

Directions:
1. Preheat oven to 400°F. Line a baking sheet with parchment paper and set it aside.
2. In a small bowl, combine the lemon juice, paprika, olive oil, pepper spices, and salt.
3. Place the fish fillets in the center of the greaseproof paper. Arrange the broccoli and asparagus around the fish fillets.
4. Pour lemon juice mixture over the fish fillets and top with parsley.
5. Bake in preheated oven for 13-15 minutes.
6. Serve and enjoy.

Nutrition: Calories 240, Fat 11 g, Carbs 6 g, Sugar 6 g, Protein 27 g, Cholesterol 56 mg

95. Sheet Pan Chicken Fajita Lettuce Wraps
Preparation Time: 15 minutes
Cooking Time: 30 minutes
Servings: 2
Ingredients:
- 1 lb. chicken breast, thinly sliced into strips
- 2 teaspoon of olive oil
- 2 bell peppers, thinly sliced into strips
- 2 teaspoon of fajita seasoning
- 6 leaves from a romaine heart
- Juice of half a lime
- ¼ cup plain of non-fat Greek yogurt

Directions:
1. Preheat your oven to about 400°F
2. Combine all of the ingredients except for lettuce in a large plastic bag that can be resealed. Mix very well to coat vegetables and chicken with oil and seasoning evenly.
3. Spread the contents of the bag evenly on a foil-lined baking sheet. Bake it for

about 25-30 minutes, until the chicken is thoroughly cooked.

4. Serve on lettuce leaves and topped with Greek yogurt if you like

Nutrition: Calories: 387, Fat: 6 g, Carbohydrates: 14 g, Protein: 18 g

96. Tomato Braised Cauliflower with Chicken

Preparation Time: 10 minutes
Cooking Time: 30 minutes
Servings: 4
Ingredients:

- 4 garlic cloves, sliced
- 3 scallions, to be trimmed and cut into 1-inch pieces
- ¼ teaspoon dried oregano
- ¼ teaspoon crushed red pepper flakes
- 4 ½ cups cauliflower
- 1 ½ cups diced canned tomatoes
- 1 cup fresh basil, gently torn
- ½ teaspoon each of pepper and salt, divided
- 1 ½ teaspoon olive oil
- 1 ½ lb. boneless, skinless chicken breasts

Directions:

1. Get a saucepan and combine the garlic, scallions, oregano, crushed red pepper, cauliflower, and tomato, and add ¼ cup of water. Get everything boil together, add ¼ teaspoon of pepper and salt for seasoning, and cover the pot with a lid. Let it simmer for 10 minutes and stir as often as possible until you observe that the cauliflower is tender. Now, wrap up the seasoning with the remaining ¼ teaspoon of pepper and salt.
2. Toss the chicken breast with oil, olive preferably, and let it roast in the oven with the heat of 4500F for 20 minutes and an internal temperature of 165°F. Allow the chicken to rest for like 10 minutes.
3. Now slice the chicken, and serve on a bed of tomato braised cauliflower.

Nutrition: Calories: 290, Fat: 10 g, Carbohydrates: 13 g, Protein: 38 g

97. Broccoli Cheddar Breakfast Bake

Preparation Time: 10 minutes
Cooking Time: 45 minutes
Servings: 4
Ingredients:

- 9 eggs - 6 cups small broccoli florets
- ¼ teaspoon salt
- 1 cup unsweetened almond milk
- ¼ teaspoon cayenne pepper
- ¼ teaspoon ground pepper
- Cooking spray
- 4 oz. of shredded, reduced-fat cheddar

Directions:

1. Preheat your oven to about 375°F.
2. In your large microwave-safe, add broccoli and 2 to 3 tablespoons of water. Microwave on high heat for 4 minutes or until it becomes tender. Now transfer the broccoli to a colander to drain excess liquid. Get a medium-sized bowl and whisk the milk, eggs, and seasonings together. Set the broccoli neatly on the bottom of a lightly greased 13 x 9-inch baking dish. Sprinkle the cheese gently on the broccoli and pour the egg mixture on top of it. Bake for about 45 minutes or until the center is set and the top forms a light brown crust.

Nutrition: Calories: 290, Protein: 25 g, Carbohydrates: 8 g, Fat: 18 g

98. Taco Zucchini Boats

Preparation Time: 20 minutes
Cooking Time: 55 minutes
Servings: 4
Ingredients:

- 4 medium zucchinis, cut in half lengthwise

- ¼ cup fresh cilantro, chopped
- ½ cup cheddar cheese, shredded
- ¼ cup water - 4 oz tomato sauce
- 2 tablespoons bell pepper, mined
- ½ small onion, minced
- ½ teaspoon oregano
- 1 teaspoon paprika
- 1 teaspoon chili powder
- 1 teaspoon cumin
- 1 teaspoon garlic powder
- 1 lb. lean ground turkey
- ½ cup salsa - 1 teaspoon kosher salt

Directions:
1. Preheat the oven to 400°F.
2. Add ¼ cup of salsa to the bottom of the baking dish.
3. Using a spoon, hollow out the center of the zucchini halves.
4. Chop the scooped-out flesh of zucchini and set aside ¾ of a cup of chopped flesh.
5. Add zucchini halves in the boiling water and cook for 1 minute. Remove zucchini halves from water.
6. Add ground turkey to a large pan and cook until meat is no longer pink. Add spices and mix well.
7. Add reserved zucchini flesh, water, tomato sauce, bell pepper, and onion. Stir well and cover, simmer over low heat for 20 minutes.
8. Stuff zucchini boats with taco meat and top each with one tablespoon of shredded cheddar cheese.
9. Place zucchini boats in the baking dish. Cover dish with foil and bake in preheated oven for 35 minutes.
10. Top with remaining salsa and chopped cilantro. Serve and enjoy.

Nutrition: Calories 297, Fat 17 g, Carbs 12 g, Sugar 3 g, Protein 30.2 g, Cholesterol 96 mg

99. Blueberry Cantaloupe Avocado Salad
Preparation Time: 5 minutes
Cooking Time: 0 minutes
Servings: 2
Ingredients:
- 1 diced cantaloupe

- 2–3 chopped avocados
- 1 package of blueberries
- ¼ cup olive oil
- 1/8 cup balsamic vinegar

Directions:
1. Mix all ingredients.

Nutrition: Calories: 406, Protein: 9 g, Carbohydrates: 32 g, Fat: 5 g

100. Beet Salad (from Israel)
Preparation Time: 5 minutes
Cooking Time: 0 minutes
Servings: 2
Ingredients:
- 2–3 fresh, raw beets grated or shredded in food processor
- 3 tablespoons olive oil
- 2 tablespoons balsamic vinegar
- ¼ teaspoon salt
- 1/3 teaspoon cumin
- Dash stevia powder or liquid
- Dash pepper

Directions:
1. Mix all ingredients together for the best raw beet salad.

Nutrition: Calories: 156, Protein: 8 g, Carbohydrates: 40 g, Fat: 5 g

101. Broccoli Salad
Preparation Time: 5 minutes
Cooking Time: 0 minutes
Servings: 2
Ingredients:
- 1 head broccoli, chopped
- 2–3 slices of fried bacon, crumbled
- 1 diced green onion
- ½ cup raisins or craisins
- ½–1 cup of chopped pecans
- ¾ cup sunflower seeds
- ½ cup of pomegranate

Dressing:
- 1 cup organic mayonnaise
- ¼ cup baking stevia
- 2 teaspoons white vinegar

Directions:
1. Mix all ingredients together. Mix dressing and fold into salad.

Nutrition: Calories: 239, Protein: 10 g, Carbohydrates: 33 g, Fat: 2 g

102. Rosemary Garlic Potatoes

Preparation Time: 5 minutes
Cooking Time: 30 minutes
Servings: 2
Ingredients:
- 5 red new potatoes, chopped
- ¼ cup olive oil
- 2–3 cloves of minced garlic
- 1 tablespoon rosemary

Directions:
1. Preheat oven to 425°F.
2. Stir all ingredients together in a bowl. Pour onto a baking sheet and bake for 30 minutes.

Nutrition: Calories: 176, Protein: 5 g, Carbohydrates: 30 g, Fat: 2 g

103. Sweet and Sour Cabbage

Preparation Time: 5 minutes
Cooking Time: 15 minutes
Servings: 2
Ingredients:
- 1 tablespoon honey or maple syrup
- 1 teaspoon baking stevia
- 2 tablespoons water
- 1 tablespoon olive oil
- ¼ teaspoon caraway seeds
- ¼ teaspoon salt
- 1/8 teaspoon pepper
- 2 cups chopped red cabbage
- 1 diced apple

Directions:
1. Cook all ingredients in a covered saucepan on the stove for 15 minutes.

Nutrition: Calories: 170, Protein: 17 g, Carbohydrates: 20 g, Fat: 8 g

104. Barley and Lentil Salad

Preparation Time: 5 minutes
Cooking Time: 0 minutes
Servings: 2
Ingredients:
- 1 head romaine lettuce
- ¾ cup cooked barley
- 2 cups cooked lentils
- 1 diced carrot
- ¼ chopped red onion
- ¼ cup olives
- ½ chopped cucumber
- 3 tablespoons olive oil
- 2 tablespoons fresh lemon juice

Directions:
1. Mix all ingredients together. Add kosher salt and black pepper to taste.

Nutrition: Calories: 213, Protein: 21 g, Carbohydrates: 6 g, Fat: 9 g

105. Taste of Normandy Salad

Preparation Time: 25 minutes
Cooking Time: 5 minutes
Servings: 4 to 6
Ingredients:
For the walnuts:
- 2 tablespoons butter
- ¼ cup sugar or honey
- 1 cup walnut piece
- ½ teaspoon kosher salt

For the dressing
- 3 tablespoons extra-virgin olive oil
- 1½ tablespoons champagne vinegar
- 1½ tablespoons Dijon mustard
- ¼ teaspoon kosher salt

For the salad:
- 1 head red leaf lettuce, torn into pieces
- 3 heads endive, ends trimmed and leaves separated
- 2 apples, cored and cut into thin wedges
- 1 (8-ounce) Camembert wheel, cut into thin wedges

Directions:
1. To make the walnuts
2. In a skillet over medium-high heat, melt the butter. Stir in the sugar and cook until it dissolves. Add the walnuts and cook for about 5 minutes, stirring,

until toasty. Season with salt and transfer to a plate to cool.

3. To make the dressing
4. In a large bowl, whisk the oil, vinegar, mustard, and salt until combined.
5. To make the salad Add the lettuce and endive to the bowl with the dressing and toss to coat. Transfer to a serving platter. Decoratively arrange the apple and Camembert wedges over the lettuce and scatter the walnuts on top. Serve immediately.

Nutrition: Calories: 699; Total fat: 52 g; Total carbs: 44 g; Cholesterol: 60 mg; Fiber: 17 g, Protein: 23 g; Sodium: 1170 mg

106. Norwegian Niçoise Salad: Smoked Salmon, Cucumber, Egg, and Asparagus

Preparation Time: 20 minutes
Cooking Time: 5 minutes
Servings: 4
Ingredients:

For the vinaigrette

- 3 tablespoons walnut oil
- 2 tablespoons champagne vinegar
- 1 tablespoon chopped fresh dill
- ½ teaspoon kosher salt
- ¼ teaspoon ground mustard
- Freshly ground black pepper

For the salad:

- Handful green beans, trimmed
- 1 (3- to 4-ounce) package spring greens
- 12 spears pickled asparagus
- 4 large soft-boiled eggs, halved
- 8 ounces smoked salmon, thinly sliced
- 1 cucumber, thinly sliced
- 1 lemon, quartered

Directions:

1. To make the dressing
2. In a small bowl, whisk the oil, vinegar, dill, salt, ground mustard, and a few grinds of pepper until emulsified. Set aside.
3. To make the salad
4. Start by blanching the green beans: Bring a pot of salted water to a boil. Drop in the beans. Cook for 1 to 2

minutes until they turn bright green, then immediately drain and rinse under cold water. Set aside.

5. Divide the spring greens among 4 plates. Toss each serving with dressing to taste. Arrange 3 asparagus spears, 1 egg, 2 ounces of salmon, one-fourth of the cucumber slices, and a lemon wedge on each plate. Serve immediately.

Nutrition: Calories: 257; Total fat: 18 g; Total carbs: 6 g; Cholesterol: 199 mg; Fiber: 2 g, Protein: 19 g; Sodium: 603 mg

107. Loaded Caesar Salad with Crunchy Chickpeas

Preparation Time: 5 minutes
Cooking Time: 20 minutes
Servings: 6
Ingredients:

For the chickpeas:

- 2 (15-ounce) cans chickpeas, drained and rinsed
- 2 tablespoons extra-virgin olive oil
- 1 teaspoon kosher salt
- 1 teaspoon garlic powder
- 1 teaspoon onion powder
- 1 teaspoon dried oregano

For the dressing:

- ½ cup mayonnaise
- 2 tablespoons grated Parmesan cheese
- 2 tablespoons freshly squeezed lemon juice
- 1 clove garlic, peeled and smashed
- 1 teaspoon Dijon mustard
- ½ tablespoon Worcestershire sauce
- ½ tablespoon anchovy paste

For the salad:

- 3 heads romaine lettuce, cut into bite-size pieces

Directions:

To make the chickpeas:

1. Preheat the oven to 450°F. Line a baking sheet with parchment paper.
2. In a medium bowl, toss together the chickpeas, oil, salt, garlic powder, onion powder, and oregano. Scatter the coated chickpeas on the prepared baking sheet. Roast for about 20

minutes, tossing occasionally, until the chickpeas are golden and have a bit of crunch.

To make the dressing:

1. In a small bowl, whisk the mayonnaise, Parmesan, lemon juice, garlic, mustard, Worcestershire sauce, and anchovy paste until combined.
2. To make the salad:
3. In a large bowl, combine the lettuce and dressing. Toss to coat. Top with the roasted chickpeas and serve.

Nutrition: Calories: 367; Total fat: 22 g; Total carbs: 35 g; Cholesterol: 9 mg; Fiber: 13 g, Protein: 12 g; Sodium: 407 mg

108. Coleslaw Worth a Second Helping

Preparation Time: 20 minutes
Cooking Time: 10 minutes
Servings: 6
Ingredients:

- 5 cups shredded cabbage
- 2 carrots, shredded
- 1/3 cup chopped fresh flat-leaf parsley
- ½ cup mayonnaise
- ½ cup sour cream
- 3 tablespoons apple cider vinegar
- 1 teaspoon kosher salt
- ½ teaspoon celery seed

Directions:

1. In a large bowl, combine the cabbage, carrots, and parsley.
2. In a small bowl, whisk the mayonnaise, sour cream, vinegar, salt, and celery seed until smooth. Pour the dressing over the vegetables and toss until coated. Transfer to a serving bowl and chill until ready to serve.

Nutrition: Calories: 192; Total fat: 18 g; Total carbs: 7 g; Cholesterol: 18 mg; Fiber: 3 g, Protein: 2 g; Sodium: 543 mg

109. Romaine Lettuce and Radicchios Mix

Preparation Time: 6 minutes
Cooking Time: 0 minutes
Servings: 4
Ingredients:

- 2 tablespoons olive oil
- A pinch of salt and black pepper
- 2 spring onions, chopped
- 3 tablespoons Dijon mustard
- Juice of 1 lime
- ½ cup basil, chopped
- 4 cups romaine lettuce heads, chopped
- 3 radicchios, sliced

Directions:

1. In a salad bowl, mix the lettuce with the spring onions and the other ingredients, toss and serve.

Nutrition: Calories: 87, Fats: 2 g, Fiber: 1 g, Carbs: 1 g, Protein: 2 g

110. Greek Salad

Preparation Time: 15 minutes
Cooking Time: 15 minutes
Servings: 5
Ingredients:

For Dressing:

- ½ teaspoon black pepper
- ¼ teaspoon salt
- ½ teaspoon oregano
- 1 tablespoon garlic powder
- 2 tablespoons Balsamic
- 1/3 cup olive oil

For Salad:

- ½ cup sliced black olives
- ½ cup chopped parsley, fresh
- 1 small red onion, thin-sliced
- 1 cup cherry tomatoes, sliced
- 1 bell pepper, yellow, chunked
- 1 cucumber, peeled, quarter and slice
- 4 cups chopped romaine lettuce
- ½ teaspoon salt
- 2 tablespoons olive oil

Directions:

1. In a small bowl, blend all of the ingredients for the dressing and let this set in the refrigerator while you make the salad.
2. To assemble the salad, mix together all the ingredients in a large-sized bowl and toss the veggies gently but thoroughly to mix.
3. Serve the salad with the dressing in amounts as desired

Nutrition: Calories: 234, Fat: 16.1 g, Protein: 5 g, Carbs: 48 g

111. Asparagus and Smoked Salmon Salad

Preparation Time: 15 minutes
Cooking Time: 10 minutes
Servings: 8
Ingredients:

- 1 lb. fresh asparagus, trimmed and cut into 1-inch pieces
- 1/2 cup pecans,
- 2 heads red leaf lettuce, rinsed and torn
- 1/2 cup frozen green peas, thawed
- 1/4 lb. smoked salmon, cut into 1-inch chunks
- 1/4 cup olive oil
- 2 tablespoons lemon juice
- 1 teaspoon Dijon mustard
- 1/2 teaspoon salt
- 1/4 teaspoon pepper

Directions:

1. Boil a pot of water. Stir in asparagus and cook for 5 minutes until tender. Let it drain; set aside.
2. In a skillet, cook the pecans over medium heat for 5 minutes, stirring constantly until lightly toasted.
3. Combine the asparagus, toasted pecans, salmon, peas, and red leaf lettuce and toss in a large bowl.
4. In another bowl, combine lemon juice, pepper, Dijon mustard, salt, and olive oil. You can coat the salad with the dressing or serve it on its side.

Nutrition: Calories: 159, Total Carbohydrates: 7 g, Cholesterol: 3 mg, Total Fat: 12.9 g, Protein: 6 g, Sodium: 304 mg

112. Shrimp Cobb Salad

Preparation Time: 25 minutes
Cooking Time: 10 minutes
Servings: 2
Ingredients:

- 4 slices center-cut bacon
- 1 lb. large shrimp, peeled and deveined
- 1/2 teaspoon ground paprika
- 1/4 teaspoon ground black pepper
- 1/4 teaspoon salt, divided
- 2 1/2 tablespoons fresh lemon juice
- 1 1/2 tablespoons Extra-virgin olive oil
- 1/2 teaspoon whole-grain Dijon mustard
- 1 (10 oz.) package romaine lettuce hearts, chopped
- 2 cups cherry tomatoes, quartered
- 1 ripe avocado, cut into wedges
- 1 cup shredded carrots

Directions:

1. In a large skillet over medium heat, cook the bacon for 4 minutes on each side till crispy.
2. Take away from the skillet and place on paper towels; let cool for 5 minutes. Break the bacon into bits. Pour out most of the bacon fat, leaving behind only 1 tablespoon in the skillet. Bring the skillet back to medium-high heat. Add black pepper and paprika to the shrimp for seasoning. Cook the shrimp for around 2 minutes on each side until it is opaque. Sprinkle with 1/8 teaspoon of salt for seasoning.
3. Combine the remaining 1/8 teaspoon of salt, mustard, olive oil, and lemon juice together in a small bowl. Stir in the romaine hearts.
4. On each serving plate, place 1 and 1/2 cups of romaine lettuce. Add on top the same amounts of avocado, carrots, tomatoes, shrimp, and bacon.

Nutrition: Calories: 528, Total Carbohydrates: 22.7 g, Cholesterol: 365 mg, Total Fat: 28.7 g, Protein: 48.9 g, Sodium: 1166 mg

113. Toast with Smoked Salmon, Herbed Cream Cheese, and Greens

Preparation Time: 10 minutes
Cooking Time: 5 minutes
Servings: 2
Ingredients:
For the herbed cream cheese:

- ¼ cup cream cheese, at room temperature
- 2 tablespoons chopped fresh flat-leaf parsley - 2 tablespoons chopped fresh chives or sliced scallion
- ½ teaspoon garlic powder
- ¼ teaspoon kosher salt

For the toast:

- 2 slices bread
- 4 ounces smoked salmon
- Small handful microgreens or sprouts
- 1 tablespoon capers, drained and rinsed
- ¼ small red onion, very thinly sliced

Directions:

1. To make the herbed cream cheese
2. In a medium bowl, combine the cream cheese, parsley, chives, garlic powder, and salt. Using a fork, mix until combined. Chill until ready to use.
3. To make the toast
4. Toast the bread until golden. Spread the herbed cream cheese over each piece of toast, then top with the smoked salmon. Garnish with microgreens, capers, and red onion.

Nutrition: Calories: 194; Total fat: 8 g; Cholesterol: 26 mg; Fiber: 2 g, Protein: 12 g; Sodium: 227 mg

114. Crab Melt with Avocado and Egg

Preparation Time: 15 minutes
Cooking Time: 15 minutes
Servings: 2
Ingredients:

- 2 English muffins, split
- 3 tablespoons butter, divided
- 2 tomatoes, cut into slices
- 1 (4-ounce) can lump crabmeat
- 6 ounces sliced or shredded cheddar cheese - 4 large eggs - Kosher salt
- 2 large avocados, halved, pitted, and cut into slices - Microgreens, for garnish

Directions:

1. Preheat the broiler.
2. Toast the English muffin halves. Place the toasted halves, cut-side up, on a baking sheet. Spread 1½ teaspoon of butter evenly over each half, allowing the butter to melt into the crevices. Top each with tomato slices, then divide the crab over each, and finish with the cheese. Broil for about 4 minutes until the cheese melts.
3. Meanwhile, in a medium skillet over medium heat, melt the remaining 1 tablespoon of butter, swirling to coat the bottom of the skillet. Crack the eggs into the skillet, giving ample space for each. Sprinkle with salt. Cook for about 3 minutes. Flip the eggs and cook the other side until the yolks are set to your liking. Place 1 egg on each English muffin half.
4. Top with avocado slices and microgreens.

Nutrition: Calories: 1221; Total fat: 84 g; Cholesterol: 94 mg; Fiber: 2 g, Protein: 12 g; Sodium: 888 mg

115. Cranberry Salad

Preparation Time: 5 minutes
Cooking Time: 5 minutes
Servings: 2
Ingredients:

- 1 sugar-free cranberry jello pack (1/2 cup for snacks allowed)
- 1/2 cup celery chopped (1 green)
- 7 half cut walnut (1 snack)

Directions:

1. Jello mixes according to the instructions of the box. Attach walnuts and celery.
2. Allow setting. Shake until serving.
3. Serve in 4-1/2 cups.

Nutrition: Fats: 11 g, Sodium: 73 mg, Potassium: 212 mg, Carbohydrates: 54 g, Protein: 4.1 g

CHAPTER 9:

Lunch Recipes

116. Easiest Tuna Cobbler Ever

Preparation Time: 15 minutes
Cooking Time: 25 minutes
Servings: 4
Ingredients:

- 1/3 cup water, cold
- 10 ounces tuna, canned, drained
- 2 tablespoons sweet pickle relish
- 1 ½ cups mixed vegetables, frozen
- 10 ¾ ounces soup, cream of chicken, condensed
- 2 ounces pimientos, sliced, drained
- 1 teaspoon lemon juice
- Paprika

Directions:

1. Preheat the air fryer at 375°F.
2. Mist cooking spray into a round casserole (1 ½ quart).
3. Mix the frozen vegetables with milk, soup, lemon juice, relish, pimientos, and tuna in a saucepan. Cook for 8 minutes over medium heat.
4. Fill the casserole with the tuna mixture.
5. Mix the biscuit mix with cold water to form a soft dough. Beat for half a minute before dropping by four spoonsful into the casserole.
6. Dust the dish with paprika before air-frying for twenty to twenty-five minutes.

Nutrition: Calories 320, Fat 10 g, Protein 20 g, Carbohydrates 30 g

117. Deliciously Homemade Pork Buns

Preparation Time: 20 minutes
Cooking Time: 25 minutes
Servings: 8
Ingredients:

- 3 pieces green onions, sliced thinly
- 1 piece egg, beaten
- Pulled pork, diced, w/ 1 cup barbecue sauce
- 16 1/3 ounces buttermilk biscuits, refrigerated
- 1 teaspoon soy sauce

Directions:

1. Preheat the air fryer at 325°F.
2. Use parchment paper to line your baking sheet.
3. Combine pork with green onions.
4. Separate and press the dough to form 8 four-inch rounds.
5. Fill each biscuit round's center with two tablespoons of pork mixture. Cover with the dough edges and seal by pinching. Arrange the buns on the sheet and brush with a mixture of soy sauce and egg.
6. Cook in the air fryer for twenty to twenty-five minutes.

Nutrition: Calories 240, Fat 0 g, Protein 0 g, Carbohydrates 20 g

118. Mouthwatering Tuna Melts

Preparation Time: 15 minutes
Cooking Time: 20 minutes
Servings: 8
Ingredients:
- 1/8 teaspoon salt
- 1/3 cup onion, chopped
- 16 1/3 ounces biscuits, refrigerated, flaky layers
- 10 ounces tuna, water-packed, drained
- 1/3 cup mayonnaise
- 1/8 teaspoon pepper
- 4 ounces cheddar cheese, shredded
- Tomato, chopped
- Sour cream
- Lettuce, shredded

Directions:
1. Preheat the air fryer at 325°F.
2. Mist cooking spray onto a cookie sheet.
3. Mix tuna with mayonnaise, pepper, salt, and onion.
4. Separate dough so you have 8 biscuits; press each into 5-inch rounds.
5. Arrange 4 biscuit rounds on the sheet. Fill at the center with tuna mixture before topping with cheese. Cover with the remaining biscuit rounds and press to seal.
6. Air-fry for 15 to 20 minutes. Slice each sandwich into halves. Serve each piece topped with lettuce, tomato, and sour cream.

Nutrition: Calories 320, Fat 10 g, Protein 10 g, Carbohydrates 20 g

119. Bacon Wings
Preparation Time: 15 minutes
Cooking Time: 30 minutes
Servings: 12
Ingredients:
- 12 pieces bacon strips
- 1 teaspoon paprika
- 1 tablespoon black pepper
- 1 teaspoon oregano
- 12 pieces chicken wings
- 1 tablespoon kosher salt
- 1 tablespoon brown sugar
- 1 teaspoon chili powder
- Celery sticks
- Blue cheese dressing

Directions:
1. Preheat the air fryer at 325°F.
2. Mix sugar, salt, chili powder, oregano, pepper, and paprika. Coat chicken wings with this dry rub.
3. Wrap a bacon strip around each wing. Arrange wrapped wings in the air fryer basket.
4. Cook for thirty minutes on each side in the air fryer. Let cool for five minutes.
5. Serve and enjoy with celery and blue cheese.

Nutrition: Calories 100, Fat 0 g, Protein 0 g, Carbohydrates 0 g

120. Pepper Pesto Lamb
Preparation Time: 15 minutes
Cooking Time: 40 minutes
Servings: 12
Ingredients:
Pesto:
- 1/4 cup rosemary leaves, fresh
- 3 pieces garlic cloves
- 3/4 cup parsley, fresh, packed firmly
- 1/4 cup mint leaves, fresh
- 2 tablespoons olive oil

Lamb:

- 7 ½ ounces red bell peppers, roasted, drained
- 5 pounds leg of lamb, boneless, rolled
- 2 teaspoons seasoning, lemon pepper

Directions:

1. Preheat the oven at 325°F.
2. Mix the pesto ingredients in the food processor.
3. Unroll the lamb and cover the cut side with pesto. Top with roasted peppers before rolling up the lamb and tying with kitchen twine.
4. Coat lamb with seasoning (lemon pepper) and air-fry for 40 minutes.

Nutrition: Calories 310, Fat 10 g, Protein 40.0 g, Carbohydrates 0 g

121. Tuna Spinach Casserole

Preparation Time: 30 minutes
Cooking Time: 25 minutes
Servings: 8
Ingredients:

- 18 ounces mushroom soup, creamy
- 1/2 cup milk
- 12 ounces white tuna, solid, in-water, drained
- 8 ounces crescent dinner rolls, refrigerated
- 8 ounces egg noodles, wide, uncooked
- 8 ounces cheddar cheese, shredded
- 9 ounces spinach, chopped, frozen, thawed, drained
- 2 teaspoons lemon peel grated

Directions:

1. Preheat the oven at 350°F.
2. Mist cooking spray onto a glass baking dish (11x7-inch).
3. Follow package directions in cooking and draining the noodles.
4. Stir the cheese (1 ½ cups) and soup together in a skillet heated on medium. Once cheese melts, stir in your noodles, milk, spinach, tuna, and lemon peel. Once bubbling, pour into the prepped dish.
5. Unroll the dough and sprinkle with remaining cheese (1/2 cup). Roll up dough and pinch at the seams to seal.

Slice into 8 portions and place over the tuna mixture.
6. Air-fry for 20 to 25 minutes.

Nutrition: Calories 400, Fat 10 g, Protein 20 g, Carbohydrates 30 g

122. Greek Style Mini Burger Pies

Preparation Time: 15 minutes
Cooking Time: 40 minutes
Servings: 6
Ingredients:

Burger mixture:

- 1 piece onion, large, chopped
- 1/2 cup red bell peppers, roasted, diced
- 1 pound ground lamb, 80% lean
- 1/4 teaspoon red pepper flakes
- 2 ounces feta cheese, crumbled

Baking mixture:

- 1/2 cup milk
- 1/2 cup biscuit mix, classic
- 2 pieces eggs

Directions:

1. Preheat oven to 350°F.
2. Grease 12 muffin cups using cooking spray.
3. Cook the onion and beef in a skillet heated on medium-high. Once the beef is browned and cooked through, drain and let cool for five minutes. Stir together with feta cheese, roasted red peppers, and red pepper flakes.
4. Whisk the baking mixture ingredients together. Fill each muffin cup with the baking mixture (1 tablespoon).
5. Air-fry for twenty-five to thirty minutes. Let cool before serving.

Nutrition: Calories 270, Fat 10 g, Protein 10 g, Carbohydrates 10 g

123. Family Fun Pizza

Preparation Time: 30 minutes
Cooking Time: 25 minutes
Servings: 16
Ingredients:

Pizza crust:

- 1 cup water, warm
- 1/2 teaspoon salt
- 1 cup flour, whole wheat

- 2 tablespoons olive oil
- 1 package dry yeast, quick active
- 1 ½ cups flour, all-purpose
- Cornmeal
- Olive oil

Filling:
- 1 cup onion, chopped
- 4 ounces mushrooms, sliced, drained
- 2 pieces garlic cloves, chopped finely
- 1/4 cup parmesan cheese, grated
- 1 pound ground lamb, 80% lean
- 1 teaspoon Italian seasoning
- 8 ounces pizza sauce
- 2 cups mozzarella cheese, shredded

Directions:
1. Mix yeast with warm water. Combine with flours, oil (2 tablespoons), and salt by stirring and then beating vigorously for half a minute. Let the dough sit for twenty minutes.
2. Preheat oven to 350ºF.
3. Prep 2 square pans (8-inch) by greasing with oil before sprinkling with cornmeal.
4. Cut the rested dough in half; place each half inside each pan. Set aside, covered, for thirty to forty-five minutes. Cook in the air fryer for twenty to twenty-two minutes.
5. Sauté the onion, beef, garlic, and Italian seasoning until beef is completely cooked. Drain and set aside.
6. Cover the air-fried crusts with pizza sauce before topping with beef mixture, cheeses, and mushrooms.
7. Return to oven and cook for twenty minutes.

Nutrition: Calories 215, Fat 0 g, Protein 10 g, Carbohydrates 20.0 g

124. Mouth-Watering Pie
Preparation Time: 15 minutes
Cooking Time: 40 minutes
Servings: 8
Ingredients:
- 3/4-pound beef; ground
- 1/2 onion; chopped.
- 1 pie crust

- 3 tablespoons taco seasoning
- 1 teaspoon baking soda
- Mango salsa for serving
- 1/2 red bell pepper; chopped.
- A handful of cilantro; chopped.
- 8 eggs
- 1 teaspoon coconut oil
- Salt and black pepper to the taste.

Directions:
1. Heat up a pan, add oil, beef, cook until it browns, and mix with salt, pepper, and taco seasoning.
2. Stir again, transfer to a bowl and leave aside for now.
3. Heat up the pan again over medium heat with cooking juices from the meat, add onion and pepper; stir and cook for 4 minutes
4. Add eggs, baking soda, and some salt and stir well.
5. Add cilantro; stir again and take off the heat.
6. Spread beef mix in pie crust, add veggies mix and spread over meat, heat oven at 350 degrees F and bake for 40 minutes
7. Leave the pie to cool down a bit, slice, divide between plates and serve with mango salsa on top.

Nutrition: Calories: 198, Fat: 11, Fiber: 1, Carbs: 12, Protein: 12

125. Special Almond Cereal
Preparation Time: 5 minutes
Cooking Time: 5 minutes
Servings: 1
Ingredients:
- 2 tablespoons almonds; chopped
- 1/3 cup coconut milk
- 1 tablespoon chia seeds
- 2 tablespoon pepitas; roasted
- A handful blueberries
- 1 small banana; chopped
- 1/3 cup water

Directions:
1. In a bowl, mix chia seeds with coconut milk and leave aside for 5 minutes

2. In your food processor, mix half of the pepitas with almonds and pulse them well.
3. Add this to chia seeds mix.
4. Also, add the water and stir.
5. Top with the rest of the pepitas, banana pieces, and blueberries, and serve

Nutrition: Calories: 200, Fat: 3, Fiber: 2, Carbs: 5, Protein: 4

126. **Awesome Avocado Muffins**
Preparation Time: 10 minutes
Cooking Time: 20 minutes
Servings: 12
Ingredients:
- 6 bacon slices; chopped
- 1 yellow onion; chopped
- 1/2 teaspoon baking soda
- 1/2 cup coconut flour
- 1 cup coconut milk
- 2 cups avocado; pitted, peeled, and chopped
- 4 eggs
- Salt and black pepper to the taste

Directions:
1. Heat up a pan, add onion and bacon; stir and brown for a few minutes
2. In a bowl, mash avocado pieces with a fork and whisk well with the eggs
3. Add milk, salt, pepper, baking soda, and coconut flour and stir everything.
4. Add bacon mixture and stir again.
5. Add coconut oil to muffin tray, divide eggs and avocado mix into the tray, heat oven at 350°F and bake for 20 minutes. Divide muffins between plates and serve them for breakfast.

Nutrition: Calories: 200, Fat: 7, Fiber: 4, Carbs: 7 Protein: 5

127. **WW Salad in A Jar**
Preparation Time: 10 minutes
Cooking Time: 5 minutes
Servings: 1
Ingredients:
- 1-ounce favorite greens
- 1-ounce red bell pepper; chopped.
- 4 ounces' rotisserie chicken; roughly chopped.

- 4 tablespoons extra virgin olive oil
- 1/2 scallion; chopped.
- 1-ounce cucumber; chopped.
- 1-ounce cherry tomatoes; halved
- Salt and black pepper to the taste.

Directions:
1. In a bowl, mix greens with bell pepper, tomatoes, scallion, cucumber, salt, pepper, and olive oil and toss to coat well.
2. Transfer this to a jar, top with chicken pieces, and serve for breakfast.

Nutrition: Calories: 180, Fat: 12, Fiber: 4, Carbs: 5, Protein: 17

128. **Yummy Smoked Salmon**

Preparation Time: 10 minutes
Cooking Time: 10 minutes
Servings: 3
Ingredients:
- 4 eggs; whisked
- 1/2 teaspoon avocado oil
- 4 ounces smoked salmon; chopped.

For the sauce:
- 1/2 cup cashews; soaked; drained
- 1/4 cup green onions; chopped.
- 1 teaspoon garlic powder
- 1 cup coconut milk
- 1 tablespoon lemon juice
- Salt and black pepper to the taste.

Directions:
1. In your blender, mix cashews with coconut milk, garlic powder, and lemon juice and blend well.
2. Add salt, pepper, and green onions, blend again well, transfer to a bowl and keep in the fridge for now.
3. Heat up a pan with the oil over medium-low heat; add eggs, whisk a bit and cook until they are almost done
4. Introduce in your preheated broiler and cook until eggs are set.
5. Divide eggs on plates, top with smoked salmon, and serve with the green onion sauce on top.

Nutrition: Calories: 200, Fat: 10, Fiber: 2, Carbs: 11, Protein: 15

129. Almond Coconut Cereal
Preparation Time: 5 minutes
Cooking Time: 5 minutes
Servings: 2
Ingredients:
- 1/3 cup water
- 1/3 cup coconut milk
- 2 tablespoons roasted sunflower seeds
- 1 tablespoon chia seeds
- ½ cup blueberries
- 2 tablespoons chopped almonds

Directions:
1. Set a medium bowl in position to add coconut milk and chia seeds, then reserve for five minutes
2. Plugin and set the blender in position to blend almond with sunflower seeds
3. Stir the combination to chia seeds mixture, then add water to mix evenly.
4. Serve topped with the remaining sunflower seeds and blueberries

Nutrition: Calories: 181, Fat: 15.2, Fiber: 4, Carbs: 10.8, Protein: 3.7

130. Almond Porridge

Preparation Time: 10 minutes
Cooking Time: 5 minutes
Servings: 1
Ingredients:
- ¼ teaspoon ground cloves
- ¼ teaspoon nutmeg
- 1 teaspoon stevia
- ¾ cup coconut cream
- ½ cup ground almonds
- ¼ teaspoon ground cardamom
- 1 teaspoon ground cinnamon

Directions:
1. Set your pan over medium heat to cook the coconut cream for a few minutes
2. Stir in almonds and stevia to cook for 5 minutes
3. Mix in nutmeg, cardamom, and cinnamon. Enjoy while still hot

Nutrition: Calories: 695, Fat: 66.7, Fiber: 11.1, Carbs: 22, Protein: 14.3

131. Asparagus Frittata Recipe
Preparation Time: 20 minutes
Cooking Time: 20 minutes
Servings: 4
Ingredients:
- 4 bacon slices, chopped:
- Salt and black pepper
- 8 eggs (whisked)
- 1 bunch asparagus (trimmed and chopped)

Directions:
1. Heat a pan, add bacon, stir and cook for 5 minutes.
2. Add asparagus, salt, and pepper, stir and cook for another 5 minutes.
3. Add the chilled eggs, spread them in the pan, let them stand in the oven, and bake for 20 minutes at 350°F.
4. Share and divide between plates and serve for breakfast.

Nutrition: Calories 251, Carbs 16, Fat 6, Fiber 8, Protein 7

132. Avocados Stuffed with Salmon
Preparation Time: 5 minutes
Cooking Time: 5 minutes
Servings: 2
Ingredients:
- 1 avocado (pitted and halved)
- 2 tablespoons olive oil
- 1 lemon juice
- 2 ounces smoked salmon (flaked)
- 1-ounce goat cheese (crumbled)
- Salt and black pepper

Directions:
1. Combine the salmon with lemon juice, oil, cheese, salt, and pepper in your food processor and pulsate well.
2. Divide this mixture into avocado halves and serve. Dish and Enjoy!

Nutrition: Calories: 300, Fat: 15, Fiber: 5, Carbs: 8, Protein: 16

133. Bacon and Brussels Sprout Breakfast

Preparation Time: 10 minutes
Cooking Time: 15 minutes
Servings: 3
Ingredients:

- 1½ tablespoons apple cider vinegar
- Salt
- 2 minced shallots
- 2 minced garlic cloves
- 3 medium eggs
- 12 oz. sliced brussels sprouts
- Black pepper
- 2 oz. chopped bacon
- 1 tablespoon melted butter

Directions:

1. Over medium heat, quickly fry the bacon until crispy, then reserve on a plate
2. Set the pan on fire again to fry garlic and shallots for 30 seconds
3. Stir in apple cider vinegar, Brussels sprouts, and seasoning to cook for five minutes
4. Add the bacon to cook for 5 minutes, then stir in the butter and set a hole at the center
5. Crash the eggs to the pan and let cook fully
6. Enjoy

Nutrition: Calories: 275, Fat: 16.5, Fiber: 4.3, Carbs: 17.2, Protein: 17.4

134. Bacon and Lemon Spiced Muffins

Preparation Time: 10 minutes
Cooking Time: 20 minutes
Servings: 12
Ingredients:

- 2 teaspoons lemon thyme
- Salt
- 3 cup almond flour
- ½ cup melted butter
- 1 teaspoon baking soda
- Black pepper
- 4 medium eggs
- 1 cup diced bacon

Directions:

1. Set a mixing bowl in place and stir in the eggs and baking soda to incorporate well.
2. Whisk in the seasonings, butter, bacon, and lemon thyme
3. Set the mixture in a well-lined muffin pan.
4. Set the oven for 20 minutes at 350°F, allow to bake
5. Allow the muffins to cool before serving

Nutrition: Calories: 186, Fat: 17.1, Fiber: 0.8, Carbs: 1.8, Protein: 7.4

135. Hot Buffalo wings

Preparation Time: 10 minutes
Cooking Time: 40 minutes
Servings: 3
Ingredients:

- ¼ cup hot sauce
- 12 chicken wings (fresh or frozen)
- 4 tablespoons coconut oil, plus more for rubbing on the wings
- 1 clove garlic, minced
- ¼ teaspoon salt
- ¼ teaspoon paprika
- ¼ teaspoon cayenne pepper
- 1 dash ground black pepper

Directions:

1. Preheat your oven to 400°F (200°C).
2. Evenly spread chicken wings on a wire rack placed on a baking dish (it will save wings to become soggy on the bottom).
3. Rub each chicken wing with olive oil and season with salt and pepper, then bake for 40 minutes or until crispy.

4. Meanwhile, in a saucepan, combine coconut oil and garlic and cook over medium heat for 1 minute or fragrant.
5. Remove from heat and stir in hot sauce, salt, paprika, cayenne pepper, and black pepper.
6. Remove wings from the oven and transfer to a large bowl.
7. Pour the hot sauce mixture over wings and toss until each wing is coated with the sauce.
8. Serve immediately.

Nutrition: Calories: 391, Carbohydrates: 1 g, Fats: 33 g, Protein: 31 g

136. Trout and Chili Nuts
Preparation Time: 10 minutes
Cooking Time: 0 minutes
Servings: 3
Ingredients:
- 1.5 kg of rainbow trout
- 300 gr shelled walnuts
- 1 bunch of parsley
- 9 cloves of garlic
- 7 tablespoons of olive oil
- 2 fresh hot peppers
- The juice of 2 lemons
- Halls

Directions:
1. Clean and dry the trout, then place them in a baking tray.
2. Chop the walnuts, parsley, and chili peppers, then mash the garlic cloves.
3. Mix the ingredients by adding olive oil, lemon juice, and a pinch of salt.
4. Stuff the trout with some of the sauce and use the rest to cover the fish.
5. Bake at 180° for 30/40 minutes.
6. Serve the trout hot or cold.

Nutrition: Calories 226, Fat 5, Fiber 2, Carbs 7, Protein 8

137. Nut Granola & Smoothie Bowl
Preparation Time: 10 minutes
Cooking Time: 40 minutes
Servings: 3
Ingredients:
- 6 cups Greek yogurt
- 4 tablespoon almond butter
- A handful of toasted walnuts
- 3 tablespoon unsweetened cocoa powder
- 4 teaspoon swerve brown sugar
- 2 cups nut granola for topping

Directions:
1. Combine the Greek yogurt, almond butter, walnuts, cocoa powder, and swerve brown sugar in a smoothie maker; puree at high speed until smooth and well mixed.
2. Share the smoothie into four breakfast bowls, top with a half cup of granola each, and serve.

Nutrition: Kcal 361, Fat 31.2 g, Net Carbs 2 g, Protein 13 g

138. Bacon and Egg Quesadillas
Preparation Time: 10 minutes
Cooking Time: 30 minutes
Servings: 3
Ingredients:
- 8 low carb tortilla shells
- 6 eggs
- 1 cup water
- 3 tablespoon butter
- 1 ½ cups grated cheddar cheese
- 1 ½ cups grated Swiss cheese
- 5 bacon slices
- 1 medium onion, thinly sliced
- 1 tablespoon chopped parsley

Directions:
1. Bring the eggs to a boil in water over medium heat for 10 minutes. Transfer the eggs to an ice water bath, peel the shells, and chop them; set aside.
2. Meanwhile, as the eggs cook, fry the bacon in a skillet over medium heat for 4 minutes until crispy. Remove and chop. Plate and set aside too.
3. Fetch out 2/3 of the bacon fat and sauté the onions in the remaining grease over medium heat for 2 minutes; set aside. Melt 1 tablespoon of butter in a skillet over medium heat.
4. Lay one tortilla in a skillet; sprinkle with some Swiss cheese. Add some chopped eggs and bacon over the cheese, top with onion, and sprinkle with some cheddar cheese. Cover with

another tortilla shell. Cook for 45 seconds, then carefully flip the quesadilla, and cook the other side too for 45 seconds. Remove to a plate and repeat the cooking process using the remaining tortilla shells.

5. Garnish with parsley and serve warm.

Nutrition: Kcal 449, Fat 48.7 g, Net Carbs 6.8 g, Protein 29.1 g

139. **Bacon and Cheese Frittata**
Preparation Time: 10 minutes
Cooking Time: 20 minutes
Servings: 3
Ingredients:
- 10 slices bacon
- 10 fresh eggs
- 3 tablespoon butter, melted
- ½ cup almond milk
- Salt and black pepper to taste
- 1 ½ cups cheddar cheese, shredded
- ¼ cup chopped green onions

Directions:
1. Preheat the oven to 400°F and grease a baking dish with cooking spray. Cook the bacon in a skillet over medium heat for 6 minutes. Once crispy, remove from the skillet to paper towels and discard grease. Chop into small pieces. Whisk the eggs, butter, milk, salt, and black pepper. Mix in the bacon and pour the mixture into the baking dish.
2. Sprinkle with cheddar cheese and green onions, and bake in the oven for 10 minutes or until the eggs are thoroughly cooked. Remove and cool the frittata for 3 minutes, slice into wedges, and serve warm with a dollop of Greek yogurt.

Nutrition: Kcal 325, Fat 28 g, Net Carbs 2 g, Protein 15 g

140. **Bacon Wrapped Asparagus**
Preparation Time: 10 minutes
Cooking Time: 20 minutes
Servings: 2
Ingredients:
- 1/3 cup heavy whipping cream
- 2 bacon slices, precooked

- 4 small spears of asparagus
- Salt, to taste
- 1 tablespoon butter

Directions:
1. Preheat the oven to 360°F and grease a baking sheet with butter.
2. Meanwhile, mix cream, asparagus and salt in a bowl.
3. Wrap the asparagus in bacon slices and arrange them in the baking dish.
4. Transfer the baking dish to the oven and bake for about 20 minutes.
5. Remove from the oven and serve hot.
6. Place the bacon-wrapped asparagus in a dish and set it aside to cool for meal prepping. Divide it into 2 containers and cover the lid. Refrigerate for about 2 days and reheat in the microwave before serving.

Nutrition: Calories: 204, Carbs: 1.4 g, Protein: 5.9 g, Fat: 19.3 g, Sugar: 0.5 g

141. **Spinach Chicken**

Preparation Time: 10 minutes
Cooking Time: 10 minutes
Servings: 2
Ingredients:
- 2 garlic cloves, minced
- 2 tablespoons unsalted butter, divided
- ¼ cup parmesan cheese, shredded
- ¾ pound chicken tenders
- ¼ cup heavy cream
- 10 ounces frozen spinach, chopped
- Salt and black pepper, to taste

Directions:
1. Heat 1 tablespoon of butter in a large skillet and add chicken, salt, and black pepper.

2. Cook for about 3 minutes on both sides and remove the chicken to a bowl.
3. Melt remaining butter in the skillet and add garlic, cheese, heavy cream, and spinach.
4. Cook for about 2 minutes and add the chicken.
5. Cook for about 5 minutes on low heat and dish out to immediately serve.
6. Place chicken in a dish and set aside to cool for meal prepping. Divide it into 2 containers and cover them. Refrigerate for about 3 days and reheat in microwave before serving.

Nutrition: Calories: 288, Carbs: 3.6 g, Protein: 27.7 g, Fat: 18.3 g, Sugar: 0.3 g

142. Lemongrass Prawns
Preparation Time: 10 minutes
Cooking Time: 15 minutes
Servings: 2
Ingredients:
- ½ red chili pepper, seeded and chopped
- 2 lemongrass stalks
- ½ pound prawns, deveined and peeled
- 6 tablespoons butter
- ¼ teaspoon smoked paprika

Directions:
1. Preheat the oven to 390°F and grease a baking dish.
2. Mix together red chili pepper, butter, smoked paprika, and prawns in a bowl.
3. Marinate for about 2 hours and then thread the prawns on the lemongrass stalks. Arrange the threaded prawns on the baking dish and transfer them to the oven. Bake for about 15 minutes and dish out to serve immediately.
4. Place the prawns in a dish and set them aside to cool for meal prepping. Divide it into 2 containers and close the lid. Refrigerate for about 4 days and reheat in microwave before serving.

Nutrition: Calories: 322, Carbs: 3.8 g, Protein: 34.8 g, Fat: 18 g, Sugar: 0.1 g, Sodium: 478 mg

143. Stuffed Mushrooms
Preparation Time: 20 minutes
Cooking Time: 25 minutes
Servings: 4
Ingredients:
- 2 ounces bacon, crumbled
- ½ tablespoon butter
- ¼ teaspoon paprika powder
- 2 portobello mushrooms
- 1 oz cream cheese
- ¾ tablespoon fresh chives, chopped
- Salt and black pepper, to taste

Directions:
1. Preheat the oven to 400°F and grease a baking dish. Heat butter in a skillet and add mushrooms.
2. Sauté for about 4 minutes and set aside. Mix together cream cheese, chives, paprika powder, salt, and black pepper in a bowl. Stuff the mushrooms with this mixture and transfer them to the baking dish.
3. Place in the oven and bake for about 20 minutes.
4. These mushrooms can be refrigerated for about 3 days for meal prepping and can be served with scrambled eggs.

Nutrition: Calories: 570, Carbs: 4.6 g, Protein: 19.9 g, Fat: 52.8 g, Sugar: 0.8 g, Sodium: 1041 mg

144. Honey Glazed Chicken Drumsticks
Preparation Time: 10 minutes
Cooking Time: 20 minutes
Servings: 2
Ingredients:
- ½ tablespoon fresh thyme, minced
- 1/8 cup Dijon mustard
- ½ tablespoon fresh rosemary, minced
- ½ tablespoon honey
- 2 chicken drumsticks
- 1 tablespoon olive oil
- Salt and black pepper, to taste

Directions:
1. Preheat the oven at 325°F and grease a baking dish. Combine all the ingredients in a bowl except the drumsticks and mix well.

2. Add drumsticks and coat generously with the mixture.
3. Cover and refrigerate to marinate overnight. Place the drumsticks in the baking dish and transfer them to the oven. Cook for about 20 minutes and dish out to immediately serve.
4. Place chicken drumsticks in a dish and set them aside to cool for meal prepping. Divide it into 2 containers and cover them. Refrigerate for about 3 days and reheat in microwave before serving.

Nutrition: Calories: 301, Carbs: 6 g, Fats: 19.7 g, Proteins: 4.5 g, Sugar: 4.5 g, Sodium: 316 mg

145. Keto Zucchini Pizza
Preparation Time: 10 minutes
Cooking Time: 15 minutes
Servings: 2
Ingredients:
- 1/8 cup spaghetti sauce
- ½ zucchini, cut in circular slices
- ½ cup cream cheese
- Pepperoni slices, for topping
- ½ cup mozzarella cheese, shredded

Directions:
1. Preheat the oven to 350°F and grease a baking dish.
2. Arrange the zucchini on the baking dish and layer with spaghetti sauce.
3. Top with pepperoni slices and mozzarella cheese.
4. Transfer the baking dish to the oven and bake for about 15 minutes.
5. Remove from the oven and serve immediately.

Nutrition: Calories: 445, Carbs: 3.6 g, Protein: 12.8 g, Fat: 42 g, Sugar: 0.3 g, Sodium: 429 mg

146. Omega-3 Salad
Preparation Time: 10 minutes
Cooking Time: 5 minutes
Servings: 2
Ingredients:
- ½ pound skinless salmon fillet, cut into 4 steaks
- ¼ tablespoon fresh lime juice

- 1 tablespoon olive oil, divided
- 4 tablespoons sour cream
- ¼ zucchini, cut into small cubes
- ¼ teaspoon jalapeño pepper, seeded and chopped finely
- Salt and black pepper, to taste
- ¼ tablespoon fresh dill, chopped

Directions:
1. Put olive oil and salmon in a skillet and cook for about 5 minutes on both sides.
2. Season with salt and black pepper, stirring well, and dish out.
3. Mix remaining ingredients in a bowl and add cooked salmon to serve.

Nutrition: Calories: 291, Fat: 21.1 g, Carbs: 2.5 g, Protein: 23.1 g, Sugar: 0.6 g, Sodium: 112 mg

147. Crab Cakes

Preparation Time: 20 minutes
Cooking Time: 10 minutes
Servings: 2
Ingredients:
- ½ pound lump crabmeat, drained
- 2 tablespoons coconut flour
- 1 tablespoon mayonnaise
- ¼ teaspoon green Tabasco sauce
- 3 tablespoons butter
- 1 small egg, beaten
- ¾ tablespoon fresh parsley, chopped
- ½ teaspoon yellow mustard
- Salt and black pepper, to taste

Directions:
1. Mix together all the ingredients in a bowl except butter.
2. Make patties from this mixture and set them aside.

3. Heat butter in a skillet over medium heat and add patties.
4. Cook for about 10 minutes on each side and dish out to serve hot.
5. You can store the raw patties in the freezer for about 3 weeks for meal prepping. Place patties in a container and place parchment paper in between the patties to avoid stickiness.

Nutrition: Calories: 153, Fat: 10.8 g, Carbs: 6.7 g, Protein: 6.4 g, Sugar: 2.4 Sodium: 46 mg

148. Low Carb Black Beans Chili Chicken

Preparation Time: 10 minutes
Cooking Time: 25 minutes
Servings: 10
Ingredients:
- 1-3/4 pounds chicken breasts, cubed (boneless skinless)
- 2 sweet red peppers, chopped
- 1 onion, chopped
- 3 tablespoons olive oil
- 1 can chopped green chiles
- 4 cloves garlic, minced
- 2 tablespoons chili powder
- 2 teaspoons ground cumin
- 1 teaspoon ground coriander
- 2 cans black beans, rinsed and drained
- 1 can Italian stewed tomatoes, cut up
- 1 cup chicken broth or beer
- 1/2 to 1 cup water

Directions:
1. Put oil into a skillet and place over medium heat. Add in the red pepper, chicken, and onion and cook until the chicken is brown, about 5 minutes.
2. Add in the garlic, chiles, chili powder, coriander, and cumin, and cook for an additional minute.
3. Next, add the tomatoes, beans, half cup of water, and broth and cook until it boils. Decrease the heat, uncover the skillet and cook while stirring for fifteen minutes.
4. Serve.

Nutrition: Calories: 236, Fat: 6 g, Protein: 22 g, Carbohydrates: 21 g

149. Quick Keto Blt Chicken Salad

Preparation Time: 20 minutes
Cooking Time: 0 minutes
Servings: 8
Ingredients:
- 1/2 cup mayonnaise
- 3 to 4 tablespoons barbecue sauce
- 2 tablespoons finely chopped onion
- 1 tablespoon lemon juice
- 1/4 teaspoon pepper
- 8 cups torn salad greens
- 2 tomatoes, chopped
- 10 strips bacon, cooked and crumbled
- 2 hard-boiled eggs, sliced
- 1-1/2 pounds boneless skinless chicken breasts, cooked and cubed

Directions:
1. Mix the first five ingredients in a bowl until combined. Cover the bowl and transfer the mixture to the refrigerator.
2. Next, put the salad greens in a bowl. Add in the chicken, tomatoes, and bacon. Top with eggs and a drizzle of the dressing.
3. Serve.

Nutrition: Calories: 281, Protein: 23 g, Fat: 19 g, Carbohydrates: 5 g

150. Quick Healthy Avocado Tuna Salad

Preparation Time: 10 minutes
Cooking Time: 0 minutes
Servings: 4
Ingredients:
- 2 avocados
- 2 tablespoons lime juice
- 4 5-oz cans of tuna, drained
- 1/4 cup fresh cilantro, chopped
- 3 tablespoons celery, finely chopped
- 3 tablespoons red onion, minced
- 1 tablespoon jalapenos, minced
- 1/2 teaspoon sea salt

Directions:
1. Crush the lime juice and avocado in a bowl. Add in the sea salt and combine.

Next, add in the cilantro, tuna, celery, red onion, and jalapenos.

2. Stir to combine. Adjust seasonings as desired and serve.

Nutrition: Calories: 169, Protein: 27 g, Fat: 14 g, Carbohydrates: 10 g

151. Flavorful Keto Taco Soup

Preparation Time: 5 minutes
Cooking Time: 15
Servings: 8
Ingredients:

- 1 lb. ground beef
- 3 tablespoons taco seasoning, divided
- 4 cup beef bone broth
- 2 14.5-oz cans diced tomatoes
- 3/4 cup ranch dressing

Directions:

1. Put the ground beef into a pot and place over medium-high heat and cook until brown, about ten minutes.
2. Add in ¾ cup of broth and two tablespoons of taco seasoning. Cook until part of the liquid has evaporated.
3. Add in the diced tomatoes, rest of the broth, and rest of the taco seasoning. Stir to mix, then simmer for ten minutes.
4. Remove the pot from heat, and add in the ranch dressing. Garnish with cilantro and cheddar cheese. Serve.

Nutrition: Calories: 309, Fat: 24 g, Protein: 13 g

152. Delicious Instant Pot Keto Buffalo Chicken Soup

Preparation Time: 10 minutes
Cooking Time: 20 minutes
Servings: 6
Ingredients:

- 1 tablespoon olive oil
- 1/2 onion, diced
- 1/2 cup celery, diced
- 4 cloves garlic, minced
- 1 lb. shredded chicken, cooked
- 4 cup chicken bone broth, or any chicken broth
- 3 tablespoons buffalo sauce
- 6 oz cream cheese
- 1/2 cup Half & half

Directions:

1. Switch the instant pot to the sauté function. Add in the chopped onion, oil, and celery. Cook until the onions are brown and translucent, about ten minutes.
2. Add in the garlic and cook until fragrant, about one minute. Switch off the instant pot.
3. Add in the broth, shredded chicken, and buffalo sauce. Cover the instant pot and seal. Switch the soup feature on and set the time to 5 minutes.
4. When cooked, release pressure naturally for 5 minutes and then quickly.
5. Scoop out one cup of the soup liquid into a blender bowl, then add in the cheese and blend until smooth. Pour the puree into the instant pot, then add in the calf and half and stir to mix.
6. Serve.

Nutrition: Calories: 270, Protein: 27 g, Fat: 16 g, Carbohydrates: 4 g

153. Creamy Low Carb Cream of Mushroom Soup

Preparation Time: 15 minutes
Cooking Time: 15 minutes
Servings: 5
Ingredients:

- 1 tablespoon olive oil
- 1/2 onion, diced
- 20 oz mushrooms, sliced
- 6 cloves garlic, minced
- 2 cup chicken broth
- 1 cup heavy cream
- 1 cup unsweetened almond milk
- 3/4 teaspoon sea salt
- 1/4 teaspoon black pepper

Directions:

1. Place a pot over medium heat and add in olive oil. Add in the mushrooms and onions and cook until browned, about fifteen minutes. Next, add in the garlic and cook for another one minute.
2. Add in the cream, chicken broth, sea salt, almond milk, and black pepper.

Cook until boil, then simmer for fifteen minutes.

3. Puree the soup using an immersion blender until smooth. Serve.

Nutrition: Calories: 229, Fat: 21 g, Protein: 5 g, Carbohydrates: 8 g

154. **Easy Keto Chicken Soup**
Preparation Time: 10 minutes
Cooking Time: 1 hour
Servings: 14
Ingredients:
- 2 cups shredded chicken, cooked
- 1 cup carrots, diced
- 1 cup celery, diced
- 1 cup onion, diced
- 10 cups chicken broth
- 1 tablespoon Italian seasoning
- 1 bay leaf
- A dash of sea salt
- A dash of black pepper
- 1 Spaghetti squash

Directions:
1. Combine all the ingredients except the spaghetti squash in a pot over medium heat. Cook until it boils, then decrease to a simmer and cover the pot. Cook for one hour.
2. Next, preheat the oven to about 375ºF, then punch holes in the spaghetti squash with a knife. Transfer to a baking sheet and bake in the oven for sixty minutes.
3. When the spaghetti squash is cooked, cut it in half and scoop out the strands using a fork. Remove the bay leaf and add in half of the spaghetti squash strands.

Nutrition: Calories: 44, Carbohydrates: 4 g, Protein: 5 g, Fat: 1 g

155. **Taco Casserole**
Preparation Time: 30 minutes
Cooking Time: 1 Hour
Servings: 8
Ingredients:
- 1 lb. ground turkey
- 1 cauliflower, small & chopped into florets
- 1 jalapeno diced

- ¼ cup red peppers, diced
- ¼ cup onion, diced
- 1 teaspoon cumin
- 1 teaspoon parsley
- 1 teaspoon garlic minced
- 1 teaspoon turmeric
- 1 teaspoon oregano
- 1 ½ cups cheddar cheese, shredded
- 1 cup sour cream

Directions:
1. Put your minced meat and cauliflower in a bowl before adding all your herbs and spices. Stir in your red peppers, jalapenos, and onions together, mixing in a cup of your cheese.
2. Pour into a casserole dish before topping with remaining cheese.
3. Bake at 350ºF for an hour and serve with sour cream.

Nutrition: Calories: 242, Protein: 18 g, Fat: 17 g, Net Carbs: 4 g

156. **Quick Keto Roasted Tomato Soup**
Preparation Time: 5 minutes
Cooking Time: 40 minutes
Servings: 6
Ingredients:
- 10 fresh Rome tomatoes, sliced into tubes
- 2 tablespoons olive oil
- 4 cloves garlic, minced
- 2 cup chicken bone broth
- 1 tablespoon herbs de Provence
- 1/2 teaspoon sea salt
- 1/4 teaspoon black pepper
- 1/4 cup heavy cream
- 2 tablespoons fresh basil

Directions:
1. First, preheat the oven to about 400ºF, then line a baking sheet with some foil, then grease the foil.
2. Mix the tomato chunks with minced garlic and olive oil. Place the tomato chunks on a baking sheet.
3. Transfer to the oven and bake until the skin wrinkles, about twenty-five minutes.

4. Remove from the heat and put the tomato chunks into the blender and blend until smooth.
5. Pour the tomato puree into the pot and place over medium-high heat. Add in the broth and season with sea salt, herbs de Provence, and black pepper. Boil for about fifteen minutes.
6. Add in the basil and cream and serve.

Nutrition: Calories: 95, Fat: 8 g, Protein: 3 g, Carbohydrates: 3 g

157. **Delicious Low Carb Chicken Caesar Salad**
Preparation Time: 10 minutes
Cooking Time: 6 minutes
Servings: 4
Ingredients:
- 1 cup parmesan crisps
- 1 head romaine lettuce, chopped
- 2 cups grape tomatoes, halved
- 2 grilled chicken breasts, sliced

For Keto Caesar Dressing:
- 1/3 cup caesar salad dressing

Directions:
1. Chill the Caesar salad dressing in the refrigerator.
2. Combine the grape tomatoes, romaine lettuce, and cooked chicken.
3. Break the cheese crisps into bits and sprinkle on the salad and drizzle with the dressing. Mix to combine.

Nutrition: Calories: 400, Protein: 33 g, Fat: 25 g, Carbohydrates: 5 g

158. **Keto Cheesy Broccoli Soup**
Preparation Time: 15 minutes
Cooking Time: 20 minutes
Servings: 8
Ingredients:
- 4 cups broccoli, chopped into florets
- 4 cloves garlic, minced
- 3 1/2 cups chicken broth
- 1 cup heavy cream
- 3 cups cheddar cheese

Directions:
1. Place a pot over medium heat, then add in the garlic and cook until fragrant. Add in the heavy cream, chicken broth, and chopped broccoli.

2. Raise the heat and cook until it boils, then decrease heat. Cook until the broccoli is tender, about 20 minutes.
3. Remove one-third of the broccoli and keep it aside. Blend the rest of the broccoli using an immersion blender. Decrease the heat to low.
4. Add in the cheddar cheese and stir until combined. Blend again to smooth.
5. Remove from the heat source, then add in the reserved broccoli florets and serve.

Nutrition: Calories: 292, Protein: 13 g, Fat: 25 g, Carbohydrates: 5 g

159. **Creamy Low Carb Zucchini Alfredo**
Preparation Time: 10 minutes
Cooking Time: 15 minutes
Servings: 4
Ingredients:
- 3 zucchini
- 1 teaspoon butter
- 2 cloves garlic, minced
- 1/4 teaspoon nutmeg
- 1/2 cup unsweetened almond milk
- 1/3 cup heavy cream
- 3/4 cup grated parmesan cheese
- 1 tablespoon arrowroot powder
- A dash of black pepper

Directions:
1. First, prepare the zucchini noodles using a julienne peeler or spiralizer. Next, put butter into a skillet and place over medium-high heat. When heated, add in the garlic and cook until fragrant and soft, about a minute.
2. Decrease the heat to low heat, then add in the heavy cream, almond milk, and nutmeg. Boil for some minutes.
3. Combine the arrowroot powder with two tablespoons of water in a bowl until dissolved, then pour into the sauce in the skillet.
4. Add in the Parmesan cheese and season with black pepper. Keep cooking while stirring frequently until the cheese melts. Transfer the sauce to a container and keep it aside.

5. Dry the zucchini using paper towels, then put the noodles into the pan and stir fry over medium-high heat. Cook until softened, about four minutes.
6. Pour in the sauce and garnish with more Parmesan cheese and parsley. Serve.

Nutrition: Calories: 209, Protein: 11 g, Fat: 16 g, Carbohydrates: 9 g

160. Amazing Low Carb Shrimp Lettuce Wraps
Preparation Time: 10 minutes
Cooking Time: 4 minutes
Servings: 4
Ingredients:
For Thai Shrimp:
- 1 lb. shrimp, peeled, deveined
- 2 tablespoons coconut aminos
- 1/4 cup olive oil, divided
- 1 tablespoon fish sauce
- 2 teaspoons lime juice
- 1/4 teaspoon crushed red pepper flakes

For Lettuce Wraps:
- 16 leaves bibb lettuce
- 1/3 fresh cucumber, julienned
- 1 avocado, diced

For Peanut Sauce:
- 1/4 cup peanut butter
- 1/4 cup coconut aminos
- 1 1/2 tablespoon lime juice
- 1/2 teaspoon crushed red pepper flakes
- 1/4 teaspoon sea salt
- 1/4 teaspoon garlic powder

For Garnish: Sliced green onions, lime wedges, roasted peanuts
Directions:
1. Combine two tablespoons of olive oil, coconut aminos, fish sauce, red peppers, and lime juice in a bowl.
2. Add in the shrimp and stir to mix. Cover the bowl and keep it aside to marinate for thirty minutes.
3. Combine the peanut sauce Ingredients: and keep aside. Pour two tablespoons of oil into a pan and place over medium heat.

4. Add in shrimp and cook until opaque, about six minutes. Share the cucumbers, shrimp, and avocados among the lettuce leaves. Add in a drizzle of peanut sauce and garnish with peanuts, green onions, and lime wedges if desired.

Nutrition: Calories: 470, Protein: 29 g, Fat: 31 g, Carbohydrates: 16 g

161. Tasty Low Carb Cucumber Salad
Preparation Time: 10 minutes
Cooking Time: 0 minutes
Servings: 6
Ingredients:
- 1/2 cup sour cream
- 2 tablespoons fresh dill, chopped
- 1 tablespoon olive oil
- 1 tablespoon lemon juice
- 1/2 teaspoon garlic powder
- 1/2 teaspoon sea salt
- 1/4 teaspoon black pepper
- 6 cups cucumber, chopped
- 1 red onion, thinly sliced

Directions:
1. Combine the dill, sour cream, olive oil, garlic powder, and lemon juice in a bowl. Season the mixture with black pepper and sea salt.
2. Add in the red onions and chopped cucumbers. Serve.

Nutrition: Calories: 86, Protein: 2 g, Fat: 6 g, Carbohydrates: 7 g

162. Classic Low Carb Cobb Salad
Preparation Time: 30 minutes
Cooking Time: 10 minutes
Servings: 6
Ingredients:
- 1/4 cup red wine vinegar
- 2 teaspoons salt
- 1 teaspoon lemon juice
- 1 clove garlic, minced
- 3/4 teaspoon coarsely ground pepper
- 3/4 teaspoon Worcestershire sauce
- 1/4 teaspoon sugar
- 1/4 teaspoon ground mustard

- 3/4 cup canola oil
- 1/4 cup olive oil

For Salad:

- 6-1/2 cups torn romaine
- 2-1/2 cups torn curly endive
- 1 bunch of watercress, trimmed, divided
- 2 chicken breasts, cooked, chopped
- 2 tomatoes, seeded and chopped
- 1 ripe avocado, peeled and chopped
- 3 boiled large eggs, chopped
- 1/2 cup crumbled blue or Roquefort cheese
- 6 cooked bacon strips, crumbled
- 2 tablespoons minced fresh chives

Directions:

1. Puree the first eight ingredients in the blender while adding in olive and canola oils until smooth.
2. Mix the endive, romaine, and half of the watercress in a bowl. Transfer to a platter, then assemble the tomatoes, chicken, eggs, avocado, bacon, and cheese on the greens.
3. Top with chives and rest of the watercress. Drizzle one cup of dressing over the salad. Serve.

Nutrition: Calories: 577, Protein:20 g, Fat:52 g, Carbohydrates: 10 g

163. Yummy Keto Mushroom Asparagus Frittata

Preparation Time: 25 minutes
Cooking Time: 20 minutes
Servings: 8
Ingredients:

- 8 eggs
- 1/2 cup whole-milk ricotta cheese
- 2 tablespoons lemon juice
- 1/2 teaspoon salt
- 1/4 teaspoon pepper
- 1 tablespoon olive oil
- 1 package of frozen asparagus spears, thawed
- 1 onion, halved and thinly sliced
- 1/4 cup baby portobello mushrooms, sliced
- 1/2 cup sweet green or red pepper, finely chopped

Directions:

1. First, preheat the oven to about 350°F, then whisk the ricotta cheese, eggs, salt, lemon juice, and pepper in a bowl.
2. Pour oil into a skillet and add onion, asparagus, mushrooms, and red pepper. Cook until pepper and onions are tender, about eight minutes.
3. Add in the egg mixture and transfer to the oven. Bake until eggs are set, about twenty-five minutes.
4. Keep aside to cool, then cut into wedges.

Nutrition: Calories: 130, Protein: 9 g, Fat: 8 g, Carbohydrates: 5 g

164. Yogurt Garlic Chicken

Preparation Time: 30 minutes
Cooking Time: 60 minutes
Servings: 6
Ingredients:

- 6 pieces Pita bread rounds, halved
- English cucumber, sliced thinly, w/ each slice halved (1 cup)

Chicken & vegetables:

- 3 tablespoons olive oil
- 1/2 teaspoon black pepper, freshly ground
- 20 ounces chicken thighs, skinless, boneless
- 1 piece bell pepper, red, sliced into half-inch portions
- 4 pieces garlic cloves, chopped finely
- 1/2 teaspoon cumin, ground
- 1 piece red onion, medium, sliced into half-inch wedges
- 1/2 cup yogurt, plain, fat-free
- 2 tablespoons lemon juice
- 1 ½ teaspoon salt
- 1/2 teaspoon red pepper flakes, crushed
- 1/2 teaspoon allspice, ground
- 1 piece bell pepper, yellow, sliced into half-inch portions

Yogurt sauce:

- 2 tablespoons olive oil
- 1/4 teaspoon salt
- 1 tablespoon parsley, flat-leaf, chopped finely

- 1 cup yogurt, plain, fat-free
- 1 tablespoon lemon juice, fresh
- 1 piece garlic clove, chopped finely

Directions:

1. Mix the yogurt (1/2 cup), garlic cloves (4 pieces), olive oil (1 tablespoon), salt (1 teaspoon), lemon juice (2 tablespoons), pepper (1/4 teaspoon), allspice, cumin, and pepper flakes. Stir in the chicken and coat well. Cover and marinate in the fridge for two hours.
2. Preheat the air fryer at 400°F.
3. Grease a rimmed baking sheet (18x13-inch) with cooking spray.
4. Toss the bell peppers and onion with remaining olive oil (2 tablespoons), pepper (1/4 teaspoon), and salt (1/2 teaspoon).
5. Arrange veggies on the baking sheets left side and the marinated chicken thighs (drain first) on the right side. Cook in the air fryer for twenty-five to thirty minutes.
6. Mix the yogurt sauce ingredients.
7. Slice air-fried chicken into half-inch strips.
8. Top each pita round with chicken strips, roasted veggies, cucumbers, and yogurt sauce.

Nutrition: Calories: 380, Fat: 10 g, Protein 20 g, Carbohydrates: 30 g

165. Lemony Parmesan Salmon

Preparation Time: 10 minutes
Cooking Time: 25 minutes
Servings: 4
Ingredients:

- 2 tablespoons butter, melted
- 2 tablespoons green onions, sliced thinly
- 3/4 cup breadcrumbs, white, fresh
- 1/4 teaspoon thyme leaves, dried
- 1 piece salmon fillet, 1 ¼-pound
- 1/4 teaspoon salt
- 1/4 cup parmesan cheese, grated
- 2 teaspoons lemon peel, grated

Directions:

1. Preheat the oven at 350°F.
2. Mist cooking spray onto a baking pan (shallow). Fill with pat-dried salmon. Brush salmon with butter (1 tablespoon) before sprinkling with salt.
3. Combine the breadcrumbs with onions, thyme, lemon peel, cheese, and remaining butter (1 tablespoon).
4. Cover salmon with the breadcrumb mixture. Air-fry for fifteen to twenty-five minutes.

Nutrition: Calories: 290, Fat: 10 g, Protein 30 g, Carbohydrates: 0 g

CHAPTER 10:

Snack Recipes

166. Fluffy Bites

Preparation Time: 20 minutes
Cooking Time: 60 minutes
Servings: 12
Ingredients:
- 2 teaspoons cinnamon
- 2/3 cup sour cream
- 2 cups heavy cream
- 1 teaspoon scraped vanilla bean
- ¼ teaspoon cardamom
- 4 egg yolks
- Stevia to taste

Directions:
1. Start by whisking your egg yolks until creamy and smooth.
2. Get out a double boiler, and add your eggs with the rest of your ingredients. Mix well.
3. Remove from heat, allowing it to cool until it reaches room temperature.
4. Refrigerate for an hour before whisking well.
5. Pour into molds, and freeze for at least an hour before serving.

Nutrition: Calories: 363, Protein: 2 g, Fat: 40 g, Carbohydrates: 1 g

167. Coconut Fudge

Preparation Time: 20 minutes
Cooking Time: 60 minutes
Servings: 12
Ingredients:
- 2 cups coconut oil

- ½ cup dark cocoa powder
- ½ cup coconut cream
- ¼ cup almonds, chopped
- ¼ cup coconut, shredded
- 1 teaspoon almond extract
- Pinch of salt
- Stevia to taste

Directions:
1. Pour your coconut oil and coconut cream in a bowl, whisking with an electric beater until smooth. Once the mixture becomes smooth and glossy, do not continue.
2. Begin to add in your cocoa powder while mixing slowly, making sure that there aren't any lumps.
3. Add in the rest of your ingredients, and mix well.
4. Line a pan with parchment paper, and freeze until it sets.
5. Slice into squares before serving.

Nutrition: Calories: 172, Fat: 20 g, Carbohydrates: 3 g

168. Nutmeg Nougat

Preparation Time: 30 minutes
Cooking Time: 60 minutes
Servings: 12
Ingredients:
- 1 cup heavy cream
- 1 cup cashew butter
- 1 cup coconut, shredded
- ½ teaspoon nutmeg
- 1 teaspoon vanilla extract, pure
- Stevia to taste

Directions:
1. Melt your cashew butter using a double boiler, and then stir in your vanilla extract, dairy cream, nutmeg, and stevia. Make sure it's mixed well.
2. Remove from heat, allowing it to cool down before refrigerating it for half an hour.
3. Shape into balls, and coat with shredded coconut. Chill for at least two hours before serving.

Nutrition: Calories: 341, Fat: 34 g, Carbohydrates: 5 g

169. Sweet Almond Bites

Preparation Time: 30 minutes
Cooking Time: 90 minutes
Servings: 12
Ingredients:

- 18 ounces butter, grass-fed
- 2 ounces heavy cream
- ½ cup Stevia
- 2/3 cup cocoa powder
- 1 teaspoon vanilla extract, pure
- 4 tablespoons almond butter

Direction:

1. Use a double boiler to melt your butter before adding in all of your remaining ingredients.
2. Place the mixture into molds, freezing for two hours before serving.

Nutrition: Calories: 350, Protein: 2 g, Fat: 38 g

170. Strawberry Cheesecake Minis

Preparation Time: 30 minutes
Cooking Time: 120 minutes
Servings: 12
Ingredients:

- 1 cup coconut oil
- 1 cup coconut butter
- ½ cup strawberries, sliced
- ½ teaspoon lime juice
- 2 tablespoons cream cheese, full fat
- Stevia to taste

Directions:

1. Blend your strawberries together.
2. Soften your cream cheese, and then add in your coconut butter.
3. Combine all ingredients together, and then pour your mixture into silicone molds.

4. Freeze for at least two hours before serving.

Nutrition: Calories: 372, Protein: 1 g, Fat: 41 g, Carbohydrates: 2 g

171. Cocoa Brownies

Preparation Time: 10 minutes
Cooking Time: 30 minutes
Servings: 12
Ingredients:

- 1 egg
- 2 tablespoons butter, grass-fed
- 2 teaspoons vanilla extract, pure
- ¼ teaspoon baking powder
- ¼ cup cocoa powder
- 1/3 cup heavy cream
- ¾ cup almond butter
- Pinch sea salt

Directions:

1. Break your egg into a bowl, whisking until smooth.
2. Add in all of your wet ingredients, mixing well.
3. Mix all dry ingredients into a bowl.
4. Sift your dry ingredients into your wet ingredients, mixing to form a batter.
5. Get out a baking pan, greasing it before pouring in your mixture.
6. Heat your oven to 350°F and bake for twenty-five minutes.
7. Allow it to cool before slicing and serve at room temperature or warm.

Nutrition: Calories: 184, Protein: 1 g, Fat: 20 g, Carbohydrates: 1 g

172. Chocolate Orange Bites

Preparation Time: 20 minutes
Cooking Time: 120 minutes
Servings: 6
Ingredients:

- 10 ounces coconut oil
- 4 tablespoons cocoa powder
- ¼ teaspoon orange extract
- Stevia to taste

Directions:

1. Melt half of your coconut oil using a double boiler, and then add in your stevia and orange extract.
2. Get out candy molds, pouring the mixture into them. Fill each mold

halfway, and then place it in the fridge until they set.

3. Melt the other half of your coconut oil, stirring in your cocoa powder and stevia, making sure that the mixture is smooth with no lumps.

4. Pour into your molds, filling them up all the way, and then allow them to set in the fridge before serving.

Nutrition: Calories: 188 g, Protein: 1 g, Fat: 21 g, Carbohydrates: 5 g

173. Caramel Cones
Preparation Time: 25 minutes
Cooking Time: 120 minutes
Servings: 6
Ingredients:
- 2 tablespoons heavy whipping cream
- 2 tablespoons sour cream
- 1 tablespoon caramel sugar
- 1 teaspoon sea salt, fine
- 1/3 cup butter, grass-fed
- 1/3 cup coconut oil
- Stevia to taste

Directions:
1. Soften your coconut oil and butter, mixing together.
2. Mix all ingredients to form a batter, and then place them in molds.
3. Top with a little salt, and keep refrigerated until serving.

Nutrition: Calories: 100, Fat: 12 g, Carbohydrates: 1 g

174. Cinnamon Bites
Preparation Time: 20 minutes
Cooking Time: 95 minutes
Servings: 6
Ingredients:
- 1/8 teaspoon nutmeg
- 1 teaspoon vanilla extract
- ¼ teaspoon cinnamon
- 4 tablespoons coconut oil
- ½ cup butter, grass-fed
- 8 ounces cream cheese
- Stevia to taste

Directions:
1. Soften your coconut oil and butter, mixing in your cream cheese.

2. Add all of your remaining ingredients, and mix well.
3. Pour into molds, and freeze until set.

Nutrition: Calories: 178, Protein: 1 g, Fat: 19 g

175. Sweet Chai Bites

Preparation Time: 20 minutes
Cooking Time: 45 minutes
Servings: 6
Ingredients:
- 1 cup cream cheese
- 1 cup coconut oil
- 2 ounces butter, grass-fed
- 2 teaspoons ginger
- 2 teaspoons cardamom
- 1 teaspoon nutmeg
- 1 teaspoon cloves
- 1 teaspoon vanilla extract, pure
- 1 teaspoon Darjeeling black tea
- Stevia to taste

Directions:
1. Melt your coconut oil and butter before adding in your black tea. Allow it to set for one to two minutes.
2. Add in your cream cheese, removing your mixture from heat.
3. Add in all of your spices, and stir to combine.
4. Pour into molds, and freeze before serving.

Nutrition: Calories: 178, Protein: 1 g, Fat: 19 g

176. Easy Vanilla Bombs
Preparation Time: 20 minutes
Cooking Time: 45 minutes
Servings: 14
Ingredients:
- 1 cup macadamia nuts, unsalted

- ¼ cup coconut oil / ¼ cup butter
- 2 teaspoons vanilla extract, sugar-free
- 20 drops liquid Stevia
- 2 tablespoons erythritol, powdered

Directions:

1. Pulse your macadamia nuts in a blender, and then combine all of your ingredients together. Mix well.
2. Get out mini muffin tins with a tablespoon and a half of the mixture.
3. Refrigerate it for a half-hour before serving.

Nutrition: Calories: 125, Fat: 5 g, Carbohydrates: 5 g

177. Marinated Eggs

Preparation Time: 2 hours and 10 minutes
Cooking Time: 7 minutes
Servings: 4
Ingredients:

- 6 eggs
- 1 and ¼ cups water
- ¼ cup unsweetened rice vinegar
- 2 tablespoons coconut aminos
- Salt and black pepper to the taste
- 2 garlic cloves, minced
- 1 teaspoon stevia 4 ounces cream cheese
- 1 tablespoon chives, chopped

Directions:

1. Put the eggs in a pot, add water to cover, bring to a boil over medium heat, cover and cook for 7 minutes.
2. Rinse eggs with cold water and leave them aside to cool down.
3. In a bowl, mix one cup of water with coconut aminos, vinegar, stevia, and garlic, and whisk well.
4. Put the eggs in this mix, cover with a kitchen towel, and leave them aside for 2 hours, rotating from time to time.
5. Peel eggs, cut in halves, and put egg yolks in a bowl.
6. Add ¼ cup water, cream cheese, salt, pepper, and chives and stir well.
7. Stuff egg whites with this mix and serve them.
8. Enjoy!

Nutrition: Calories: 289, Protein: 15.86 g, Fat: 22.62 g, Carbohydrates: 4.52 g, Sodium: 288 mg

178. Sausage and Cheese Dip

Preparation Time: 10 minutes
Cooking Time: 130 minutes
Servings: 28
Ingredients:

- 8 ounces cream cheese
- A pinch of salt and black pepper
- 16 ounces sour cream
- 8 ounces pepper jack cheese, chopped
- 15 ounces canned tomatoes mixed with habaneros
- 1-pound Italian sausage, ground
- ¼ cup green onions, chopped

Directions:

1. Heat up a pan over medium heat, add sausage, stir and cook until it browns.
2. Add tomatoes mix, stir and cook for 4 minutes more.
3. Add a pinch of salt, pepper, and the green onions, stir and cook for 4 minutes.
4. Spread pepper jack cheese on the bottom of your slow cooker.
5. Add cream cheese, sausage mix, and sour cream, cover, and cook on High for 2 hours.
6. Uncover your slow cooker, stir dip, transfer to a bowl, and serve.
7. Enjoy!

Nutrition: Calories: 132, Protein: 6.79 g, Fat: 9.58 g, Carbohydrates: 6.22 g, Sodium: 362 mg

179. Tasty Onion and Cauliflower Dip

Preparation Time: 20 minutes
Cooking Time: 30 minutes
Servings: 24
Ingredients:

- 1 and ½ cups chicken stock
- 1 cauliflower head, florets separated
- ¼ cup mayonnaise
- ½ cup yellow onion, chopped
- ¾ cup cream cheese
- ½ teaspoon chili powder

- ½ teaspoon cumin, ground
- ½ teaspoon garlic powder
- Salt and black pepper to the taste

Directions:

1. Put the stock in a pot, add cauliflower and onion, heat up over medium heat, and cook for 30 minutes.
2. Add chili powder, salt, pepper, cumin, and garlic powder and stir.
3. Also, add cream cheese and stir a bit until it melts.
4. Blend using an immersion blender and mix with the mayo.
5. Transfer to a bowl and keep in the fridge for 2 hours before you serve it.
6. Enjoy!

Nutrition: Calories: 40, Protein: 1.23 g, Fat: 3.31 g, Carbohydrates: 1.66 g, Sodium: 72 mg

180. Pesto Crackers

Preparation Time: 10 minutes
Cooking Time: 17 minutes
Servings: 6
Ingredients:

- ½ teaspoon baking powder
- Salt and black pepper to the taste
- 1 and ¼ cups almond flour
- ¼ teaspoon basil, dried
- 1 garlic clove, minced
- 2 tablespoons basil pesto
- A pinch of cayenne pepper
- 3 tablespoons ghee

Directions:

1. In a bowl, mix salt, pepper, baking powder, and almond flour.
2. Add garlic, cayenne, and basil and stir.
3. Add pesto and whisk.
4. Also, add ghee and mix your dough with your finger.
5. Spread this dough on a lined baking sheet, introduce it in the oven at 325°F and bake for 17 minutes.
6. Leave aside to cool down, cut your crackers, and serve them as a snack.
7. Enjoy!

Nutrition: Calories: 9, Protein: 0.41 g, Fat: 0.14 g, Carbohydrates: 1.86 g, Sodium: 2 mg

181. Pumpkin Muffins

Preparation Time: 10 minutes
Cooking Time: 15 minutes
Servings: 18
Ingredients:

- ¼ cup sunflower seed butter
- ¾ cup pumpkin puree
- 2 tablespoons flaxseed meal
- ¼ cup coconut flour
- ½ cup erythritol
- ½ teaspoon nutmeg, ground
- 1 teaspoon cinnamon, ground
- ½ teaspoon baking soda
- 1 egg ½ teaspoon baking powder
- A pinch of salt

Directions:

1. In a bowl, mix butter with pumpkin puree and egg and blend well.
2. Add flaxseed meal, coconut flour, erythritol, baking soda, baking powder, nutmeg, cinnamon, and a pinch of salt and stir well.
3. Spoon this into a greased muffin pan, introduce it in the oven at 350°F and bake for 15 minutes.
4. Leave muffins to cool down and serve them as a snack.
5. Enjoy!

Nutrition: Calories: 65, Protein: 2.82 g, Fat: 5.42 g, Carbohydrates: 2.27 g, Sodium: 57 mg

182. Cheeseburger Pie

Preparation Time: 20 minutes
Cooking Time: 90 minutes
Servings: 4
Ingredients:

- 1 large spaghetti squash
- 1 lb. lean ground beef

- 1/4 cup diced onion
- 2 eggs
- 1/3 cup low-fat, plain Greek yogurt
- 2 tablespoons tomato sauce
- 1/2 teaspoons Worcestershire sauce
- 2/3 cup reduced-fat, shredded cheddar cheese - 2 oz. dill pickle slices
- Cooking spray

Directions:

1. Preheat oven to 400°F. Slice spaghetti squash in half lengthwise; dismiss pulp and seeds. Spray insides with cooking spray.
2. Place squash halves cut-side- down onto a foil-lined baking sheet, and bake for 30 minutes.
3. Once cooked, let cool to before scraping squash flesh with a fork to remove spaghetti-like strands; set aside. Push squash strands in the bottom and up sides of the greased pie pan, creating an even layer.
4. Meanwhile, set up pie filling.
5. In a lightly greased, medium-sized skillet, cook beef and onion over medium heat for 8 to 10 minutes, sometimes stirring, until meat is brown. Drain and remove from heat.
6. In a medium-sized bowl, whisk together eggs, tomato paste, Greek yogurt, and Worcestershire sauce. Stir in ground beef mixture.
7. Pour pie filling over squash crust.
8. Sprinkle meat filling with cheese, and then top with dill pickle slices.
9. Bake for 40 minutes.

Nutrition: Calories: 409, Fat: 24.49 g, Carbohydrates: 15.06 g, Protein: 30.69 g

---

183. Chicken Enchilada Bake

Preparation Time: 20 minutes
Cooking Time: 50 minutes
Servings: 5
Ingredients:

- 5 oz. Shredded chicken breast (boil and shred ahead) or 99% fat-free white chicken can be used in a pan.
- 1 can tomato paste
- 1 low sodium chicken broth can be fat-free
- 1/4 cup cheese with low-fat mozzarella
- 1 tablespoon oil
- 1 tablespoon of salt
- Ground cumin, chili powder, garlic powder, oregano, and onion powder (all to taste)
- 1 to 2 zucchinis sliced longways (similar to lasagna noodles) into thin lines
- Sliced (optional) olives

Directions:

1. Add olive oil in a saucepan over medium/high heat, stir in tomato paste and seasonings, and heat in chicken broth for 2-3 min.
2. Stirring regularly to boil, turn heat to low for 15 min.
3. Set aside and cool to ambient temperature.
4. Pull-strip of zucchini through enchilada sauce and lay flat on the pan's bottom in a small baking pan.
5. Next, add the chicken a little less than 1/4 cup of enchilada sauce and mix it.
6. Attach chicken to the cover ends to the end of the baking tray.
7. Sprinkle some bacon over the chicken.
8. Add another layer of the pulled zucchini via enchilada sauce (similar to lasagna making).
9. When needed, cover with the remaining cheese and olives on top. Bake for 35 to 40 minutes.
10. Keep an eye on them.
11. When the cheese starts getting golden, cover with foil.
12. Serve and enjoy!

Nutrition: Calories: 312, Carbohydrates: 21.3 g, Protein: 27 g, Fat: 10.2 g

Edith Rose

CHAPTER 11:

Dinner Recipes

184. Zucchini Salmon Salad

Preparation Time: 5 minutes
Cooking Time: 10 minutes
Servings: 3
Ingredients:

- 2 salmon fillets - 2 tablespoons soy sauce - 2 zucchinis, sliced
- Salt and pepper to taste
- 2 tablespoons extra virgin olive oil
- 2 tablespoons sesame seeds
- Salt and pepper to taste

Directions:

1. Drizzle the salmon with soy sauce.
2. Heat a grill pan over a medium flame. Cook salmon on the grill on each side for 2–3 minutes.
3. Season the zucchini with salt and pepper and place it on the grill as well. Cook on each side until golden.
4. Place the zucchini, salmon, and the rest of the ingredients in a bowl.
5. Serve the salad fresh.

Nutrition: Calories: 224, Fat: 19 g, Protein: 18 g, Carbohydrates: 0 g

185. Pan Fried Salmon

Preparation Time: 5 minutes
Cooking Time: 20 minutes
Servings: 4

Ingredients:

- 4 salmon fillets - Salt and pepper to taste - 1 teaspoon dried oregano
- 1 teaspoon dried basil
- 3 tablespoons extra virgin olive oil

Directions:

1. Season the fish with salt, pepper, oregano, and basil.
2. Heat the oil in a pan and place the salmon in the hot oil, with the skin facing down. Fry on each side for 2 minutes until golden brown and fragrant.
3. Serve the salmon warm and fresh.

Nutrition: Calories: 327, Fat: 25 g, Protein: 36 g, Carbs: 0.3 g

186. Grilled Salmon with Pineapple Salsa

Preparation Time: 5 minutes
Cooking Time: 30 minutes
Servings: 4
Ingredients:

- 4 salmon fillets
- Salt and pepper to taste
- 2 tablespoons Cajun seasoning
- 1 fresh pineapple, peeled and diced
- 1 cup cherry tomatoes, quartered
- 2 tablespoons cilantro, chopped
- 2 tablespoons parsley, chopped
- 1 teaspoon mint, dried
- 2 tablespoons lemon juice
- 2 tablespoons extra virgin olive oil
- 1 teaspoon honey
- Salt and pepper to taste

Directions:

1. Add salt, pepper, and Cajun seasoning to the fish. Heat a grill pan over a medium flame. Cook fish on the grill

on each side for 3–4 minutes. For the salsa, mix the pineapple, tomatoes, cilantro, parsley, mint, lemon juice, olive oil, and honey in a bowl. Season with salt and pepper.
2. Serve the grilled salmon with pineapple salsa.

Nutrition: Calories: 332, Fat: 12 g, Protein: 34 g, Carbs: 0 g

187. Mediterranean Chickpea Salad

Preparation Time: 5 minutes
Cooking Time: 20 minutes
Servings: 6
Ingredients:
- 1 can chickpeas, drained
- 1 fennel bulb, sliced
- 1 red onion, sliced
- 1 teaspoon basil, dried
- 1 teaspoon oregano, dried
- 2 tablespoons parsley, chopped
- 4 garlic cloves, minced
- 2 tablespoons lemon juice
- 2 tablespoons extra virgin olive oil
- Salt and pepper to taste

Directions:
1. Combine the chickpeas, fennel, red onion, herbs, garlic, lemon juice, and oil in a salad bowl.
2. Add salt and pepper and serve the salad fresh.

Nutrition: Calories: 200, Fat: 9 g, Protein: 4 g, Carbs: 28 g

188. Warm Chorizo Chickpea Salad

Preparation Time: 5 minutes
Cooking Time: 20 minutes
Servings: 6
Ingredients:
- 1 tablespoon extra-virgin olive oil
- 4 chorizo links, sliced
- 1 red onion, sliced
- 4 red bell peppers, chopped, roasted
- 1 can chickpeas, drained
- 2 cups cherry tomatoes
- 2 tablespoons balsamic vinegar
- Salt and pepper to taste

Directions:
1. Heat the oil in a skillet and add the chorizo. Cook briefly just until fragrant, then add the onion, bell peppers, and chickpeas and cook for 2 additional minutes.
2. Transfer the mixture to a salad bowl, then add the tomatoes, vinegar, salt, and pepper. Mix well and serve the salad right away.

Nutrition: Calories: 359, Fat: 18 g, Protein: 15 g, Carbs: 21 g

189. Greek Roasted Fish

Preparation Time: 5 minutes
Cooking Time: 30 minutes
Servings: 4
Ingredients:
- 4 salmon fillets
- 1 tablespoon oregano, chopped
- 1 teaspoon basil, dried
- 1 zucchini, sliced - 1 red onion, sliced
- 1 carrot, sliced - 1 lemon, sliced
- 2 tablespoons extra virgin olive oil
- Salt and pepper to taste

Directions:
1. Add all the ingredients to a deep-dish baking pan.
2. Season with salt and pepper and cook in the preheated oven at 350°F for 20 minutes. Serve the fish and vegetables warm.

Nutrition: Calories: 328, Fat: 13 g, Protein: 38 g, Carbs: 8 g

190. Tomato Fish Bake

Preparation Time: 5 minutes
Cooking Time: 30 minutes
Servings: 4
Ingredients:
- 4 cod fillets

- 4 tomatoes, sliced
- 4 garlic cloves, minced
- 1 shallot, sliced
- 1 celery stalk, sliced
- 1 teaspoon fennel seeds
- 1 cup vegetable stock
- Salt and pepper to taste

Directions:
1. Layer the cod fillets and tomatoes in a deep-dish baking pan.
2. Add the rest of the ingredients and add salt and pepper.
3. Cook in the preheated oven at 350°F for 20 minutes.
4. Serve the dish warm or chilled.

Nutrition: Calories: 299, Fat: 3 g, Protein: 64 g, Carbs: 2 g

191. **Garlicky Tomato Chicken Casserole**

Preparation Time: 5 minutes
Cooking Time: 50 minutes
Servings: 4
Ingredients:

- 4 chicken breasts
- 2 tomatoes, sliced
- 1 can tomatoes, diced
- 2 garlic cloves, chopped
- 1 shallot, chopped
- 1 bay leaf
- 1 thyme sprig
- 1/2 cup dry white wine
- 1/2 cup chicken stock
- Salt and pepper to taste

Directions:
1. Combine the chicken and the remaining ingredients in a deep-dish baking pan.
2. Adjust the taste with salt and pepper and cover the pot with a lid or aluminum foil.
3. Cook in the preheated oven at 330°F for 40 minutes.
4. Serve the casserole warm.

Nutrition: Calories: 313, Fat: 8 g, Protein: 47 g, Carbs: 6 g

192. **Chicken Cacciatore**

Preparation Time: 5 minutes
Cooking Time: 45 minutes
Servings: 6
Ingredients:

- 2 tablespoons extra virgin olive oil
- 6 chicken thighs
- 1 sweet onion, chopped
- 2 garlic cloves, minced
- 2 red bell peppers, cored and diced
- 2 carrots, diced
- 1 rosemary sprig
- 1 thyme sprig
- 4 tomatoes, peeled and diced
- 1/2 cup tomato juice
- 1/4 cup dry white wine
- 1 cup chicken stock
- 1 bay leaf
- Salt and pepper to taste

Directions:
1. Heat the oil in a heavy saucepan.
2. Cook chicken on all sides until golden.
3. Stir in the onion and garlic and cook for 2 minutes.
4. Stir in the rest of the ingredients and season with salt and pepper.
5. Cook on low heat for 30 minutes.
6. Serve the chicken cacciatore warm and fresh.

Nutrition: Calories: 363, Fat: 14 g, Protein: 42 g, Carbs: 9 g

193. **Fennel Wild Rice Risotto**

Preparation Time: 5 minutes
Cooking Time: 35 minutes
Servings: 6
Ingredients:

- 2 tablespoons extra virgin olive oil
- 1 shallot, chopped
- 2 garlic cloves, minced
- 1 fennel bulb, chopped
- 1 cup wild rice
- 1/4 cup dry white wine
- 2 cups chicken stock
- 1 teaspoon orange zest, grated
- Salt and pepper to taste

Directions:

1. Heat the oil in a heavy saucepan.
2. Add the garlic, shallot, and fennel, then cook for a few minutes until softened.
3. Stir in the rice and cook for 2 additional minutes, then add the wine, stock, and orange zest, with salt and pepper to taste.
4. Cook on low heat for 20 minutes.
5. Serve the risotto warm and fresh.

Nutrition: Calories: 162, Fat: 2 g, Protein: 8 g, Carbohydrates: 20 g

194. Wild Rice Prawn Salad

Preparation Time: 5 minutes
Cooking Time: 35 minutes
Servings: 6
Ingredients:

- 3/4 cup wild rice
- 1 3/4 cups chicken stock
- 1 lb. prawns
- Salt and pepper to taste
- 2 tablespoons lemon juice
- 2 tablespoons extra virgin olive oil
- 2 cups arugula

Directions:

1. Combine the rice and chicken stock in a saucepan, and cook until the liquid has been absorbed entirely.
2. Transfer the rice to a salad bowl.
3. Season the prawns with salt and pepper and drizzle them with lemon juice and oil.
4. Heat a grill pan over a medium flame.
5. Place the prawns on the hot pan and cook on each side for 2–3 minutes.
6. For the salad, combine the rice with arugula and prawns and mix well.
7. Serve the salad fresh.

Nutrition: Calories: 207, Fat: 4 g, Protein: 20.6 g, Carbs: 17 g

195. Chicken Broccoli Salad with Avocado Dressing

Preparation Time: 5 minutes
Cooking Time: 40 minutes
Servings: 6
Ingredients:

- 2 chicken breasts
- 1 lb. broccoli, cut into florets
- 1 avocado, peeled and pitted
- 1/2 lemon, juiced
- 2 garlic cloves
- 1/4 teaspoons chili powder
- 1/4 teaspoons cumin powder
- Salt and pepper to taste
- 4 to 5 cups of water

Directions:

1. Cook the chicken in a large pot of water.
2. Drain and cut the chicken into small cubes. Place in a salad bowl.
3. Add the broccoli and mix well.
4. Combine the avocado, lemon juice, garlic, chili powder, cumin powder, salt, and pepper in a blender. Pulse until smooth.
5. Spoon the dressing over the salad and mix well.
6. Serve the salad fresh.

Nutrition: Calories: 195, Fat: 11 g, Protein: 14 g, Carbs: 3 g

196. Seafood Paella

Preparation Time: 5 minutes
Cooking Time: 45 minutes
Servings: 8
Ingredients:

- 2 tablespoons extra virgin olive oil
- 1 shallot, chopped
- 2 garlic cloves, chopped
- 1 red bell pepper, cored and diced
- 1 carrot, diced
- 2 tomatoes, peeled and diced
- 1 cup wild rice
- 1 cup tomato juice
- 2 cups chicken stock
- 1 chicken breast, cubed
- Salt and pepper to taste
- 2 monkfish fillets, cubed
- 1/2 lb. fresh shrimps, peeled and deveined
- 1/2 lb. prawns
- 1 thyme sprig
- 1 rosemary sprig

Directions:

1. Heat the oil in a skillet and stir in the shallot, garlic, bell pepper, carrot, and

tomatoes. Cook for a few minutes until softened.

2. Stir in the rice, tomato juice, stock, chicken, salt, and pepper, and cook on low heat for 20 minutes.
3. Add the rest of the ingredients and cook for 10 additional minutes.
4. Serve the paella warm and fresh.

Nutrition: Calories: 245, Fat: 8 g, Protein: 27 g, Carbs: 20.6 g

197. Herbed Roasted Chicken Breasts

Preparation Time: 5 minutes
Cooking Time: 50 minutes
Servings: 4
Ingredients:
- 2 tablespoons extra virgin olive oil
- 2 tablespoons parsley, chopped
- 2 tablespoons cilantro, chopped
- 1 teaspoon oregano, dried
- 1 teaspoon basil, dried
- 2 tablespoons lemon juice
- Salt and pepper to taste
- 4 chicken breasts

Directions:
1. Combine the oil, parsley, cilantro, oregano, basil, lemon juice, salt, and pepper in a bowl.
2. Spread this mixture over the chicken and rub it well into the meat.
3. Place in a deep-dish baking pan and cover with aluminum foil.
4. Cook in the preheated oven at 350°F for 20 minutes, then remove the foil and cook for 25 additional minutes.
5. Serve the chicken warm and fresh with your favorite side dish.

Nutrition: Calories: 330, Fat: 15 g, Protein: 40.7 g, Carbs: 1 g

198. Mediterranean Chicken Salad

Preparation Time: 15 minutes
Cooking Time: 30 minutes
Servings: 4
Ingredients:
For Chicken:
- 1 3/4 lb. boneless, skinless chicken breast
- 1/4 teaspoons each pepper and salt (or as desired)
- 1 1/2 tablespoons butter, melted

For Mediterranean Salad:
- 1 cup cucumber, sliced
- 6 cups romaine lettuce, torn or roughly chopped
- 10 pitted Kalamata olives
- 1-pint cherry tomatoes
- 1/3 cup reduced-fat feta cheese
- 1/4 teaspoons each pepper and salt (or lesser)
- 1 small lemon juice (About 2 tablespoons)

Directions:
1. Preheat your oven or grill to about 350°F.
2. Season the chicken with salt, butter, and black pepper
3. Roast or grill chicken until it reaches an internal temperature of 165°F in about 25 minutes.
4. Once your chicken breasts are cooked, remove and keep them aside to rest for about 5 minutes before you slice them.
5. Combine all the salad ingredients you have and toss everything together very well.
6. Serve the chicken with a Mediterranean salad.

Nutrition: Calories: 340, Protein: 45 g, Carbs: 9 g, Fat: 14 g

199. Jalapeno Lentil Burgers

Preparation Time: 15 minutes
Cooking Time: 10 minutes
Servings: 5
Ingredients:
- 1/2 cup dried red lentils; rinsed
- 1–12 oz. can chickpeas; rinsed
- 1 teaspoon ground cumin;
- 1 teaspoon chili powder
- 1 teaspoon sea salt
- 1/2 cup packed cilantro
- Garlic cloves, minced
- Jalapeno, finely chopped
- 1/2 small red onion; minced
- Red bell pepper
- Carrot; shredded

- 1/4 cup oat bran/oat flour; (gluten-free)
- Lettuce
- Hamburger buns
- 2 cups of water
- 2 tablespoons of olive oil (optional)

For pico:

- 1 ripe mango, diced
- 1 ripe avocado, diced
- 1/2 small red onion; finely diced
- 1/2 cup cilantro; chopped
- 1/2 teaspoons fresh lime juice
- Sea salt

Directions:

1. Put all ingredients in a large bowl and mix.
2. Stir in the salt to compare.
3. Put a medium saucepan on medium heat, add lentils plus 1 1/2 cups of water, then bring water to a boil, cover it afterward, lower the heat to low, and then simmer lentils until the water is absorbed.
4. Drain, and set aside some extra water.
5. In a food processor, put the cooked lentils, chickpeas, garlic, sea salt, cilantro, chili powder, and cumin, and blend until the beans and lentils are smooth.
6. Add tomato, red pepper, jalapeno, and carrot to compare.
7. Divide into 6 equal parts and use your hands to create dense patties.
8. Heat skillet over a medium-high flame; apply 1/2 tablespoons of olive oil.
9. Place a few burgers in at a time and cook on either side for a couple of minutes, just until crisp and golden brown.
10. Repeat with remaining patties and add olive oil whenever desired.
11. Place the patties in a bun or lettuce and finish with mango avocado pico.

Nutrition: Calories: 225, Carbs: 34.9 g, Sugar: 7.7 g, Fats: 6.1 g

200. Mozzarella Sticks

Preparation Time: 8 minutes
Cooking Time: 2 minutes
Servings: 2
Ingredients:

- 1 large whole egg
- 3 sticks Mozzarella cheese in half (frozen overnight)
- 2 tablespoons Parmesan cheese, grated
- 1/2 cup almond flour
- 1/4 cup coconut oil
- 2 1/2 teaspoons Italian seasoning blend
- 1 tablespoon parsley, chopped
- 1/2 teaspoons salt
- ½ cup keto marinara sauce (optional)

Directions:

1. Heat the coconut oil in a cast-iron skillet of medium size over low-medium heat.
2. Crack the egg in a small bowl in the meantime and beat it well.
3. Take another bowl of medium size and add Parmesan cheese, almond flour, and seasonings to it. Whisk together the ingredients until a smooth mixture is prepared.
4. Take the overnight frozen Mozzarella stick, dip it in the beaten egg, and coat it well with the dry mixture. Do the same with all the remaining cheese sticks.
5. Place all the coated sticks in the preheated skillet and cook them for 2 minutes or until they start giving a golden-brown look from all sides.

6. Remove from the skillet once cooked properly and place over a paper towel so that any extra oil gets absorbed.
7. Sprinkle parsley over the sticks, if you desire, and serve with keto marinara sauce.

Nutrition: Calories: 430, Fat: 39 g, Carbohydrates: 10 g. Protein: 20 g.

201. Avocado Taco Boats
Preparation Time: 5 minutes
Cooking Time: 20 minutes
Servings: 4
Ingredients:
- 4 grape tomatoes
- 2 large avocados
- 1 lb. ground beef
- 4 tablespoons taco seasoning
- 3/4 cup Cheddar cheese, shredded sharp
- 4 slices of pickled jalapeno
- 1/4 cup salsa
- 3 romaine leaves, shredded
- 1/4 cup sour cream
- 2/3 cup water

Directions:
1. Take a skillet of large size, grease it with oil, and heat it over medium-high heat. Cook the ground beef in it for 10–15 minutes or until it gives a brownish look.
2. Once the beef gets brown, drain the grease from the skillet and add the water and the taco seasoning.
3. Reduce the heat once the taco seasoning gets mixed well and simmer for 8–10 minutes.
4. Take both avocados and prepare their halves using a sharp knife.
5. Take each avocado shell and fill it with 1/4 of the shredded romaine leaves.
6. Fill each shell with 1/4 of the cooked ground beef.
7. Do the topping with sour cream, cheese, jalapeno, salsa, and tomato before you serve the delicious avocado taco boats.

Nutrition: Calories: 430, Fat: 35 g, Carbs: 5 g, Protein: 32 g

202. Cauliflower Rice
Preparation Time: 5 minutes
Cooking Time: 20 minutes
Servings: 1
Ingredients:
Round 1:
- 1/2 teaspoons of turmeric
- 1/2 cup of diced carrot
- 1/8 cup of diced onion
- 1/2 tablespoons of low-sodium soy sauce
- 1/8 block of extra firm tofu

Round 2:
- 1/2 cup of frozen peas
- 1/4 minced garlic cloves
- 1/2 cup of chopped broccoli
- 1/2 tablespoons of minced ginger
- 1/4 tablespoons of rice vinegar
- 1/4 teaspoons of toasted sesame oil
- 1/2 tablespoons of reduced-sodium soy sauce
- 1/2 cup of diced cauliflower

Directions:
1. Crush tofu in a large bowl and toss with all the Round one ingredients.
2. Lock the air fryer lid—preheat the instant crisp air fryer to 370°F. Also, set the temperature to 370°F, set the time to 10 minutes, and cook for 10 minutes, making sure to shake once.
3. In another bowl, toss ingredients from Round 2 together.
4. Add Round 2 mixture to instant crisp air fryer and cook for another 5 to 10 minutes.
5. Enjoy!

Nutrition: Calories: 67, Fat: 8 g, Protein: 3 g, Sugar: 0 g

203. Jarlsberg Lunch Omelet
Preparation Time: 5 minutes
Cooking Time: 10 minutes
Servings: 2
Ingredients:
- 4 medium mushrooms; sliced, 2 oz.
- 1 green onion; sliced
- 2 eggs; beaten
- 1 oz. Jarlsberg or Swiss cheese; shredded

- 1 oz. ham; diced

Directions:
1. In a skillet, cook the mushrooms and scallion until soft.
2. Add the eggs and blend well.
3. Sprinkle with salt and top with the mushroom mixture, cheese, and ham.
4. When the egg is settled, fold the plain side of the omelet on the filled side.
5. Turn off the heat and let it stand until the cheese has melted.
6. Serve!

Nutrition: Calories: 288, Carbs: 22 g, Fat: 12 g, Protein: 27 g, Fiber: 6 g

204. Jalapeno Cheese Balls
Preparation Time: 10 minutes
Cooking Time: 8 minutes
Servings: 1
Ingredients:
- 1-ounce cream cheese
- 1/6 cup shredded mozzarella cheese
- 1/6 cup shredded Cheddar cheese
- 1/2 jalapeños; finely chopped
- 1/2 cup breadcrumbs
- 2 eggs
- 1/2 cup all-purpose flour
- Salt
- Pepper
- Cooking oil

Directions:
1. Mix the cream cheese, mozzarella, Cheddar cheese, and jalapeños in a medium bowl. Mix very well.
2. Form the cheese mixture into balls about an inch thick. You can also use a little ice cream scoop. It works well.
3. Arrange the cheese balls on a sheet pan and place them in the freezer for 15 minutes. It can help the cheese balls maintain their shape while frying.
4. Spray the instant Crisp Air Fryer basket with olive oil.
5. Place the breadcrumbs in a small bowl. Beat the eggs in another small bowl. In a third small bowl, mix the flour with salt and pepper to taste, and blend well.
6. Remove the cheese balls from the freezer. Plunge the cheese balls in the flour, then the eggs, then the breadcrumbs.
7. Place the cheese balls in the Instant Crisp Air Fryer. Spray with olive oil. Lock the air fryer lid. Cook for 8 minutes.
8. Open the instant Crisp Air Fryer and flip the cheese balls. I would like to recommend flipping them rather than shaking, so the balls maintain their form. Cook for more than 4 minutes.
9. Cool before serving.

Nutrition: Calories: 96, Fat: 6 g, Protein: 4 g, Sugar: 0 g

205. Zucchini Omelet
Preparation Time: 10 minutes
Cooking Time: 10 minutes
Servings: 1
Ingredients:
- 1/2 teaspoon of butter
- 1/2 zucchini; julienned
- 1 egg
- 1/8 teaspoon of fresh basil; chopped
- 1/8 teaspoon of red pepper flakes, crushed
- Salt and newly ground black pepper, to taste

Directions:
1. Preheat the instant Crisp Air Fryer to 355°F.
2. Melt butter on a medium heat using a skillet.
3. Add zucchini and cook for about 3-4 minutes.
4. In a bowl, add the eggs, basil, red pepper flakes, salt, black pepper, and beat well.
5. Add cooked zucchini and gently stir to mix.
6. Transfer the mixture into the instant Crisp Air Fryer pan. Lock the air fryer lid.
7. Cook for about 10 minutes. Also, you might prefer to wait until it is thoroughly done.

Nutrition: Calories: 285, Fat: 20.5 g, Protein: 8.6 g

206. Courgettes Risotto

Preparation Time: 10 minutes
Cooking Time: 5 minutes
Servings: 8
Ingredients:

- 2 tablespoons olive oil
- 4 cloves garlic; finely chopped
- 1.5 pounds Arborio rice
- 6 tomatoes; chopped
- 2 teaspoons chopped rosemary
- 6 courgettes; finely diced
- 1 ¼ cups peas; fresh or frozen
- 12 cups hot vegetable stock
- Salt to taste
- Freshly ground pepper

Directions:

1. Place a large, heavy-bottomed pan over medium heat. Add oil. When the oil is heated, add onion and sauté until translucent.
2. Stir in the tomatoes and cook until soft.
3. Stir in the rice and rosemary. Mix well.
4. Add half the stock and cook until dry. Stir frequently.
5. Add remaining stock and cook for 3-4 minutes.
6. Add courgettes and peas and cook until rice becomes soft. Add salt and pepper to taste.
7. Stir in the basil. Let it sit for 5 minutes.

Nutrition: Calories: 406, Fats: 5 g, Carbohydrates: 82 g, Proteins: 14 g

207. Cheesy Cauliflower Fritters

Preparation Time: 10 minutes
Cooking Time: 7 minutes
Servings: 1
Ingredients:

- 1/2 cup chopped parsley
- 1 cup Italian breadcrumbs
- 1/3 cup shredded mozzarella cheese
- 1/3 cup shredded sharp cheddar cheese
- 1 egg
- 2 minced garlic cloves
- 3 chopped scallions

- 1 head of cauliflower

Directions:

1. Cut the cauliflower up into florets. Wash well and pat dry. Place into a food processor and pulse for 20-30 seconds or till it's like rice.
2. Place the cauliflower rice in a bowl and blend with pepper, salt, egg, cheeses, breadcrumbs, garlic, and scallions.
3. Make 15 patties of the mixture with your hands, then add more breadcrumbs if needed.
4. Spritz patties with vegetable oil, and put the fitters into your Instant Crisp Air Fryer. Pile it into a single layer. Lock the air fryer lid. Set temperature to 390°F, and set time to 7 minutes, flipping after 7 minutes.

Nutrition: Calories: 209, Fat: 17 g, Protein: 6 g, Sugar: 0.5 g

208. Bell-Pepper Corn Wrapped in Tortilla

Preparation Time: 5 minutes
Cooking Time: 15 minutes
Servings: 1
Ingredients:

- 1/4 small red bell pepper; chopped
- 1/4 small yellow onion; diced
- 1/4 tablespoon of water
- 1/2 cob of grilled corn kernels
- 1 large tortilla
- One-piece commercial vegan nuggets, chopped
- Mixed greens for garnish

Directions:

1. Preheat the Crisp Air Fryer to 400°F.
2. In a skillet heated over medium heat, sauté the vegan nuggets, onions, bell peppers, and corn kernels. Set aside.
3. Place filling inside the corn tortillas.
4. Lock the air fryer lid. Fold the tortillas and place inside the moment Crisp Air Fryer. Cook for 15 minutes or until the tortilla wraps are crispy.
5. Serve with mixed greens on top.

Nutrition: Calories: 548, Fat: 20.7 g, Protein: 46 g

209. Zucchini Parmesan Chips

Preparation Time: 10 minutes
Cooking Time: 8 minutes
Servings: 1
Ingredients:
- 1/2 teaspoons paprika
- 1/2 cup grated parmesan cheese
- 1/2 cup Italian breadcrumbs
- 1 lightly beaten egg
- 2 thinly sliced zucchinis

Directions:
1. Use a really sharp knife or mandolin slicer to slice the zucchini as thinly as you can. Pat off extra moisture.
2. Beat the egg with a pinch of pepper, salt, and a bit of water.
3. Combine paprika, cheese, and breadcrumbs in a bowl.
4. Dip slices of zucchini into the egg mixture and then into the breadcrumb mixture. Press gently to coat.
5. Mist encrusted zucchini slices with vegetable oil cooking spray. Put them into your Instant Crisp Air Fryer in a single layer. Latch the air fryer lid. Set temperature to 350°F and set time to 8 minutes.
6. Sprinkle with salt and serve with salsa.

Nutrition: Calories: 211, Fat: 16 g, Protein: 8 g, Sugar: 0 g

210. Prosciutto Spinach Salad

Preparation Time: 5 minutes
Cooking Time: 5 minutes
Servings: 2
Ingredients:
- 2 cups baby spinach
- 1/3 lb. prosciutto
- 1 cantaloupe
- 1 avocado
- ¼ cup diced red onion
- Handful of raw, unsalted walnuts

Directions:
1. Put a cup of spinach on each plate.
2. Top with the diced prosciutto, cubes of melon, slices of avocado, a couple of purple onion, and a couple of walnuts.
3. Add some freshly ground pepper, if you wish.

4. Serve!

Nutrition: Calories: 348, Carbs: 11 g, Fat: 9 g, Protein: 26 g, Fiber: 22 g

211. Crispy Roasted Broccoli

Preparation Time: 10 minutes
Cooking Time: 8 minutes
Servings: 1
Ingredients:
- 1/4 teaspoons Masala
- 1/2 teaspoons red chili powder
- 1/2 teaspoons salt
- 1/4 teaspoons turmeric powder
- 1 tablespoon chickpea flour
- 1 tablespoon yogurt
- 1/2-pound broccoli

Directions:
1. Cut broccoli up into florets. Immerse in a bowl of water with two teaspoons of salt for at least half an hour to get rid of impurities.
2. Take out broccoli florets from water and allow them to drain. Wipe down thoroughly.
3. Mix all other ingredients to make a marinade.
4. Toss broccoli florets into the marinade. Cover and chill for 15-30 minutes.
5. Preheat the instant Crisp Air Fryer to 390°F. Place marinated broccoli florets into the fryer, lock the air fryer lid, set the temperature to 350°F, and set time to 10 minutes. Florets are going to be crispy when done.

Nutrition: Calories: 96, Fat: 1.3 g, Protein: 7 g, Sugar: 4.5 g

212. Grilled Ham and Cheese

Preparation Time: 15 minutes
Cooking Time: 30 minutes
Servings: 2
Ingredients:
- 3 low-carb buns
- 4 slices medium-cut deli ham
- 1 tablespoon salted butter
- 1 oz. flour
- 3 slices cheddar cheese
- 3 slices muenster cheese

Directions:

Bread:

1. Preheat your fryer to 350°F/175°C.
2. Mix the flour, salt, and baking powder in a bowl. Set aside.
3. Add in the butter and coconut oil to a skillet.
4. Melt for 20 seconds and pour into another bowl.
5. In this bowl, mix in the dough.
6. Scramble 2 eggs and add to the dough.
7. Add ½ tablespoon of coconut flour to thicken, and place evenly in a cupcake tray. Fill about ¾ inch.
8. Bake for 20 minutes or until browned.
9. Allow to chill for 15 minutes and cut each in half for the buns.

Sandwich:

1. Fry the deli meat in a skillet on high heat.
2. Put the ham and cheese between the buns.
3. Heat the butter on medium-high.
4. When brown, turn heat to low and add the dough to the pan.
5. Press down with weight until you smell burning, then flip to crisp each side.
6. Enjoy!

Nutrition: Calories: 188, Carbs: 12 g, Fat: 16 g, Protein: 14 g, Fiber: 18 g

213. Mashed Garlic Turnips

Preparation Time: 5 minutes
Cooking Time: 10 minutes
Servings: 2
Ingredients:

- 3 cups diced turnip
- 2 cloves garlic; minced
- ¼ cup heavy cream
- 3 tablespoons melted butter
- Salt and pepper to season

Directions:

1. Boil the turnips until it is soft.
2. Drain and mash the turnips.
3. Add the cream, butter, salt, pepper, and garlic. Mix very well.
4. Serve!

Nutrition: Calories: 488, Carbs: 32 g, Fat: 19 g, Protein: 34 g, Fiber: 20 g

214. Air Fryer Asparagus

Preparation Time: 5 minutes
Cooking Time: 8 minutes
Servings: 1
Ingredients:

- Nutritional yeast
- Olive oil non-stick spray
- 1 bunch of asparagus

Directions:

1. Wash the asparagus. Don't forget to trim off the thick, woody ends.
2. Spray with olive oil spray and sprinkle with yeast.
3. In your Instant Crisp Air Fryer, lay the asparagus in a singular layer. Set the temperature to 360°F. Set the time to 8 minutes.

Nutrition: Calories: 17, Fat: 4 g, Protein: 9 g

215. Avocado Fries

Preparation Time: 10 minutes
Cooking Time: 7 minutes
Servings: 1
Ingredients:

- 1 avocado
- 1/8 teaspoons of salt
- 1/4 cup of panko breadcrumbs
- Bean liquid (aquafaba) from a 15-ounce can of white or garbanzo beans

Directions:

1. Peel, pit, and slice avocado.
2. Toss salt and breadcrumbs together in a bowl. Place the aquafaba into another bowl.
3. Dredge slices of avocado first in the aquafaba then in the panko, ensuring you are evenly coating.

4. Place coated avocado slices into one layer in the Instant Crisp Air Fryer. Set temperature to 390°F and set time to 5 minutes.
5. Serve with your favorite Keto dipping sauce!

Nutrition: Calories: 102, Fat: 22 g, Protein: 9 g, Sugar: 1 g

216. Diced Cauliflower & Curry Chicken

Preparation Time: 15 minutes
Cooking Time: 30 minutes
Servings: 6
Ingredients:
- 2 lbs. chicken (4 breasts)
- 1 packet of curry paste
- 3 tablespoons ghee (can substitute with butter)
- ½ cup heavy cream
- 1 head of cauliflower (around 1 kg)

Directions:
1. In a large skillet, melt the ghee.
2. Add the curry paste and blend.
3. Once mixed, add a cup of water and simmer for 5 minutes.
4. Add the chicken, cover the skillet and simmer for 18 minutes.
5. Cut a cauliflower head into florets and blend in a food processor to form the diced cauliflower.
6. When the chicken is cooked, uncover, add the cream and cook for more than 7 minutes.
7. Serve!

Nutrition: Calories: 267, Carbs: 42 g, Fat: 31 g, Protein: 34 g, Fiber: 32 g

217. Jalapeno Coins

Preparation Time: 10 minutes
Cooking Time: 5 minutes
Servings: 1
Ingredients:
- 1 egg
- 2/3 tablespoons coconut flour
- 1 sliced and seeded jalapeno
- Pinch of garlic powder
- Pinch of onion powder
- Bit of Cajun seasoning (optional)
- Pinch of pepper and salt

Directions:
1. Ensure your Instant Crisp Air Fryer is preheated to 400°F.
2. Mix all dry ingredients.
3. Pat jalapeno slices dry. Dip them into the egg wash and then into the dry mixture. Toss to coat thoroughly.
4. Add coated jalapeno slices to Instant Crisp Air Fryer in a singular layer. Spray with vegetable oil.
5. Lock the air fryer lid. Set temperature to 350°F and set time to 5 minutes. Cook till just crispy.

Nutrition: Calories: 128, Fat: 8 g, Protein: 7 g, Sugar: 0 g

218. Lasagna Spaghetti Squash

Preparation Time: 30 minutes
Cooking Time: 90 minutes
Servings: 6
Ingredients:
- 25 slices mozzarella cheese
- 1 large jar (40 oz.) of Rao's Marinara sauce
- 30 oz. whole-milk ricotta cheese
- 2 large spaghetti squash; cooked (44 oz.)
- 4 lbs. ground beef

Directions:
1. Preheat your fryer to 375°F/190°C.
2. Slice the spaghetti squash and place it face down inside a fryer-proof dish. Fill with water until covered.
3. Heat for 45 minutes or until the skin is soft.
4. Roast the meat until it browns.
5. In a large skillet, heat the browned meat and marinara sauce. Put aside when warm.
6. Scrape the flesh off the cooked squash to resemble strands of spaghetti.
7. Layer the lasagna in a large greased pan in alternating layers of spaghetti squash, meat sauce, mozzarella, and ricotta. Repeat until all are layered.
8. Bake for 30 minutes and serve!

Nutrition: Calories: 508, Carbs: 32 g, Fat: 8 g, Protein: 22 g, Fiber: 21 g

219. Monkey Salad

Preparation Time: 4 minutes
Cooking Time: 7 minutes
Servings: 1
Ingredients:

- 2 tablespoons butter
- 1 cup unsweetened coconut flakes
- 1 cup raw, unsalted cashews
- 1 cup 90% dark chocolate shavings

Directions:

1. In a skillet, melt the butter on medium heat.
2. Add the coconut flakes and sauté until it becomes lightly browned or for 4 minutes.
3. Add the cashews and sauté for 3 minutes. Remove from the heat and sprinkle with bittersweet chocolate shavings.
4. Serve!

Nutrition: Calories: 321, Carbs: 5 g, Fat: 12 g, Protein: 6 g, Fiber: 5 g

220. Mu Shu Lunch Pork

Preparation Time: 5 minutes
Cooking Time: 10 minutes
Servings: 2
Ingredients:

- 4 cups coleslaw mix, with carrots
- 1 small onion; sliced thin
- 1 lb. cooked roast pork; cut into ½" cubes
- 2 tablespoons hoisin sauce
- 2 tablespoons soy sauce

Directions:

1. In a large skillet, heat the oil on high heat.
2. Stir-fry the cabbage and onion for 4 minutes or until they are soft.
3. Add the pork, hoisin, and soy sauce.
4. Cook until browned.
5. Enjoy!

Nutrition: Calories: 388, Carbs: 16 g, Fat: 21 g, Protein: 25 g, Fiber: 16 g

CHAPTER 12:

Desserts Recipes

221. Greek Yogurt Muesli Parfaits

Preparation Time: 10 minutes
Cooking Time: 0 minutes
Servings: 4
Ingredients:
- 4 cups Greek yogurt
- 1 cup whole wheat muesli
- 2 cups fresh berries of your choice

Directions:
1. Layer the four classes with Greek yogurt at the bottom, muesli on top, and berries.
2. Repeat the layers until the glass is filled.
3. Place in the fridge for at least hours to chill.

Nutrition Calories 280, Fat 36 g, Protein 23 g, Carbs 4 g

222. Lemon Cream

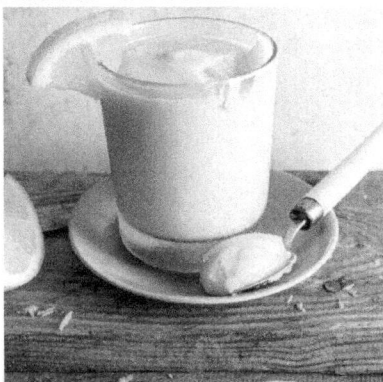

Preparation Time: 10 minutes
Cooking Time: 10 minutes
Servings: 6
Ingredients:
- 2 eggs, whisked

- 1 and ¼ cup stevia
- 10 tablespoons avocado oil
- 1 cup heavy cream
- Juice of 2 lemons
- Zest of 2 lemons, grated

Directions:
1. In a pan, combine the cream with the lemon juice and the other ingredients, whisk well, cook for 10 minutes, divide into cups and keep in the fridge for 1 hour before serving.

Nutrition: Calories 200, Fat 8.5 g, Protein 4.5 g, Carbs 8.6 g, Fiber 4.5 g

223. Peanut Banana Yogurt Bowl

Preparation Time: 15 minutes
Cooking Time: 0 minutes
Servings: 4
Ingredients:
- 4 cups Greek yogurt
- 2 medium bananas, sliced
- ¼ cup creamy natural peanut butter
- ¼ cup flax seed meal
- 1 teaspoon nutmeg

Directions:
1. Divide the yogurt between four bowls and top with banana, peanut butter, and flaxseed meal.

Nutrition: Calories 370, Fat 10.6 g, Protein 22.7 g, Carbs 47.7 g

224. Sweet Tropical Medley Smoothie

Preparation Time: 15 minutes
Cooking Time: 0 minutes
Servings: 4
Ingredients:
- 1 banana, peeled
- 1 sliced mango

- 1 cup fresh pineapple
- ½ cup coconut water

Directions:
1. Place all ingredients in a blender.
2. Blend until smooth.
3. Pour in a glass container and allow to chill in the fridge for at least 30 minutes.

Nutrition: Calories 73, Fat 0,5 g, Protein 0.8 g, Carbs 18.6 g

225. Mediterranean Fruit Tart
Preparation Time: 15 minutes
Cooking Time: 30 minutes
Servings: 1/8 of tart
Ingredients:
- ¼ cups all-purpose flour
- ½ teaspoon salt
- 2 TB. sugar
- 1 cup cold butter
- ½ cup shortening
- 5 TB. ice water
- 2 cups Ashta Custard
- 10 strawberries, sliced
- 2 kiwis, peeled and sliced
- 1 cup blueberries
- 1 cup peach or apricot jam
- 3 TB. water

Directions:
1. In a food processor fitted with a chopping blade, pulse 2 cups of all-purpose flour, salt, and sugar 5 times.
2. Add butter and shortening, and blend for 1 minute or until mixture crumbles. Transfer mixture to a medium bowl.
3. Add ice enter to the batter, and mix just until combined.
4. Place dough on a piece of plastic wrap, form into a flat disc, and refrigerate for 20 minutes.
5. Preheat the oven to 450°F.
6. Dust your workspace with flour, and using a rolling pin, roll out dough to 1/8-inch thickness. Place rolled-out dough into a 9-inch tart pan, press to mold into the pan, and cut off excess dough. Bake for 13 minutes.
7. Let the tart cool for 10 minutes.
8. Place tart shell on a serving dish and fill with Ashta Custard. Arrange strawberry slices, kick slices, and blueberries on top of the tart.
9. In a small saucepan over medium heat, heat peach jam and enter, stirring for 2 minutes.
10. Using a pastry brush, brush the top of the fruit and tart with warmed jam.
11. Serve chilled and store in the refrigerator.

Nutrition: Calories 644, Fat 39 g, Carbs 70 g, Fiber 2 g, Protein 6 g

226. Green Tea and Vanilla Cream
Preparation Time: 10 minutes
Cooking Time: 0 minutes
Servings: 4
Ingredients:
- 14 ounces almond milk, hot
- 2 tablespoons green tea powder
- 14 ounces heavy cream
- 3 tablespoons stevia
- 1 teaspoon vanilla extract
- 1 teaspoon gelatin powder

Directions:
1. In a bowl, combine the almond milk with the green tea powder and the rest of the ingredients, whisk well, cool down, divide into cups and keep in the fridge for 2 hours before serving.

Nutrition: Calories 120, Fat 3 g, Protein 4 g, Carbs 7 g, Fiber 3 g

227. Warm Peach Compote
Preparation Time: 10 minutes
Cooking Time: 5 minutes
Servings: 4
Ingredients:
- 4 peaches, peeled and chopped
- 1 tablespoon water
- ½ tbsp cornstarch
- 1 teaspoon vanilla

Directions:
1. Add water, vanilla, and peaches into the instant pot.
2. Seal pot with lid and cook on high for 1 minute.
3. Once done, allow to release pressure naturally. Remove lid.

4. In a small bowl, whisk together 1 tablespoon of water and cornstarch and pour into the pot and stir well.
5. Serve and enjoy.

Nutrition: Calories 66, Fat 0.4 g, Protein 1.4 g, Carbs 15 g, Sugar 14 g

228. Honey Walnut Bars

Preparation Time: 30 minutes
Cooking Time: 25 minutes
Servings: 8
Ingredients:

- 5 oz puff pastry
- ½ cup water
- 3 tablespoons of liquid honey
- 1 teaspoon Erythritol
- 1/'3 cup butter, softened
- ½ cup walnuts, chopped
- 1 teaspoon olive oil

Directions:

1. Roll up the puff paste and cut it on 6 sheets. Then brush the tray with olive oil and arrange the first puff pastry sheet inside. Grease it with butter gently and sprinkle it with walnuts.
2. Repeat the same steps with 4 puff pastry sheets.
3. Then sprinkle the last layer with walnuts and Erythritol and cove with the sixth puff past sheet.
4. Cut the baklava on the servings. Bake the baklava for 30 minutes.
5. Meanwhile, bring to boil liquid honey and water
6. When the baklava is cooked, remove it from the oven.
7. Pour hot honey liquid over baklava and let it cool till room temperature.

Nutrition: Calories 243, Fat 19.6 g, Protein 3.3 g, Carbs 15.9 g

229. Lime Vanilla Fudge

Preparation Time: 10 minutes
Cooking Time: 0 minutes
Servings: 6
Ingredients:

- 1/3 cup cashew butter
- 5 tablespoons lime juice
- ½ teaspoon lime zest, grated
- 1 tablespoons stevia

Directions:

1. In a bowl, mix the cashew butter with the other ingredients and whisk well.
2. Line a muffin tray with parchment paper, scoop 1 tablespoon of lime fudge, mix in each of the muffin tins and keep in the freezer for 3 hours before serving.

Nutrition: Calories 200, Fat 4.5 g, Protein 5 g, Carbs 13.5 g, Fiber 3.4 g

230. Pear Sauce

Preparation Time: 15 minutes
Cooking Time: 10 minutes
Servings: 6
Ingredients:

- 10 pears, sliced
- 1 cup apple juice
- 1 ½ teaspoon cinnamon
- ¼ teaspoon nutmeg

Directions:

1. Add all ingredients into the instant pot and stir well.
2. Seal pot with lid and cook on high for 15 minutes. Once done, allow to release pressure naturally for 10 minutes, then release remaining using quick release. Remove lid. Blend the pear mixture using an immersion blender until smooth.
3. Serve and enjoy.

Nutrition: Calories 222, Fat 0.6 g, Protein 1.3 g, Carbs 58.2 g, Sugar 38 g, Chol 0 mg

231. Honey Cream

Preparation Time: 5 minutes
Cooking Time: 10 minutes
Servings: 2
Ingredients:

- ½ cup cream

- ¼ cup milk
- 2 teaspoons honey
- 1 teaspoon vanilla extract
- 1 tablespoons gelatin
- 2 tablespoons orange juice

Directions:

1. Mix up together milk and gelatin and leave it for 5 minutes.
2. Meanwhile, pour cream into the saucepan and bring it to a boil.
3. Add honey and vanilla extract.
4. Remove the cream from the heat and stir well until honey is dissolved.
5. After this, add gelatin mixture (milk+ gelatin) and mix it up until gelatin is dissolved. After this, place 1 tablespoon of orange juice in every serving glass. Add the cream mixture over the orange juice.
6. Refrigerate the pannacotta for 30-50 minutes in the fridge or until it is solid.

Nutrition: Calories 100, Fat 4 g, Protein 4.6 g, Carbs 11 g

232. Dragon Fruit, Pear, and Spinach Salad

Preparation Time: 3 minutes
Cooking Time: 0 minute
Servings: 4
Ingredients:

- 5 ounces spinach leaves, torn
- 1 dragon fruit, peeled and cubed
- 2 pears, peeled and cubed
- 10 ounces organic goat cheese
- 1 cup pecan, halves
- 6 ounces blackberries
- 6 ounces raspberries
- 8 tablespoons olive oil
- 8 tablespoons red wine vinegar
- 1 tablespoon poppy seeds

Directions:

1. In a mixing bowl, combine all ingredients except for the poppy seeds.
2. Place inside the fridge and allow to chill before seizing.
3. Sprinkle with poppy seeds on top before serving.

Nutrition: Calories 321, Fat 3 g, Protein 3.3 g, Carbs 27.2 g

233. Kataifi

Preparation Time: 30 minutes
Cooking Time: 25 minutes
Servings: 8-10
Ingredients:

- 1 kg almonds, blanched and then chopped
- 1 teaspoon cinnamon
- ¼ kg kataifi phyllo
- 2 eggs
- 4 tablespoons sugar
- 400 g butter
- 1 ½ kilograms sugar
- 1 lemon rind
- 1 teaspoon lemon juice
- 5 cups water

Directions:

1. Preheat the oven to 340ºF.
2. Put the sugar, eggs, cinnamon, and almonds in a bowl.
3. With your fingers, open the kataifi past gently. Lay it on a piece of marble and wood. Put 1 tablespoon of the almond mixture in one end and then roll the pasts into a log or a cylinder. Make sure you fold the pasts a little tight so that way the filling is enclosed securely. Repeat the process with the remaining past and almond mixture.
4. Melt the butter and put it into a baking dish.
5. Brush the kataifi rolls with the melted butter, covering all the sides.
6. Place into baking sheets and bake for about 30 minutes.
7. Meanwhile, prepare the syrup.
8. Except for the lemon juice, cook the rest of the syrup ingredients for about 5-10 minutes. Add the lemon juice and let cook for a few minutes until the syrup is slightly thick.
9. After baking the kataifi, pour the syrup over the still warm rolls.
10. Cover the pastry with a clean towel. Let cool as the kataifi absorbs the syrup.

Nutrition: Calories 1085, Fat 83.3 g, Protein 22.6 g, Carbs 76.6 g, Sugar 59 g, Chol 119 mg, Sodium 248, Pot 759 mg

234. Walnuts Kataifi
Preparation Time: 50 minutes
Cooking Time: 30 minutes
Servings: 2
Ingredients:
- 7 oz kataifi dough
- 1/3 cup walnuts, chopped
- ½ teaspoon ground cinnamon
- ¾ teaspoon vanilla extract
- 4 tablespoons butter, melted
- ¼ teaspoon ground clove
- 1/3 cup water
- 3 tablespoons honey

Directions:
1. For the filling: mix up together walnuts, ground cinnamon, and vanilla extract. Add ground clove and blend the mixture until smooth.
2. Make the kataifi dough: grease the casserole mold with butter and place ½ part of the kataifi dough.
3. Then sprinkle the filling over the kataifi dough.
4. After this, sprinkle the filling with 1 tablespoon of melted butter.
5. Sprinkle the filling with the remaining kataifi dough.
6. Make the roll from ½ part of kataifi dough and cut it. Gently arrange the kataifi roll in the tray.
7. Repeat the same steps with the remaining dough. In the end, you should get 2 kataifi rolls.
8. Preheat the oven to 355°F and place the tray with kataifi rolls inside.
9. Bake the dessert for 50 minutes or until it is crispy.
10. Meanwhile, make the syrup: bring the water to a boil.
11. Add honey and heat it up until the honey is dissolved.
12. When the kataifi rolls are cooked, pour the hot syrup over the hot kataifi rolls.
13. Cut every kataifi roll into 2 pieces.
14. Serve the dessert with the remaining syrup.

Nutrition: Calories 120, Fat 1.5 g, Protein 3 g, Carbs 22 g

235. Mediterranean Biscotti
Preparation Time: 1 Hour
Cooking Time: 45 minutes
Servings: 3
Ingredients:
- 2 eggs
- 1 cup whole-wheat flour
- 1 cup all-purpose flour
- ¾ cup parmesan cheese, grated
- 2 teaspoons baking powder
- 2 tablespoons sugar
- ¼ cup sun-dried tomato, finely chopped
- ¼ cup kalamata olive, finely chopped
- 1/3 cup olive oil
- ½ teaspoon salt
- ½ teaspoon black pepper, cracked
- 1 teaspoon dried oregano (preferably Greek)
- 1 teaspoon dried basil

Directions:
1. Into a large-sized bowl, beat the eggs and the sugar together. Pour in the olive, beat until smooth.
2. In another bowl, combine the flours, baking powder, pepper, salt, oregano, and basil. Stir the flour mix into the egg mixture, stirring until blended.
3. Stir in the cheese, tomatoes, and olives, stirring until thoroughly combined.
4. Divide the dough into 2 portions; shape each into 10-inch-long logs. Place the logs into a parchment-lined cookie sheet, flatten the low tops slightly.
5. Bake for about 30 minutes in a preheated 375°F oven or until the loss are pale golden and not quite firm to the touch.
6. Remove from the oven; let cool on the baking sheet for 3 minutes, transfer the logs into a cutting board, slice each log into 1/2-inch diagonal slices using a serrated knife.

7. Place the biscotti slices on the baking sheet, return them into the 325°F oven and bake for about 20 to 25 minutes until dry and firm. Flip the slices halfway through baking. Remove from the oven, transfer on a ride rack and let cool.

Nutrition: Calories 731, Fat 36.5 g, Protein 23.3 g, Carbs 77.8 g, Sugar 10.7, Fiber 3.5 g, Chol 146 mg, Sodium 1238.4 mg

236. Semolina Pie

Preparation Time: 1 Hour
Cooking Time: 45 minutes
Servings: 6
Ingredients:
- ½ cup milk
- 3 tablespoons semolina
- ½ cup butter, softened
- 8 Phyllo sheets
- 2 eggs, beaten
- 3 tablespoons Erythritol
- 1 teaspoon lemon rind
- 1 tablespoon lemon juice
- 1 teaspoon vanilla extract
- 2 tablespoons liquid honey
- 1 teaspoon ground cinnamon
- ¼ cup of water

Directions:
1. Melt ½ part of all butter.
2. Then brush the casserole glass mold with the butter and place 1 Phyllo sheet inside.
3. Brush the Phyllo sheet with butter and cover it with a second Phyllo sheet.
4. Blake the dessert filling: heat up milk and add semolina.
5. Stir it carefully.

6. After this, add the remaining softened butter. Erythritol and vanilla extract.
7. Bring the mixture to a boil and simmer it for 2 minutes.
8. Remove it from the heat and cool to room temperature.
9. Then add beaten eggs and mix up well.
10. Pour the semolina mixture in the mold over the Phyllo sheets, flatten it if needed.
11. When covering the semolina mixture with remaining Phyllo sheets and brush with remaining melted butter.
12. Cut the dessert on the bars.
13. Bake galaktoboureko for 1 hour at 365°F.
14. Then make the syrup: bring to boil lemon juice, honey and water and remove the liquid from the heat.
15. Pour the syrup over the hot dessert and let it chill well.

Nutrition: Calories 304, Fat 18 g, Protein 6 g, Carbs 39.5 g

237. Vanilla Apple Compote

Preparation Time: 15 minutes
Cooking Time: 20 minutes
Servings: 6
Ingredients:
- 3 cups apples, cored and cubed
- 1 teaspoon vanilla
- ¾ cup coconut sugar
- 1 cup water
- 2 tablespoons fresh lime juice

Directions:
1. Add all ingredients into the inner pot of the instant pot and stir well.
2. Seal pot with lid and cook on high for 15 minutes.
3. Once done, allow to release pressure naturally for 10 minutes, then release remaining using quick release. Remove lid.
4. Stir and serve.

Nutrition: Calories 76, Fat 0.2 g, Protein 0.5 g, Carbs 19 g, Sugar 11.9 g

238. Cold Lemon Squares
Preparation Time: 10 minutes
Cooking Time: 0 minutes
Servings: 4
Ingredients:
- 1 cup avocado oil + a drizzle
- 2 bananas, peeled and chopped
- 1 tablespoon honey
- ¼ cup lemon juice
- A pinch of lemon zest, grated

Directions:
1. In your food processor, mix the bananas with the rest of the ingredients, pulse well, and spread on the bottom of a pan greased with a drizzle of oil.
2. Introduce in the fridge for 30 minutes, slice into squares and serve.

Nutrition: Calories 136, Fat 11.2 g, Protein 1.1 g, Carbs 0.2 g, Fiber 0.2 g

239. Minty Coconut Cream
Preparation Time: 10 minutes
Cooking Time: 0 minutes
Ingredients
- 1 banana, peeled
- 2 cups coconut flesh, shredded
- 3 tablespoons mint, chopped
- 1 and ½ cups coconut water
- 2 tablespoons stevia
- ½ avocado, pitted and peeled

Directions:
1. In a blender, combine the coconut with the banana and the rest of the ingredients, pulse well, divide into cups and serve cold.

Nutrition: Calories 193, Fat 5.4 g, Fiber 3.4 g, Carbs 7.6 g, Protein 3.4 g

240. Cherry Cream

Preparation Time: 15 minutes
Cooking Time: 0 minutes
Servings: 4
Ingredients:
- 2 cups cherries, pitted and chopped
- 1 cup almond milk
- ½ cup whipping cream
- 3 eggs, whisked
- 1/3 cup stevia
- 1 teaspoon lemon juice
- ½ teaspoon vanilla extract

Directions:
1. In your food processor, combine the cherries with the milk and the rest of the ingredients, pulse well, divide into cups and keep in the fridge for 2 hours before serving.

Nutrition: Calories 200, Fat 4.5 g, Protein 3.4 g, Carbs 5.6 g, Fiber 3.3 g

241. Tiny Orange Cardamom Cookies
Preparation Time: 12 minutes
Cooking Time: 15 minutes
Servings: 8
Ingredients:
- ½ cup whole-wheat flour
- ½ cup all-purpose flour
- 1 large egg
- 1 tablespoon sesame seeds, toasted, optional (salted roasted pistachios, chopped)
- 1 teaspoon orange zest
- 1 teaspoon vanilla extract
- ½ cup butter, softened
- ½ cup sugar
- ¼ teaspoon ground cardamom

Directions:
1. Preheat the oven to 375°F.
2. In a medium bowl, blend the orange zest and the sugar thoroughly and blend in the cardamom. Add the butter and with a mixer, beat until the mixture is flux and light. Beat in the egg and the vanilla into the mixture. With the mixer on low speed, mix the flours into the mixture.
3. Line 3 baking sheets with parchment paper. Using a lead teaspoon measure,

drop the batter of the cookie mixture onto the sheets. Top each cookie with a pinch of sesame seeds or nuts, if desired, bake for 10-12 minutes or until the cookies are brown at the edges and crisp. When baked, transfer the cookies to a cooling rack and let them cool completely.

Nutrition: Calories 113, Fat 6.5 g, Protein 1.4 g, Carbs 12 g, Fiber 0.3 g, Sodium 46 mg, Chol 29 mg

242. Sparkling Limoncello
Preparation Time: 5 minutes
Cooking Time: 15 minutes
Servings: 1
Ingredients:
- 4 ounces club soda
- 1-ounce vodka
- 1-ounce Limoncello
- 1 ½ teaspoon simple syrup
- Ice, as needed
- Lemon peels for garnish
- Splash lemon juice

Directions:
1. Combine the lemon juice, simple syrup, club soda, vodka, and limoncello in a cocktail shaker. Fill the shaker 2/3 full with ice. Stir for about 10 to 15 minutes to chill. Strain the ice into a cocktail glass, garnish with the lemon peel, and serve.

Nutrition: Calories 98, Fat 0 g, Protein 0 g, Carbs 8.4 g

243. Mast-O Khiar (Persian Yogurt)
Preparation Time: 10 minutes
Cooking Time: 10 minutes
Servings: 8
Ingredients:
- 4 cup yogurt, plain Greek
- 2 teaspoon mints, dried
- 2 teaspoon dills, dried
- ¼ teaspoon black pepper, ground
- ½ teaspoon salt
- 1 ½ cup Persian cucumbers, diced

Directions:
1. Combine all the ingredients in a medium-sized bowl.

Nutrition: Calories 62, Fat 4 g, Protein 0.8 g, Carbs 7.2 g, Sugar 5.5 g

244. Mediterranean Martini
Preparation Time: 10 minutes
Cooking Time: 10 minutes
Servings: 2
Ingredients:
- 4 pieces fresh strawberries
- 30 ml vodka
- 2 pieces fresh gooseberries
- Chilled sparkling wine, to top
- Few pieces of mint leaves
- Splash of lime juice
- Splash of sugar syrup

Directions:
1. Put the gooseberries, strawberries, and mint leaves into a mixing glass; muddle the ingredients to release the juices.
2. Put ice into a mixing glass until full. Add in the lime, sugar, and vodka. Shake and then stir into chilled martini glasses. Top with the sparkling wine and then garnish, serve.

Nutrition: Calories 51, Fat 0.1 g, Protein 0.3 g, Carbs 4.6 g, Sugar 1.2 g, Fiber 1 g

245. Greek Mountain Tea
Preparation Time: 5 minutes
Cooking Time: 10 minutes
Servings: 1
Ingredients:
- Greek Mountain Tea
- 1 cup water
- Honey or sugar, optional

Directions:
1. Get about 1 to 2 Greek Mountain Tea leaves and break them into thirds.
2. Fill a pot with water. Turn the flame or heat on to medium-high. Put the tea leaves into the pot from the heat and let the tea steep for 7 minutes.

3. After steeping, pour the tea into a cup over a strainer to catch the tea leaves.
4. If desired, sweeten with honey and sugar. Enjoy!

Nutrition: Calories 3, Fat 0 g, Protein 0 g, Carbs 0.9 g, Sugar 0.7 g

246. Santorini Sunrise

Preparation Time: 5 minutes
Cooking Time: 5 minutes
Servings: 1
Ingredients:

- 2 1/4 cups vodka, unflavored, plus more
- 1 pink grapefruit, sliced
- 1 ounce Campari
- 2-ounce Pink Grapefruit-infused vodka
- 2 slices pink grapefruit, quartered (8 total pieces)
- 2 teaspoons honey (or Greek honey, if available)
- 3 ounces freshly squeezed pink grapefruit juice
- 4 mint leaves, plus more for garnish

Directions:
For the grapefruit-infused vodka:
1. Put the grapefruit in a sterilized 1-quart glass jar, stuffing them tight. Pour the vodka over the grapefruit.
2. Add more vodka, if needed, to submerge the grapefruit completely. Seal the jar with tight lit; let sit at room temperature for 3 days. After 3 days, strain the infused vodka through a coffee filter into another sterilized glass jar; store with other spirits for up to 2 months.

For the cocktail:
1. In a highball glass, muddle 7 pieces of the quartered grapefruit slices with the honey and mint leaves. Add ice until the glass is filled. Add the vodka, Campari, and grapefruit juice. Stir. Garnish with the remaining 1 grapefruit slice and mint leaves: serve.

Nutrition: Calories 284, Fat 0.6 g, Fiber 6.2 g, Carbs 38.3 g, Sugar 7.3 g, Iron 31%, Calcium 12%, Protein 3.3 g

247. Yogurt Mint

Preparation Time: 5 minutes
Cooking Time: 10 minutes
Servings: 2
Ingredients:

- 1 cup water
- 5 cups milk
- ¾ cup plain yogurt
- ¼ cup fresh mint
- 1 tablespoon maple syrup

Directions:
1. Add 1 cup water to the Instant Pot Pressure Cooker.
2. Press the steam function button and adjust to 1 minute.
3. Once done, add the milk, then press the yogurt function button and allow boiling.
4. Add yogurt and fresh mint, and then stir well.
5. Pour into a glass and add maple syrup.
6. Enjoy.

Nutrition: Calories: 25, Fat: 0.5 g, Carbs: 5 g, Protein: 2 g

248. Chocolate Fondue

Preparation Time: 5 minutes
Cooking Time: 10 minutes
Servings: 2
Ingredients:

- 1 cup water
- ½ teaspoon sugar
- ½ cup coconut cream
- ¾ cup dark chocolate, chopped

Directions:
1. Pour the water into your Instant Pot.
2. To a heatproof bowl, add the chocolate, sugar, and coconut cream.
3. Place in the Instant Pot.
4. Seal the lid, select manual, and cook for 2 minutes. When ready, do a quick release and carefully open the lid. Stir well and serve immediately.

Nutrition: Calories: 216, Fat: 17 g, Carbs: 11 g, Protein: 2 g

249. Rice Pudding
Preparation Time: 5 minutes
Cooking Time: 12 minutes
Servings: 2
Ingredients:
- ½ cup short grain rice
- ¼ cup sugar
- 1 cinnamon stick
- 1½ cup milk
- 1 slice lemon peel
- Salt to taste

Directions:
1. Rinse the rice under cold water.
2. Put the milk, cinnamon stick, sugar, salt, and lemon peel inside the Instant Pot Pressure Cooker.
3. Close the lid, lock it in place, and make sure to seal the valve. Press the Pressure button and cook for 10 minutes on High.
4. When the timer beeps, choose the Quick Pressure release. This will take about 2 minutes.
5. Remove the lid. Open the pressure cooker and discard the lemon peel and cinnamon stick. Spoon in a serving bowl and serve.

Nutrition: Calories: 111, Fat: 6 g, Carbs: 21 g, Protein: 3 g

250. Braised Apples
Preparation Time: 5 minutes
Cooking Time: 12 minutes
Servings: 2
Ingredients:
- 2 cored apples
- ½ cup water
- ½ cup red wine
- 3 tablespoons sugar
- ½ teaspoon. ground cinnamon

Directions:
1. In the bottom of the Instant Pot, add the water and place apples.
2. Pour wine on top and sprinkle with sugar and cinnamon. Close the lid carefully and cook for 10 minutes at high pressure.
3. When done, do a quick pressure release?

4. Transfer the apples onto serving plates and top with cooking liquid.
5. Serve immediately.
Nutrition: Calories: 245, Fat: 0.5 g, Carbs: 53 g, Protein: 1 g

251. Wine Figs
Preparation Time: 5 minutes
Cooking Time: 3 minutes
Servings: 2
Ingredients:
- ½ cup pine nuts
- 1 cup red wine
- 1 lb. figs
- Sugar, as needed

Directions:
1. Slowly pour the wine and sugar into the Instant Pot.
2. Arrange the trivet inside it; place the figs over it. Close the lid and lock. Ensure that you have sealed the valve to avoid leakage.
3. Press manual mode and set the timer to 3 minutes.
4. After the timer reads zero, press cancel and quick-release pressure.
5. Carefully remove the lid.
6. Divide figs into bowls, and drizzle wine from the pot over them.
7. Top with pine nuts and enjoy.

Nutrition: Calories: 95, Fat: 3 g, Carbs: 5 g, Protein: 2 g

252. Lemon Curd
Preparation Time: 10 minutes
Cooking Time: 10 minutes
Servings: 2
Ingredients:
- 4 tablespoons butter
- 1 cup sugar - 2/3 cup lemon juice
- 3 eggs - 2 teaspoons lemon zest
- 1 ½ cups of water

Directions:
1. Whisk the butter and sugar thoroughly until smooth.
2. Add 2 whole eggs and incorporate just the yolk of the other egg.
3. Add the lemon juice.
4. Transfer the mixture into the two jars and tightly seal the tops

5. Pour 1 ½ cups of water into the bottom of the Instant Pot and place in the steaming rack. Put the jars on the rack and cook on High Pressure for 10 minutes. Natural-release the pressure for 10 minutes before quickly releasing the rest. Stir in the zest and put the lids back on the jars.

Nutrition: Calories: 45, Fat: 1 g, Carbs: 8 g, Protein: 1 g

253. **Rhubarb Dessert**
Preparation Time: 4 minutes
Cooking Time: 5 minutes
Servings: 2
Ingredients:
- 3 cups rhubarb, chopped
- 1 tablespoon ghee, melted
- 1/3 cup water - 1 tablespoon stevia
- 1 teaspoon vanilla extract

Directions:
1. Put all the listed Ingredients: in your Instant Pot, cover, and cook on High for 5 minutes.
2. Divide into small bowls and serve cold.
3. Enjoy!

Nutrition: Calories: 83, Fat: 2 g, Carbs: 2 g, Protein: 2 g

254. **Raspberry Compote**

Preparation Time: 11 minutes
Cooking Time: 30 minutes
Servings: 2
Ingredients:
- 1 cup raspberries
- ½ cup Swerve
- 1 teaspoon freshly grated lemon zest
- 1 teaspoon vanilla extract

- 2 cups water

Directions:
1. Press the sauté button on your Instant Pot, and then add all the listed ingredients. Stir well and pour in 1 cup of water. Cook for 5 minutes, continually stirring, then pour in 1 more cup of water and press the cancel button. Secure the lid properly, press the manual button, and set the timer to 15 minutes on low pressure.
2. When the timer buzzes, press the cancel button and release the pressure naturally for 10minutes.
3. Move the pressure handle to the "venting" position to release any remaining pressure and open the lid.
4. Let it cool before serving.

Nutrition: Calories: 48, Fat: 0.5 g, Carbs: 5 g, Protein: 1 g

255. **Poached Pears**
Preparation Time: 8 minutes
Cooking Time: 10 minutes
Servings: 2
Ingredients:
- 1 tablespoon lime juice
- 2 teaspoons lime zest
- 1 cinnamon stick
- 2 whole pears, peeled
- 1 cup water
- Fresh mint leaves for garnish

Directions:
1. Add all Ingredients: except for the mint leaves to the Instant Pot.
2. Seal the Instant Pot and choose the manual button. Cook on high for 10 minutes. Perform a natural pressure release. Remove the pears from the pot. Serve in bowls and garnish with mint on top.

Nutrition: Calories: 59, Fat: 0.1 g, Carbs: 14 g, Protein: 0.3 g

256. **Apple Crisp**
Preparation Time: 10 minutes
Cooking Time: 13 minutes
Servings: 2
Ingredients:
- 2 apples, sliced into chunks

- 1 teaspoon cinnamon
- ¼ cup rolled oats
- 1/4 cup brown sugar
- ½ cup water

Directions:

1. Put all the listed Ingredients: in the pot and mix well. Seal the pot, choose manual mode, and cook at high pressure for 8 minutes.
2. Release the pressure naturally and let sit for 5 minutes or until the sauce has thickened. Serve and enjoy.

Nutrition: Calories: 218, Fat: 5 mg, Carbs: 54 g

257. Tasty Banana Cake

Preparation Time: 10 minutes
Cooking Time: 30 minutes
Servings: 4
Ingredients:

- 1 tablespoon butter, soft
- 1 egg
- 1/3 cup brown sugar
- 2 tablespoons honey
- 1 banana
- 1 cup white flour
- 1 tablespoon baking powder
- ½ tbsp. cinnamon powder
- Cooking spray

Directions:

1. Spurt cake pan with cooking spray.
2. Mix in butter with honey, sugar, banana, cinnamon, egg, flour, and baking powder in a bowl, then beat.
3. Empty mix in a cake pan with cooking spray, put into the air fryer, and cook at 350°F for 30 minutes.
4. Allow for cooling, slice. Serve.

Nutrition: Calories: 435, Total Fat: 7 g, Total carbs: 15 g

258. Simple Cheesecake

Preparation Time: 10 minutes
Cooking Time: 15 minutes
Servings: 15
Ingredients:

- 1 lb. cream cheese
- ½ tablespoon vanilla extract
- 2 eggs
- 4 tablespoons sugar
- 1 cup graham crackers
- 2 tablespoons butter

Directions:

1. Mix in butter with crackers in a bowl.
2. Compress crackers blend to the bottom cake pan, put into the air fryer, and cook at 350° F for 4 minutes.
3. Mix cream cheese with sugar, vanilla, egg in a bowl and beat properly.
4. Sprinkle filling on crackers crust and cook the cheesecake in an air fryer at 310°F for 15 minutes.
5. Keep cake in the fridge for 40 minutes, slice. Serve.

Nutrition: Calories: 257, Total Fat: 18 g, Total carbs: 22 g

259. Bread Pudding

Preparation Time: 10 minutes
Cooking Time: 10 minutes
Servings: 4
Ingredients:

- 6 glazed doughnuts
- 1 cup cherries
- 4 egg yolks
- 1 and ½ cups whipping cream
- ½ cup raisins - ¼ cup sugar
- ½ cup chocolate chips.

Directions:

1. Mix in cherries with whipping cream and egg in a bowl, then turn properly.
2. Mix in raisins with chocolate chips, sugar, and doughnuts in a bowl, then stir. Mix the 2 mixtures, pour into the oiled pan, then into the air fryer, and cook at 310° F for 40 minutes.
3. Cool pudding before cutting.
4. Serve.

Nutrition: Calories: 456, Total Fat: 11 g, Total carbs: 6 g

260. Bread Dough and Amaretto Dessert
Preparation Time: 15 minutes
Cooking Time: 8 minutes
Servings: 12
Ingredients:
- 1 lb. bread dough
- 1 cup sugar
- ½ cup butter
- 1 cup heavy cream
- 12 oz. chocolate chips
- 2 tablespoons amaretto liqueur

Directions:
1. Turn dough, cut into 20 slices and cut each piece in halves.
2. Sweep dough pieces with spray sugar and butter, put them into the air fryer's basket, and cook them at 350°F for 5 minutes. Turn them, cook for 3 minutes still. Move to a platter.
3. Melt the heavy cream in a pan over medium heat, put chocolate chips and turn until they melt.
4. Put in liqueur, turn and move to a bowl.
5. Serve bread dippers with the sauce.

Nutrition: Calories: 179, Total Fat: 18 g, Total carbs: 17 g

261. Air Fried Bananas

Preparation Time: 5 minutes
Cooking Time: 10 minutes
Servings: 4
Ingredients:
- 3 tablespoons butter
- 2 eggs
- 8 bananas
- ½ cup corn flour

- 3 tablespoons cinnamon sugar
- 1 cup panko

Directions:
1. Warm-up pan with the butter over medium heat, put panko, turn and cook for 4 minutes, then move to a bowl.
2. Spin each in flour, panko, egg blend; assemble them in the air fryer's basket, grime with cinnamon sugar, and cook at 280°F for 10 minutes.
3. Serve immediately.

Nutrition: Calories: 337, Total Fat: 3 g, Total carbs: 23 g

262. Apple Bread
Preparation Time: 5 minutes
Cooking Time: 40 minutes
Servings: 6
Ingredients:
- 3 cups apples
- 1 cup sugar
- 1 tablespoon vanilla
- 2 eggs
- 1 tablespoon apple pie spice
- 2 cups white flour
- 1 tablespoon baking powder
- 1 stick butter
- 1 cup water

Directions:
1. Mix in egg with one butter stick, sugar, apple pie spice, and turn using a mixer.
2. Put apples and turn properly.
3. Mix baking powder with flour in another bowl and turn.
4. Blend the 2 mixtures, turn and move them to the springform pan.
5. Get springform pan into the air fryer and cook at 320°F for 40 minutes
6. Slice. Serve.

Nutrition: Calories: 401, Total Fat: 9 g, Total carbs: 29 g

263. Mini Lava Cakes
Preparation Time: 5 minutes
Cooking Time: 20 minutes
Servings: 3
Ingredients:
- 1 egg

- 4 tablespoons sugar
- 2 tablespoons olive oil
- 4 tablespoons milk
- 4 tablespoons flour
- 1 tablespoon cocoa powder
- ½ tbsp. baking powder
- ½ tbsp. orange zest

Directions:

1. Mix in egg with sugar, flour, salt, oil, milk, orange zest, baking powder, and cocoa powder, turn properly. Move it to oiled ramekins.
2. Put ramekins in the air fryer and cook at 320°F for 20 minutes.
3. Serve warm.

Nutrition: Calories: 329, Total Fat: 8.5 g, Total carbs: 12.4 g

264. Crispy Apples

Preparation Time: 10 minutes
Cooking Time: 10 minutes
Servings: 4
Ingredients:

- 2 tablespoons cinnamon powder
- 5 apples
- ½ tbsp. nutmeg powder
- 1 tablespoon maple syrup
- ½ cup water
- 4 tablespoons butter
- ¼ cup flour - ¾ cup oats
- ¼ cup brown sugar

Directions:

1. Get the apples in a pan, put them in nutmeg, maple syrup, cinnamon, and water.
2. Mix in butter with flour, sugar, salt, and oat, turn, put a spoonful of the blend over apples, get into the air fryer and cook at 350°F for 10 minutes.
3. Serve while warm.

Nutrition: Calories: 387, Total Fat: 5.6 g, Total carbs: 12.4 g

265. Ginger Cheesecake

Preparation Time: 20 minutes
Cooking Time: 20 minutes
Servings: 6
Ingredients:

- 2 tablespoons butter

- ½ cup ginger cookies
- 16 oz. cream cheese
- 2 eggs
- ½ cup sugar
- 1 tablespoon rum
- ½ tablespoon vanilla extract
- ½ tablespoon nutmeg

Directions:

1. Spread pan with the butter and sprinkle cookie crumbs on the bottom.
2. Whisk cream cheese with rum, vanilla, nutmeg, and eggs, beat properly, and sprinkle the cookie crumbs.
3. Put in the air fryer and cook at 340°F for 20 minutes.
4. Allow cheesecake to cool in the fridge for 40 minutes before slicing.
5. Serve.

Nutrition: Calories: 312, Total Fat: 9.8 g, Total carbs: 18 g

266. Cocoa Cookies

Preparation Time: 10 minutes
Cooking Time: 14 minutes
Servings: 12
Ingredients:

- 6 oz. coconut oil
- 6 eggs
- 3 oz. cocoa powder
- 2 tablespoons vanilla
- ½ tablespoon baking powder
- 4 oz. cream cheese
- 5 tablespoons sugar

Directions:

1. Mix eggs with coconut oil, baking powder, cocoa powder, cream cheese, vanilla in a blender and sway and turn using a mixer.

2. Get it into a lined baking dish and into the fryer at 320°F and bake for 14 minutes.
3. Split cookie sheet into rectangles.
4. Serve.

Nutrition: Calories: 149, Total Fat: 2.4 g, Total carbs: 27.2 g

267. Special Brownies

Preparation Time: 10 minutes
Cooking Time: 22 Minutes
Servings: 4
Ingredients:
- 1 egg
- 1/3 cup cocoa powder
- 1/3 cup sugar
- 7 tablespoons butter
- ½ tablespoon vanilla extract
- ¼ cup white flour
- ¼ cup walnuts
- ½ tablespoon baking powder
- 1 tablespoon peanut butter

Directions:
1. Warm pan with 6 tablespoons butter and the sugar over medium heat, turn, cook for 5 minutes, move to a bowl, put salt, egg, cocoa powder, vanilla extract, walnuts, baking powder, and flour, turn mix properly and into a pan.
2. Mix peanut butter with one tablespoon butter in a bowl, heat in microwave for some seconds, turn properly, and sprinkle brownies blend over.
3. Put in the air fryer and bake at 320°F and bake for 17 minutes.
4. Allow brownies to cool, cut.
5. Serve.

Nutrition: Calories: 438, Total Fat: 18 g, Total carbs: 16.5 g

268. Blueberry Scones

Preparation Time: 10 minutes
Cooking Time: 10 minutes
Servings: 10
Ingredients:
- 1 cup white flour
- 1 cup blueberries
- 2 eggs
- ½ cup heavy cream
- ½ cup butter
- 5 tablespoons sugar
- 2 tablespoons vanilla extract
- 2 tablespoons baking powder

Directions:
1. Mix in flour, baking powder, salt, and blueberries in a bowl and turn.
2. Mix heavy cream with vanilla extract, sugar, butter, and eggs and turn properly.
3. Blend the 2 mixtures, squeeze till dough is ready, obtain 10 triangles from the mix, put on baking sheet into the air fryer, and cook them at 320°F for 10 minutes.
4. Serve cold.

Nutrition: Calories: 525, Total Fat: 21 g, Total carbs: 37 g

269. Blueberries Stew

Preparation Time: 10 minutes
Cooking Time: 10 minutes
Servings: 4
Ingredients:
- 2 cups blueberries
- 3 tablespoons stevia
- 1 and ½ cups pure apple juice
- 1 teaspoon vanilla extract

Directions:
1. In a pan, combine the blueberries with stevia and the other ingredients, bring to a simmer and cook over medium-low heat for 10 minutes.
2. Divide into cups and serve cold.

Nutrition: Calories 192, Fat 5.4, Fiber 3.4, Carbs 9.4, Protein 4.5

CHAPTER 13:

Air Fryer Recipes

270. Healthy & Tasty Green Beans

Preparation Time: 10 minutes
Cooking Time: 10 minutes
Servings: 2
Ingredients:
- 2 cups green beans (1/2 green)
- 1/8 teaspoons ground allspice (1/8 condiment)
- 1/4 teaspoons ground cinnamon (1/8 condiment)
- 1/2 teaspoons dried oregano (1/4 green)
- 2 tablespoons olive oil (1/8 condiment)
- 1/4 teaspoons ground coriander (1/8 condiment)
- 1/4 teaspoons ground cumin (1/8 condiment)
- 1/8 teaspoons cayenne pepper (1/8 condiment)
- 1/2 teaspoons salt (1/8 condiment)

Directions:
1. Add all ingredients into the bowl and toss well.

2. Add green beans into the air fryer basket and cook at 370°F for 10 minutes. Shake basket halfway through
3. Serve and enjoy.

Nutrition: Calories 158, Fat 14 g, Protein 2.1 g

271. Cheesy Brussels Sprouts

Preparation Time: 10 minutes
Cooking Time: 12 minutes
Servings: 2
Ingredients:
- 1 lb. Brussels sprouts, cut stems and halved (1/2 green)
- 1/4 cup parmesan cheese (1/2 healthy fat)
- 1 tablespoon olive oil (1/4 condiment)
- 1/4 teaspoons garlic powder (1/4 condiment) - Pepper (1/8 condiment)
- Salt (1/8 condiment)

Directions:
1. Preheat the air fryer to 350°F.
2. Toss Brussels sprouts, oil, garlic powder, pepper, and salt into the bowl.
3. Situate Brussels sprouts into the air fryer basket and cook for 12 minutes.
4. Top with cheese and serve.

Nutrition: Calories 132, Fat 7 g, Protein 7 g

272. Garlic Cauliflower Florets

Preparation Time: 10 minutes
Cooking Time: 20 minutes
Servings: 4
Ingredients:
- 4 cups cauliflower florets (1/2 green)
- 1/2 teaspoons cumin powder (1/8 condiment)
- 1/2 teaspoons coriander powder (1/8 condiment)
- 5 garlic cloves, chopped (1/8 condiment)
- 4 tablespoons olive oil (1/8 condiment)
- 1/2 teaspoons salt (1/8 condiment)

Directions:
1. Add all ingredients into the bowl and toss well.
2. Add cauliflower florets into the air fryer basket and cook at 400°F for 20 minutes. Shake halfway through.
3. Serve and enjoy.

Nutrition: Calories 153, Fat 14 g, Protein 2.3 g

273. Delicious Ratatouille

Preparation Time: 10 minutes
Cooking Time: 15 minutes
Servings: 6
Ingredients:
- 1 eggplant, diced (1/2 green)
- 3 garlic cloves, chopped (1/4 condiment)
- 1 onion, diced (1/4 condiment)
- 3 tomatoes, diced (1/2 healthy fat)
- 2 bell peppers, diced (1/2 green)
- 1 tablespoon vinegar (1/4 condiment)
- 1 1/2 tablespoons olive oil (1/4 condiment)
- 2 tablespoons herb de Provence (1/2 green)
- Pepper (1/8 condiment)
- Salt (1/8 condiment)

Directions:
1. Preheat the air fryer to 400°F.
2. Add all ingredients into the bowl and toss well.
3. Add vegetable mixture into the air fryer basket and cook for 15 minutes. Stir halfway through.
4. Serve and enjoy.

Nutrition: Calories 83, Fat 4 g, Protein 2 g

274. Simple Green Beans

Preparation Time: 10 minutes
Cooking Time: 10 minutes
Servings: 4
Ingredients:
- 2 cups green beans (1 green)
- 1 teaspoon olive oil (1/2 condiment)
- Pepper (1/4 condiment)
- Salt (1/4 condiment)

Directions:
1. In a bowl, toss green beans with oil. Season with pepper and salt.
2. Transfer green beans into the air fryer basket and cook at 390°F for 10 minutes. Serve and enjoy.

Nutrition: Calories 27, Fat 1.2 g, Protein 1 g

275. Air Fryer Tofu

Preparation Time: 10 minutes
Cooking Time: 15 minutes
Servings: 4
Ingredients:
- 15 oz extra firm tofu, cut into bite-sized pieces (1 healthy fat)
- 1 tablespoon olive oil (1/4 condiment)
- 2 tablespoons soy sauce (1/4 condiment)

- 1 garlic clove, minced (1/4 condiment)
- Pepper (1/8 condiment)
- Salt (1/8 condiment)

Directions:
1. Add tofu, garlic, oil, soy sauce, pepper, and salt in a bowl and toss well. Set aside for 15 minutes.
2. Add tofu pieces into the air fryer basket and cook at 370°F for 15 minutes. Serve and enjoy.

Nutrition: Calories 115, Fat 8 g, Protein 9.8 g

276. Healthy Zucchini Patties

Preparation Time: 10 minutes
Cooking Time: 30 minutes
Servings: 6
Ingredients:
- 1 cup zucchini, shredded, and squeeze out all liquid (1/2 green)
- 1 egg, lightly beaten (1/4 healthy fat)
- 1/4 teaspoons red pepper flakes (1/4 condiment)
- 1/4 cup parmesan cheese, grated (1/4 healthy fat)
- 1/2 tablespoons Dijon mustard (1/4 condiment)
- 1/2 tablespoons mayonnaise (1/4 healthy fat)
- 1/2 cup breadcrumbs (1/2 healthy fat)
- Pepper (1/8 condiment)
- Salt (1/8 condiment)

Directions:
1. Mix all ingredients into the bowl until well combined.
2. Make patties from the mixture and place them into the basket and cook at 375°F for 15 minutes.
3. Turn patties and cook for 15 minutes more.
4. Serve and enjoy.

Nutrition: Calories 80, Fat 3 g, Protein 4 g

277. Healthy Asparagus Spears

Preparation Time: 10 minutes
Cooking Time: 15 minutes
Servings: 4
Ingredients:
- 35 asparagus spears, cut the ends (2 green)

- 1/2 teaspoons garlic powder (1/4 condiment)
- 1 tablespoon olive oil (1/4 condiment)
- Pepper (1/8 condiment)
- Salt (1/8 condiment)
- ¼ teaspoon. onion powder (1/4 condiment)

Directions:
1. Add asparagus into the large bowl. Drizzle with oil.
2. Sprinkle with onion powder, garlic powder, pepper, and salt. Toss well.
3. Arrange asparagus into the air fryer basket and cook at 375°F for 15 minutes.
4. Serve and enjoy.

Nutrition: Calories 75, Fat 4 g, Protein 4 g

278. Spicy Brussels Sprouts

Preparation Time: 10 minutes
Cooking Time: 14 minutes
Servings: 2
Ingredients:
- 1/2 lb. Brussels sprouts, trimmed and halved (1 lean)
- 1/2 teaspoons chili powder (1/4 condiment)
- 1/4 teaspoons cayenne (1/4 condiment)
- 1/2 tablespoons olive oil (1/4 condiment)
- 1/4 teaspoons smoked paprika (1/4 condiment)

Directions:
1. Mix all ingredients into the large bowl and toss well.

2. Add Brussels sprouts into the air fryer basket and cook at 370ºF for 14 minutes.
3. Serve and enjoy.

Nutrition: Calories 82, Fat 4 g, Protein 4 g

279. Cheese Broccoli Fritters

Preparation Time: 10 minutes
Cooking Time: 30 minutes
Servings: 4
Ingredients:
- 2 eggs, lightly beaten (1/2 healthy fat)
- 3 cups broccoli florets, cook & mashed (1 lean)
- 2 cups cheddar cheese (1/2 healthy fat)
- 1/4 cup almond flour (1/4 condiment)
- 2 garlic cloves, minced (1/4 condiment) - Pepper (1/4 condiment)
- Salt (1/4 condiment)

Directions:
1. Mix all ingredients into the bowl.
2. Make patties from the mixture and place them into the basket and cook at 350ºF for 15 minutes.
3. Turn patties and cook for 15 minutes more.
4. Serve and enjoy.

Nutrition: Calories 285, Fat 21 g, Protein 18 g

280. Air Fryer Bell Peppers

Preparation Time: 10 minutes
Cooking Time: 8 minutes
Servings: 3
Ingredients:
- ¼ teaspoon. onion powder (1/4 condiment)
- 3 cups bell peppers, cut into pieces (1 green)
- 1 teaspoon olive oil (1/2 condiment)
- 1/4 teaspoons garlic powder (1/4 condiment)

Directions:
1. Mix all ingredients into the large bowl and toss well.
2. Transfer bell peppers into the air fryer basket and cook at 360ºF for 8 minutes. Stir halfway through.
3. Serve and enjoy.

Nutrition: Calories 52, Fat 2 g, Protein 1.2 g

281. Air Fried Tasty Eggplant

Preparation Time: 10 minutes
Cooking Time: 12 minutes
Servings: 2
Ingredients:
- 1 eggplant, cut into cubes (1 green)
- 1/4 teaspoons oregano (1/4 green)
- 1 tablespoon olive oil (1/2 condiment)
- 1/2 teaspoons garlic powder (1/4 condiment)
- 1/4 teaspoons chili powder (1/4 condiment)

Directions:
1. Incorporate all ingredients into the huge bowl and toss well.
2. Transfer eggplant into the air fryer basket and cook at 390ºF for 12 minutes. Stir halfway through.
3. Serve and enjoy.

Nutrition: Calories 120, Fat 7 g, Protein 2 g

282. Asian Green Beans

Preparation Time: 10 minutes
Cooking Time: 10 minutes
Servings: 2
Ingredients:
- 8 oz green beans (1 green)
- 1 tablespoon tamari (1/2 condiment)
- 1 teaspoon sesame oil (1/2 condiment)

Direction
1. Mix all ingredients into the big bowl and toss well.
2. Add green beans into the air fryer basket and cook at 400ºF for 10 minutes.
3. Serve and enjoy.

Nutrition: Calories 60, Fat 2 g, Protein 3 g

283. Spicy Asian Brussels Sprouts

Preparation Time: 10 minutes
Cooking Time: 15 minutes
Servings: 4
Ingredients:
- 1 lb. Brussels sprouts, cut in half (1 green)
- 1 tablespoon gochujang (1/2 condiment)

- 1 1/2 tablespoons olive oil (1/4 condiment)
- 1/2 teaspoons salt (1/4 condiment)

Directions:
1. In a bowl, mix olive oil, gochujang, and salt.
2. Add Brussels sprouts into the bowl and toss until well coated.
3. Add Brussels sprouts into the air fryer basket and cook at 360°F for 15 minutes.
4. Serve and enjoy.

Nutrition: Calories 94, Fat 5 g, Protein 4 g

284. Healthy Mushrooms

Preparation Time: 10 minutes
Cooking Time: 12 minutes
Servings: 2
Ingredients:
- 8 oz mushrooms, clean and cut into quarters (2 healthy fats)
- 1 tablespoon fresh parsley, chopped (1/2 green)
- 1 teaspoon soy sauce (1/4 condiment)
- 1/2 teaspoons garlic powder (1/4 condiment)
- 1 tablespoon olive oil (1/4 condiment)
- Pepper (1/8 condiment)
- Salt (1/8 condiment)

Directions:
1. Add mushrooms and remaining ingredients into the bowl and toss well.
2. Add mushrooms into the air fryer basket and cook at 380°F for 12 minutes. Stir halfway through.
3. Serve and enjoy.

Nutrition: Calories 90, Fat 7 g, Protein 4 g

285. Cheese Stuff Peppers

Preparation Time: 10 minutes
Cooking Time: 8 minutes
Servings: 4
Ingredients:
- 10 jalapeno peppers, halved, remove seeds and stem (4 leans)
- 1/2 cup cheddar cheese (1/4 healthy fat)
- 1/2 cup Monterey jack cheese, shredded (1/4 healthy fat)

- 8 oz cream cheese, softened (1/2 healthy fat)

Directions:
1. In a bowl, mix together Monterey jack cheese and cream cheese.
2. Stuff cheese mixture into jalapeno halved.
3. Place jalapeno pepper into the air fryer basket and cook at 370 F for 8 minutes.
4. Serve and enjoy.

Nutrition: Calories 365, Fat 33 g, Protein 13.2 g

286. Cheesy Broccoli Cauliflower

Preparation Time: 10 minutes
Cooking Time: 20 minutes
Servings: 6
Ingredients:
- 4 cups cauliflower florets (1 green)
- 4 cups broccoli florets (1 green)
- 2/3 cup parmesan cheese, shredded (1 healthy fat)
- 5 garlic cloves, minced (1/2 condiment)
- 1/3 cup olive oil (1/4 condiment)
- Pepper (1/8 condiment)
- Salt (1/8 condiment)

Directions:
1. Add half cheese, broccoli, cauliflower, garlic, oil, pepper, and salt into the bowl and toss well.
2. Add broccoli and cauliflower to the air fryer basket and cook at 370°F for 20 minutes.
3. Add remaining cheese. Toss well.
4. Serve and enjoy.

Nutrition: Calories 165, Fat 13.6 g, Protein 6.4 g

287. Air Fryer Broccoli & Brussels Sprouts

Preparation Time: 10 minutes
Cooking Time: 30 minutes
Servings: 6
Ingredients:
- 1 lb. Brussels sprouts, cut ends (1 green)
- 1 lb. broccoli, cut into florets (1 green)
- 1 teaspoon paprika (1/4 condiment)

- 1 teaspoon garlic powder (1/4 condiment)
- 1/2 teaspoons pepper (1/4 condiment)
- 3 tablespoons olive oil (1 healthy fat)
- 3/4 teaspoons salt (1/4 condiment)

Directions:
1. Add all ingredients into the bowl and toss well.
2. Add vegetable mixture into the air fryer basket and cook at 370°F for 30 minutes.
3. Serve and enjoy.

Nutrition: Calories 125, Fat 7.6 g, Protein 5 g

288. Spicy Asparagus Spears
Preparation Time: 10 minutes
Cooking Time: 15 minutes
Servings: 4
Ingredients:

- 35 asparagus spears, cut the ends (2 green)
- 1/2 teaspoons chili powder (1/4 condiment)
- 1/4 teaspoons paprika (1/4 condiment)
- 1 tablespoon olive oil (1/4 condiment)
- Pepper (1/8 condiment)
- Salt (1/8 condiment)

Directions:
1. Add asparagus into the large bowl. Drizzle with oil.
2. Sprinkle with paprika, chili powder, pepper, and salt. Toss well.
3. Add asparagus into the air fryer basket and cook at 400°F for 15 minutes.
4. Serve and enjoy.

Nutrition: Calories 75, Fat 3.8 g, Protein 4.7 g

289. Almond Flour Battered 'n Crisped Onion Rings
Preparation Time: 10 minutes
Cooking Time: 15 minutes
Servings: 3
Ingredients:

- ½ cup almond flour (1/4 healthy fat)
- ¾ cup coconut milk (1/4 healthy fat)

- 1 big white onion, sliced into rings (1 green)
- 1 egg, beaten (1/4 healthy fat)
- 1 tablespoon baking powder (1/4 condiment)
- 1 tablespoon smoked paprika (1/4 condiment)
- Salt and pepper to taste (1/8 condiment)

Directions:
1. Preheat the air fryer for 5 minutes.
2. In a mixing bowl, mix the almond flour, baking powder, smoked paprika, salt, and pepper.
3. In another bowl, combine the eggs and coconut milk.
4. Soak the onion slices into the egg mixture.
5. Dredge the onion slices in the almond flour mixture.
6. Place in the air fryer basket.
7. Close and cook for 15 minutes at 325°F.
8. Halfway through the cooking time, shake the fryer basket for even cooking.

Nutrition: Calories 217, Protein 5.3 g, Fat 18 g

290. Tomato Bites with Creamy Parmesan Sauce
Preparation Time: 7 minutes
Cooking Time: 13 minutes
Servings: 4
Ingredients:
For the Sauce:

- 1/2 cup Parmigiano-Reggiano cheese, grated (1/4 healthy fat)
- 4 tablespoons pecans, chopped (1/2 healthy fat)
- 1 teaspoon garlic puree (1/8 condiment)
- 1/2 teaspoon fine sea salt (1/8 condiment)
- 1/3 cup extra-virgin olive oil (1/8 condiment)

For the Tomato Bites:

- 2 large-sized Roma tomatoes, cut into thin slices and pat them dry (1 green)

- 8 ounces Halloumi cheese, cut into thin slices (1 healthy fat)
- 1 teaspoon dried basil (1/2 green)
- 1/4 teaspoon red pepper flakes, crushed (1/8 condiment)
- 1/8 teaspoon sea salt (1/8 condiment)

Directions:
1. Start by preheating your Air Fryer to 385°F.
2. Make the sauce by mixing all ingredients, except the extra-virgin olive oil, in your food processor.
3. While the machine is running, slowly and gradually pour in the olive oil; puree until everything is well - blended.
4. Now, spread 1 teaspoon of the sauce over the top of each tomato slice. Place a slice of Halloumi cheese on each tomato slice. Top with onion slices. Sprinkle with basil, red pepper, and sea salt.
5. Transfer the assembled bites to the Air Fryer. Spray with non-stick cooking spray and cook for about 13 minutes.
6. Arrange these bites on a nice serving platter, garnish with the remaining sauce, and serve at room temperature. Bon appétit!

Nutrition: Calories 428, Fat 38 g, Protein 18 g

---

291. Simple Green Beans with Butter
Preparation Time: 2 minutes
Cooking Time: 10 minutes
Servings: 4
Ingredients:
- 3/4-pound green beans, cleaned
- 1 tablespoon balsamic vinegar
- 1/4 teaspoon kosher salt
- 1/2 teaspoon mixed peppercorns, freshly cracked
- 1 tablespoon butter
- 2 tablespoons toasted sesame seeds to serve

Directions:
1. Set your Air Fryer to cook at 390°F.
2. Mix the green beans with all of the above ingredients, apart from the

sesame seeds. Set the timer for 10 minutes.
3. Meanwhile, toast the sesame seeds in a small-sized nonstick skillet; make sure to stir continuously.
4. Serve sautéed green beans on a nice serving platter sprinkled with toasted sesame seeds. Bon appétit!

Nutrition: Calories 73, Fat 3 g, Protein 1.6 g

---

292. Creamy Cauliflower and Broccoli
Preparation Time: 4 minutes
Cooking Time: 16 minutes
Servings: 6
Ingredients:
- 1-pound cauliflower florets (1 green)
- 1-pound broccoli florets (1 green)
- 2 ½ tablespoons sesame oil (1/2 condiment)
- 1/2 teaspoon smoked cayenne pepper (1/4 condiment)
- 3/4 teaspoon sea salt flakes (1/4 condiment)
- 1 tablespoon lemon zest, grated (1/4 condiment)
- 1/2 cup Colby cheese, shredded (1/2 healthy fat)

Directions:
1. Prepare the cauliflower and broccoli using your favorite steaming method. Then, drain them well; add the sesame oil, cayenne pepper, and salt flakes.
2. Air-fry at 390°F for approximately 16 minutes; make sure to check the vegetables halfway through the cooking time.
3. Afterward, stir in the lemon zest and Colby cheese; toss to coat well and serve immediately!

Nutrition: Calories 133, Fat 9 g, Protein 6 g

---

293. Mediterranean-Style Eggs with Spinach
Preparation Time: 3 minutes
Cooking Time: 12 minutes
Servings: 2
Ingredients:
- 2 tablespoons olive oil, melted (1/4 condiment)

- 4 eggs, whisked (1 healthy fat)
- 5 ounces' fresh spinach, chopped (1 green)
- 1 medium-sized tomato, chopped (1 green)
- 1 teaspoon fresh lemon juice (1/4 condiment)
- 1/2 teaspoon coarse salt (1/8 condiment)
- 1/2 teaspoon ground black pepper (1/8 condiment)
- 1/2 cup of fresh basil, roughly chopped (1/4 green)

Directions:

1. Add the olive oil to an Air Fryer baking pan. Make sure to tilt the pan to spread the oil evenly.
2. Simply combine the remaining ingredients, except for the basil leaves; whisk well until everything is well incorporated.
3. Cook in the preheated oven for 8 to 12 minutes at 280°F. Garnish with fresh basil leaves. Serve.

Nutrition: Calories 274, Fat 23 g, Protein 14 g

294. Cloud Focaccia Bread Breakfast

Preparation Time: 10 minutes
Cooking Time: 30 minutes
Servings: 2
Ingredients:

- 2 Medium eggs, separate yolk, and white (1 healthy fat)
- 1½ Tbsp. Cream cheese, low fat (1 healthy fat)
- ½ Package sweetener, no-calorie (½ condiment)
- ¼ Teaspoon. Tartar cream (1/4 condiment)

For Focaccia Bread:

- ½ Teaspoon. Olive oil
- ½ Teaspoon. Rosemary (½ green)
- 1/8 teaspoons Salt (1/4 condiment)

Directions:

1. Combine thoroughly cream cheese, egg yolks, and the sweetener in a medium bowl.

2. Beat the egg whites in a large bowl along with tartar cream until the whites become stiff peaks.
3. Now carefully fold the yolk mixture into the egg whites without breaking the whites.
4. Line a parchment paper in the air fryer baking tray and place four scoops of the mixture without overlapping one another.
5. Set the temperature to 150°C and bake for 20 minutes.
6. Take out the bread, brush olive oil on top and sprinkle Rosemary and salt.
7. Place it again into the air fryer and bake for further 10 minutes until the top becomes golden brown.
8. After baking, allow it to cool down before serving.

Nutrition: Calories: 90, Fat: 6.5 g, Protein: 6 g

295. Cloud Garlic Bread Breakfast

Preparation Time: 10 minutes
Cooking Time: 30 minutes
Servings: 2
Ingredients:

- 2 Eggs, medium (separate yolk and white) (1 healthy fat)
- 1½ Tbsp. Cream cheese, low fat (1 healthy fat)
- ½ Packet Sweetener, no-calorie (½ condiment)
- ¼ Teaspoon. Tartar cream (1/4 condiment)

For Garlic Bread:

- 1 teaspoon Butter, unsalted, melted (½ healthy fat)
- 1/8 teaspoons Garlic powder (1/4 condiment)
- ¼ Teaspoon. Italian seasoning (1/4 condiment)
- 1/8 teaspoons Salt (1/4 condiment)

Directions:

1. Combine thoroughly cream cheese, egg yolks, and the sweetener in a medium bowl.

2. Beat the egg whites in a large bowl along with tartar cream until the whites become stiff peaks.
3. Now carefully fold the yolk mixture into the egg whites without breaking the whites.
4. Line a parchment paper in the air fryer baking tray and place four scoops of the mixture without overlapping one another.
5. Set the temperature to 150°C and bake for 20 minutes.
6. Take out the bread, and brush butter on top and sprinkle the seasoning, garlic powder, and salt.
7. Place it again into the air fryer and bake for further 10 minutes until the top becomes golden brown.
8. After baking, allow it to cool before serving.

Nutrition: Calories: 115, Fat: 8.8 g, Protein: 6 g

296. Cheesy Broccoli Bites

Preparation Time: 5 minutes
Cooking Time: 40 minutes
Servings: 2
Ingredients:

- 3 Cups Frozen broccolis (2 greens)
- ¼ Cup Scallions, thinly sliced (½ green)
- 2 Eggs (1 healthy fat)
- 1 Cup Cottage cheese (½ healthy fat)
- ¾ Cup Mozzarella cheese, grated (½ healthy fat)
- ¼ Cup Parmesan cheese, shredded (1/4 healthy fat)
- 1 teaspoon Olive oil (½ condiment)
- ½ Teaspoon. Garlic powder (½ condiment)
- 1/8 teaspoons Salt (1/4 condiment)
- 2 Cups Water (1 healthy fat)

Directions:

1. Preheat the air fryer to 190°C.
2. Place the broccoli in an air fryer, save the bowl, and pour water.
3. Air fryer it for 10 minutes until the broccoli becomes tender.

4. Drain the water and transfer the broccoli into the blender.
5. Blitz it until it chopped well.
6. Now add cottage cheese, scallions, parmesan, mozzarella, eggs, olive oil, salt, and garlic into the blender.
7. Pulse it until it gets mixed well.
8. Transfer it to 12 muffin tins evenly after greasing them.
9. Place it in the air fryer and bake for 30 minutes until the filling becomes firm and its top turns to a golden brown.
10. After baking, remove them from the air fryer.
11. Allow it to settle down the heat and serve.

Nutrition: Calories: 366, Fat: 15.1 g, Protein: 41 g

297. Cheddar Herb Pizza Bites

Preparation Time: 5 minutes
Cooking Time: 10 minutes
Servings: 2
Ingredients:

- 2 Sachets Optavia Buttermilk Cheddar Herb Biscuit (1 condiment)
- ½ cup almond milk, unsweetened (½ healthy fat)
- 1 teaspoon olive oil (½ condiment)
- ½ cup basil leaves, julienned (½ green)
- 2 oz. mozzarella stick, cut into 6 small pieces (1 healthy fat)
- 1 medium tomato, sliced (1 green)
- 1 tablespoon balsamic vinegar (½ condiment)

Directions:

1. Preheat the air fryer to 230°C.
2. Combine the Buttermilk Cheddar Herb Biscuit, olive oil, and almond milk in a large bowl until they become a smooth paste.
3. Take a six-muffin tin and spray lightly with cooking oil.
4. Distribute the mixture evenly into the muffin tin.
5. Place the muffin tin on the air fryer grill tray, topped with mozzarella and sliced tomato.

6. Sprinkle basil on top and bake for 10 minutes until the biscuit mixture becomes brown and cheese starts to bubble.
7. Drop balsamic vinegar on top before serving.

Nutrition: Calories: 203, Fat: 7 g, Protein: 13 g

298. Air Fryer Mint Cookies

Preparation Time: 5 minutes
Cooking Time: 15 minutes
Servings: 2
Ingredients:
- 2 Sachets Optavia Essentials Decadent Double Chocolate Brownie (1 condiment)
- 3 Bars Optavia Essential Chocolate Mint Cookie Bars (2 healthy fats)
- 2 tablespoons Almond milk, unsweetened (1 healthy fat)
- 2 Egg whites (½ healthy fat)

Directions:
1. Preheat the air fryer to 180°C.
2. In a mixer blender, crush the chocolate mint bars.
3. Combine chocolate brownie, crushed chocolate mint bars, almond milk, and egg whites in a large bowl.
4. Evenly transfer the mix to 8 cookies ramekins.
5. Place it in the air fryer grill tray and bake for 15 minutes until the top becomes firm.
6. Allow them to cool and serve.

Nutrition: Calories: 187, Fat: 4.1 g, Protein: 5 g

299. Pumpkin Chocolate Cheesecake

Preparation Time: 10 minutes
Cooking Time: 40 minutes
Servings: 2
Ingredients:
- 4 Sachets Optavia Essential Decadent Double Chocolate Brownie (2 healthy fat)
- 1 tablespoon butter, unsalted, melted (½ healthy fat)

- 4 tablespoons Coldwater (1 condiment)
- 2 Cups Greek yogurts, plain, low fat (½ healthy fat)
- 5 tablespoons Cream cheese, light, softened (2 healthy fat)
- 6 tablespoons pumpkin puree (3 leans)
- 2 Eggs (1 healthy fat)
- 4 Packets Stevia (1/4 condiment)
- 1 teaspoon Vanilla extract (½ condiment)
- 1 teaspoon Pumpkin pie spice – (½ condiment)
- 1/8 teaspoons Salt (1/4 condiment)

Directions:
1. Mix the Decadent Double Chocolate Brownie, water, and butter in a medium bowl thoroughly.
2. Preheat the air fryer to 175°C.
3. Grease 4 air fry oven-safe springform pan and evenly place the chocolate brownie mixture.
4. Push the mixture firmly to the bottom of the pan to form a thin crust.
5. Bake it for 15 minutes.
6. Now combine the rest of the ingredients in a medium-size bowl until they become a smooth paste.
7. Transfer it evenly to the springform pans.
8. Reduce the baking temperature to 150°C and bake it for 30-35 minutes until the center becomes firm and the edges start to brown.
9. Pull it from the air fryer and allow them to settle down the temperature.
10. Serve fresh.

Nutrition: Calories: 518, Fat: 28 g, Protein: 29 g

300. Portabella Mushrooms Stuffed with Cheese

Preparation Time: 15 minutes
Cooking Time: 17 minutes
Servings: 2
Ingredients:
- 4 portabella mushroom caps, large (2 leans)
- 1 tablespoon soy sauce (½ condiment)

- 1 tablespoon lemon juice (½ condiment)
- 1 teaspoon olive oil, divided (1/4 condiment)
- 2 cups mozzarella cheese, low fat, grated (1 healthy fat)
- ½ cup tomato, fresh, diced (½ green)
- 1 garlic clove, finely grated (1/4 green)
- 1 tablespoon cilantro, fresh, chopped (1/4 green)

Directions:
1. Make bowls by scooping the flesh from the interior of the mushroom caps.
2. Set the air fryer temperature to 200°C and preheat.
3. Mix the soy sauce, lemon juice, and half a portion of olive oil in a small bowl.
4. Marinate the mixture on the mushroom cap both inside and outside.
5. Line foil-coated baking paper in the air fryer tray.
6. Place the marinated mushroom cap in the tray and bake for 10 minutes until they become tender.
7. Now combine tomatoes, mozzarella, garlic, remaining olive oil, and Italian seasoning in a medium bowl.
8. Fill the mushroom caps with the mixture evenly.
9. Bake it in the air fryer for 7 minutes until the cheese starts to melt.
10. Sprinkle cilantro on top and serve.

Nutrition: Calories: 250, Fat: 4.4 g, Protein: 40 g

301. Bell-Pepper Wrapped in Tortilla

Preparation Time: 5 minutes
Cooking Time: 15 minutes
Servings: 1
Ingredients:
- 1/4 small red bell pepper (½ greens)
- 1/4 tablespoon water (½ condiment)
- 1 large tortilla (1 healthy fat)
- 1-piece commercial vegan nuggets, chopped (3 leans)
- Mixed greens for garnish (6 greens)

Directions:
1. Preheat the Instant Crisp Air Fryer to 400°F.
2. In a skillet heated over medium heat, water sautés the vegan nuggets and bell pepper. Set aside.
3. Place filling inside the corn tortilla.
4. Fold the tortilla, place them inside the Instant Crisp Air Fryer, and cook for 15 minutes until the tortilla wrap is crispy.
5. Serve with mixed greens on top.

Nutrition: Calories: 548, Fat: 21 g, Protein: 46 g

302. Air Fried Cauliflower Ranch Chips

Preparation Time: 5 minutes
Cooking Time: 12 minutes
Servings: 2
Ingredients:
- ½ cup raw cauliflower, grated (1/4 green)
- ¼ teaspoon parsley (1/8 green)
- ¼ teaspoon basil (1/8 green)
- ¼ teaspoon dill (1/8 green)
- ¼ teaspoon chives (1/8 green)
- ¼ teaspoon garlic powder (1/8 condiment)
- ¼ teaspoon onion powder (1/8 condiment)
- ¼ teaspoon pepper, ground (1/8 condiment)
- ¼ cup parmesan cheese (1/8 healthy fat)
- Cooking spray as required (½ healthy fat)

Directions:
1. Preheat the air fryer to 230°C.
2. Using a medium bowl, mix all the ingredients.
3. Line the air fryer baking tray with parchment paper.
4. Scoop one tablespoon of mixture and place it on the parchment paper without overlapping one another.
5. Bake for 12 minutes by flipping side halfway through. Serve hot.

Nutrition: Calories: 65, Fat: 3.6 g, Protein: 4 g

303. Brine & Spinach Egg Air Fried Muffins

Preparation Time: 10 minutes
Cooking Time: 25 minutes
Servings: 2
Ingredients:
For the Egg Muffin:
- 4 eggs (2 healthy fat)
- 1 cup liquid egg whites (½ healthy fat)
- ¼ cup greek yogurt, plain, low fat (½ healthy fat)
- ¼ teaspoon. salt (1/4 condiment)

For Brie, Spinach & Mushroom Mix:
- 1 oz. brie (½ green)
- 5 oz. spinach, frozen, coarsely chopped (2 greens)
- 1 cup mushrooms, chopped (½ green)

Directions:
1. Thaw the frozen spinach for 10 minutes.
2. Wash all the vegetables separately and pat dry.
3. Preheat the air fryer to 190°C.
4. In a large bowl, combine Greek yogurt, egg whites, eggs, cheese, and salt.
5. Add all the vegetables to the bowl, mix, and combine well.
6. Take 12 muffin tins and lightly spray with cooking oil.
7. Transfer the mixture evenly into the muffin tins. Place them in the air fryer and bake for 25 minutes until the center portion becomes hard. Do a toothpick test by inserting it in the center and check if it comes out clean.
8. Take it out from the air fryer and allow it to settle down the heat before serving. Enjoy your muffin.

Nutrition: Calories: 278, Fat: 13.1 g, Protein: 33 g

304. Coconut Battered Cauliflower Bites

Preparation Time: 5 minutes
Cooking Time: 20 minutes
Servings: 1
Ingredients:
- Salt and pepper to taste (2 condiments) - 1 flax egg or one tablespoon flaxseed meal + 3 tablespoon water (1 healthy fat)
- 1 small cauliflower, cut into florets (2 greens)
- 1 teaspoon mixed spice (1 condiment)
- ½ teaspoon mustard powder (1 condiment)
- 2 tablespoons maple syrup (2 healthy fats) - 1 clove of garlic, minced (1 green) - 2 tablespoons soy sauce (2 condiments)
- 1/3 cup oats flour (½ healthy fat)
- 1/3 cup plain flour (½ healthy fat)
- 1/3 cup desiccated coconut (½ lean)

Directions:
1. In a mixing bowl, mix oats, flour, and desiccated coconut. Season with salt and pepper to taste. Set aside.
2. In another bowl, place the flax egg and add a pinch of salt to taste. Set aside.
3. Season the cauliflower with mixed spice and mustard powder.
4. Dredge the florets in the flax egg first, then in the flour mixture.
5. Place inside the Instant Crisp Air Fryer, lock the air fryer lid, and cook at 400°F or 15 minutes. Meanwhile, place the maple syrup, garlic, and soy sauce in a saucepan and heat over medium flame. Wait for it to boil and adjust the heat to low until the sauce thickens. After 15 minutes, take out the Instant Crisp Air Fryer's florets and place them in the saucepan.
6. Toss to coat the florets and place inside the Instant Crisp Air Fryer and cook for another 5 minutes.

Nutrition: Calories: 154, Fat: 2.3 g, Protein: 4.6 g

305. Brownie Pies in Peanut Butter

Preparation Time: 10 minutes
Cooking Time: 20 minutes
Servings: 2
Ingredients:
- 2 Packets Optavia Decadent Double Chocolate Brownie (1 condiment)
- ¼ teaspoon baking powder (1/4 condiment)

- 3 tablespoons liquid egg substitute (1 healthy fat)
- 6 tablespoons vanilla almond milk, unsweetened, divided (2 healthy fats)
- 1 teaspoon vegetable oil (1/4 condiment)
- ¼ cup peanut butter, powdered (½ healthy fat)

Directions:
1. Preheat the air fryer to 180°C.
2. Mix the Decadent Double Chocolate Brownie mixture, egg substitute, baking powder, oil, half of the milk in a large bowl until it becomes a smooth paste. Take a four-muffin tin and spray cooking oil.
3. Evenly fill 3/4 portion of the muffin tin and bake in the air fryer for 20 minutes. When the center becomes firm, insert a toothpick and check whether it comes out clean so that you can confirm the doneness of the muffin. Remove it from the air fryer and allow them to cool down.
4. Now mix the remaining milk and powdered peanut butter in a medium bowl. Slice the muffin horizontally and spread the peanut butter paste onto one half.
5. Situate the other half on top and serve.

Nutrition: Calories: 281, Fat: 9.8 g, Protein: 7 g

306. Crispy Cauliflowers

Preparation Time: 10 minutes
Cooking Time: 10 minutes
Servings: 4
Ingredients:
- 2 cup cauliflower florets, diced (6 greens)

- ½ cup almond flour (1 healthy fat)
- ½ cup coconut flour (1 healthy fat)
- Salt and pepper to taste (½ condiment)
- 1 teaspoon mixed herbs (1 green)
- 1 teaspoon chives, chopped (1 green)
- 1 egg (1 lean)
- 1 teaspoon cumin (1 condiment)
- ½ teaspoon. garlic powder (1 condiment)
- 1 cup water (1 condiment)
- Oil for frying (1 condiment)

Directions:
1. Combine the egg, salt, garlic, water, cumin, chives, mixed herbs, pepper, and flour in a mixing bowl.
2. Stir in the cauliflower to the mixture and then fry them in oil until they become golden in color.
3. Serve.

Nutrition: Calories: 259, Protein: 3.3 g, Fat: 10.4 g

307. Red Pepper & Kale Air Fried Egg Muffins
Preparation Time: 10 minutes
Cooking Time: 25 minutes
Servings: 2
Ingredients:
For the Egg Muffin:
- 4 eggs (1 healthy fat)
- 1 cup liquid egg whites (½ healthy fat)
- ¼ cup greek yogurt, plain, low fat (1/4 healthy fat)
- ¼ teaspoon. salt (1/4 condiment)

For the Red Bell Pepper, Goat Cheese & Kale Mix:
- 6 oz. red bell pepper, cored and chopped (3 greens)
- 5 oz. kale, frozen, chopped (2 greens)
- 1 oz. goat cheese (½ healthy fat)

Directions:
1. Thaw the frozen cauliflower rice for 10 minutes.
2. Preheat the air fryer to 190°C.
3. In a large bowl, combine Greek yogurt, egg whites, eggs, cheese, and salt.
4. Add all the vegetables to the bowl mix to combine well.

5. Take 12 muffin tins and lightly spray with cooking oil.
6. Transfer the mixture evenly into the muffin tins.
7. Place them in the air fryer and bake for 25 minutes until the center portion becomes hard.
8. Do a toothpick test by inserting it in the center and check if it comes out clean.
9. Take it out from the air fryer and allow it to settle down the heat before serving.
10. Enjoy your muffin.

Nutrition: Calories: 323, Fat: 15.4 g, Protein: 34 g

308. Asparagus Risotto with Chicken

Preparation Time: 20 minutes
Cooking Time: 38 minutes
Servings: 2
Ingredients:

- 1 lb. chicken breast (2 leans)
- ½ teaspoon pepper ground (1/4 condiment)
- ¼ teaspoon salt (1/4 condiment)
- 1 tablespoon butter, melted (½ healthy fat)
- ¾ lb. cauliflower, finely grated (1 green)
- ¼ lb. asparagus, finely chopped (½ green)
- ¼ cup chicken stock (½ condiment)
- 2 tablespoons nutritional yeast flakes (1 condiment)

Directions:

1. Soak the chicken in running water and pat dry.
2. Preheat the air fryer to 180°C.
3. Season the chicken with pepper and salt.
4. Place it in an air fryer-safe casserole and pour melted butter over it.
5. Air fry it for 30 minutes until the internal temperature of the meat reaches 70°C.
6. Pull it out from the air fryer and let it cool.

7. Now place the asparagus and cauliflower rice in the air fryer tray.
8. Pour the chicken stock over it and air fry for 8 minutes until the veggies become tender.
9. After cooking, remove the risotto and mix the yeast.
10. Cut the chicken and serve along with the risotto.

Nutrition: Calories: 382, Fat: 8.6 g, Protein: 60 g

309. Chicken Continental Salad

Preparation Time: 15 minutes
Cooking Time: 40 minutes
Servings: 2
Ingredients:
Salad making:

- ½ cup eggplant, chopped (½ green)
- ½ cup zucchini, chopped (½ green)
- ½ cup cherry tomatoes halved (½ green)
- 3 cups romaine lettuce (2 greens)
- ¼ cup parmesan cheese, shredded (1/4 healthy fat)
- ¾ lb. chicken breast (1 lean)
- ¼ teaspoon salt (1/4 condiment)
- ¼ teaspoon pepper ground (1/4 condiment)

Dressing:

- ½ teaspoon fresh lemon juice (½ condiment)
- ¼ teaspoon dijon mustard (1/4 condiment)
- ½ teaspoon worcestershire sauce (1/4 condiment)
- 1 clove garlic (1/4 condiment)
- ½ teaspoon salt (1/4 condiment)
- ¼ teaspoon pepper ground (1/4 condiment)
- 1 tablespoon parmesan cheese, shredded (½ healthy fat)
- 1 tablespoon mayonnaise, light (½ healthy fat)
- 1½ teaspoon olive oil, extra virgin (1 condiment)

Directions:
1. Preheat the air fryer to 200°C.
2. Clean, wash and drain the chicken breast.
3. Rub salt, pepper on the chicken breast, and keep aside for 15 minutes for marinating.
4. Line a baking paper in the air fryer tray and spray some cooking oil onto it.
5. Place the zucchini and eggplant on the baking paper.
6. Start baking and shaking intermittently for 20 minutes until they become tender.
7. For preparing the dressing, combine all the ingredients in the dressing section in a medium bowl.
8. Put the tomatoes, lettuce, air fried veggies in the dressing mixture, and toss well.
9. Place the marinated chicken on the air fryer grill tray and broil for 20 minutes until the inside meat temperature reaches 75°C.
10. After cooking, remove it and allow it to cool down.
11. Slice the chicken and serve along with the dressing.

Nutrition: Calories: 370, Fat: 14.3 g, Protein: 45 g

310. Lemon Garlic Oregano Boneless Chicken

Preparation Time: 5 minutes
Cooking Time: 44 minutes
Servings: 2
Ingredients:
- ½ lb. chicken breast boneless, skinless (1 lean)
- 1 tablespoon lemon juice (½ condiment)
- 1 clove garlic, minced (½ condiment)
- 1 tablespoon oregano fresh, minced (½ green)
- ¼ teaspoon black pepper, ground (1/4 condiment)
- ¼ teaspoon salt (1/4 condiment)
- 1 lb. asparagus ends trimmed (2 greens)
- 1 cup water (½ condiment)

Directions:
1. Soak, wash, and pat dry the chicken.
2. Place the chicken in a big bowl and marinate with pepper, lemon juice, salt, garlic, and oregano.
3. Place the marinated chicken in the air fry grill tray.
4. Broil at 175°C for 40 minutes until the meat's internal temperature reaches 70°C.
5. After broiling, remove it from the air fryer and set it aside.
6. Now place the asparagus in the air fry tray and pour 1 cup water.
7. Air fry at 175°C for 4 minutes until the asparagus becomes tender.
8. Remove it from the air fryer and drain the water.
9. Slice the chicken and serve it along with asparagus.

Nutrition: Calories: 258, Fat: 11 g, Protein: 29 g

CHAPTER 14:

Fueling Hacks Recipes

311. Rosemary

Preparation Time: 25 minutes
Cooking Time: 20 minutes
Servings: 5
Ingredients:
- 1 1/4 cups plain flour sifted
- 1 teaspoon ground cinnamon myrtle
- 1 cup rolled oats
- 3/4 cup shredded coconut
- 1/4 cup caster sugar
- 4 blood limes zested
- Long sprigs of sea rosemary coarsely chopped, stems removed and discarded.
- 1/2 teaspoons Murray river pink salt
- 1 tablespoon golden syrup
- 1 tablespoon honey
- 150 g unsalted butter, chopped
- 1/2 teaspoons bicarbonate of soda
- 1 1/2 tablespoons water

Directions:
1. Preheat the oven to 400ºF. Line 2 baking trays with baking paper.
2. In a big bowl, add the flour, cinnamon myrtle, oats, coconut, sugar, lime zest, sea rosemary, salt, and stir to combine.
3. In a small saucepan, place the golden syrup, honey, and butter, and stir over low heat until the butter has melted.
4. Remove from the heat. Mix the bicarbonate of soda with the water and add to the golden syrup mixture.
5. Pour into the dry ingredients and mix until thoroughly combined.
6. Roll tablespoonfuls of the mixture into balls and place on baking trays, pressing down on the top to flatten.
7. Sprinkle with a little salt to taste.
8. Bake for 12-20 minutes, depending on the thickness of your biscuit.

Nutrition: Fat: 41 g, Protein: 12 g, Cholesterol: 20 mg, Carbohydrates: 20 g, Sodium: 504 mg

312. Baked Cheesy Eggplant
Preparation Time: 20 minutes
Cooking Time: 1 hour and 15 minutes
Servings: 6
Ingredients:
- 1 eggplant, fresh
- 1,16 can tomato, chopped
- 2,8 oz. can tomato sauce
- 6 oz. cheddar cheese, shredded
- 1 onion, chopped
- Oregano, dried
- 2 teaspoons Salt
- Italian seasoning
- Basil, dried for taste
- Thyme, dried for flavor
- 2-3 teaspoons garlic, powdered
- 1/2 teaspoons black pepper

Directions:
1. Slice eggplant (fresh) into thin slices, then season using a dash of salt.
2. Next, set aside in a colander for roughly 30 minutes, then pat dry using a few paper towels.
3. Rinse under warm running water and thoroughly slice eggplant into quarters.
4. Place a layer of the eggplant (quartered) into a baking dish (large).
5. Cover layer using the tomatoes (chopped) and tomato sauce (1 can).

6. Add 1/2 of the cheese over the top and repeat layers with the remaining cheese (shredded) over the top.

7. Place eggplant into the oven to bake for approximately 45 minutes at 350°F until eggplant is soft.

Nutrition: Protein: 11.7 g, Carbohydrates: 15.4 g, Dietary Fiber: 5.4 g

313. Tabasco Anzac

Preparation Time: 25 minutes
Cooking Time: 3 hours and 45 minutes
Servings: 4
Ingredients:

- 85 g porridge oats
- 85 g desiccated coconut
- 85 g sultanas
- 100 g plain flour
- 100 g caster sugar
- 100 g butter
- 1 tablespoon golden syrup
- 2 teaspoons tabasco
- 2 tablespoons hot water
- 1 teaspoon bicarbonate of soda

Directions:

1. Preheat fan-assisted oven to 350°F.
2. Pour the oats, raisins, coconut, flour, and sugar into a bowl.
3. Soften the butter in a small pan and stir inside the golden syrup, Tabasco sauce, and water.
4. Add the bicarbonate of soda and mix well.
5. Add the liquid to the bowl and mix well until all the ingredients are combined.
6. Using a dessert spoon, spoon the mixture onto a buttered baking sheet. Leave about 2.5 cm in between each spoonful to allow room for spreading.
7. Bake in batches for 8-10 minutes until golden.
8. Place the cooked biscuits onto a wire rack to cool.

Nutrition: Fat: 41 g, Protein: 12 g, Cholesterol: 20 mg, Carbohydrates: 20 g, Sodium: 504 mg

314. Sweet Potato Casserole

Preparation Time: 20 minutes
Cooking Time: 1 hour
Servings: 8
Ingredients:

- 3 lbs. potatoes, sweet, peeled, chopped
- 1 cup Greek yogurt, nonfat
- 1/2 tablespoons cinnamon, ground
- 1/8 teaspoons nutmeg, ground
- 1/4 teaspoons sea salt
- 6 tablespoons egg whites
- 1 tablespoon butter, melted
- 1/2 cup pecans, chopped
- 1/2 cup marshmallows, miniature
- sugar (dash, light brown, for sprinkling)

Directions:

1. Heat your oven to 375°F.
2. Place the potatoes (sweet) into a saucepan (large) over medium-high heat.
3. Cover potatoes using water, then bring to a boil, boil for approximately 30 minutes until soft.
4. Drain potatoes, then place potatoes back into the saucepan.
5. Add the Greek yogurt, cinnamon (ground), nutmeg (base), and sea salt (dash) into the potatoes.
6. Stir well until coated (evenly).
7. Add in the butter (melted) and egg whites, then bring to a stir once more.
8. Transfer potato mixture into a casserole dish (large).

9. Place into the oven, then bake for approximately 30 minutes. Remove from heat, then top with the pecans (chopped) and miniature marshmallows.
10. Place back into the oven to bake for an additional 10 minutes until marshmallows are browned.

Nutrition: Protein: 2.9 g, Carbohydrates: 30.1 g, Dietary Fiber: 1.9 g

315. Easter Bunny

Preparation Time: 25 minutes
Cooking Time: 30 minutes
Servings: 12
Ingredients:

- 170 g butter
- 1 1/4 cups icing sugar mixture
- 1 teaspoon vanilla extract
- 1 pinch salt
- 3 egg yolks
- 2 1/2 cups plain flour
- 12 Marshmallows
- 24 Nestle Smarties pink
- 72 Ferrero Tic Tacs pink
- 3 Drops liquid food coloring pink

Royal Icing

- 2 egg whites
- 2 teaspoons lemon juice
- 3 cups icing sugar sifted

Directions:

1. Preheat the oven to a hundred and 158°F.
2. Whisk the butter using hand until it is smooth and creamy.
3. Blend within the icing sugar, then add the egg yolks, vanilla, and salt. Stir until blended.
4. Add the flour and blend it loosely with a wooden spoon till the dough comes together.
5. Turn it out onto a floured surface and knead until the dough is smooth.
6. Shape it into a disc and wrap it in cling wrap.
7. Refrigerate the dough for 30 minutes.
8. Roll out the dough to about 1 cm thick. Use a 5-6cm round cookie cutter to cut 12 bunny butt shapes out of the dough.

Then use a small egg-shaped cookie cutter to create 24 bunny feet.

9. Place the cookies onto two baking trays lined with baking paper.
10. Bake in the oven for 10-15 minutes until the edges turn brown.
11. Cool on a cooling rack while you make some royal icing.
12. Divide the icing into two halves. Color one half with a few drops of rose food coloring to make it very light pink bunnies.
13. Ice half of your biscuits with pink and half white. Add two bunny's feet to each circle. Add a marshmallow tail and then a Smartie as a paw pad and three tic tacs for the paw toes.

Icing:

1. Use an electric-powered mixer, whisk egg whites with the lemon juice till blended.
2. Regularly upload in sifted icing sugar at a low pace till clean.
3. Add the color of the meal of your preference.
4. Pipe onto bunny biscuits.
5. Leave for 2-3 hours to set difficult.

Nutrition: Fat: 41 g, Protein: 12 g, Cholesterol: 20 mg, Carbohydrates: 20 g, Sodium: 504 mg

316. High Protein Chipotle Cheddar Quesadilla

Preparation Time: 5 minutes
Cooking Time: 10 minutes
Servings: 4
Ingredients:

- 4 tortillas, low carb
- 2 cups cottage cheese, low sodium
- 2 cups cheddar cheese, low fat, shredded
- 1 red bell pepper, thinly sliced
- 1 onion, thinly sliced
- 1 cup portobello mushrooms, thinly sliced
- 2-3 tablespoons chipotle seasoning
- mild salsa for dipping

Directions:

1. Add the bell pepper (sliced, red), onion (sliced), and mushrooms (sliced) into a large grill pan over medium heat.
2. Cook for approximately 10 minutes until soft. Remove, then transfer into a bowl (medium). Set aside.
3. Add the chipotle seasoning and cottage cheese to a small bowl. Stir well to incorporate.
4. Place tortillas onto the grill pan and pour vegetable mixture over tortillas.
5. Sprinkle cottage cheese mixture over the top, then top off using the cheddar cheese (shredded).
6. Place an additional tortilla over the top of the filling.
7. Cook for roughly 2 minutes, then flip and continue cooking for a minute.
8. Repeat process with remaining tortillas and filling.
9. Serve immediately with the salsa (mild).

Nutrition: Calories: 287, Protein: 32.6 g, Carbohydrates: 29.8 g, Fats: 10.6 g

317. Zucchini Boats with Beef and Pimiento Rojo

Preparation Time: 10 minutes
Cooking Time: 30 minutes
Servings: 4
Ingredients:

- 4 zucchinis
- 2 tablespoons olive oil
- 1 1/2 lb. ground beef
- 1 medium red onion, chopped
- 2 tablespoons chopped pimiento
- Pink salt and black pepper to taste
- 1 cup grated yellow cheddar cheese

Directions:

1. Preheat oven to 350°F.
2. Lay the zucchinis on a flat surface, trim off the ends and cut in half lengthwise. Scoop out the pulp from each half with a spoon to make shells. Chop the pulp. Heat oil in a skillet; add the ground beef, red onion, pimiento, zucchini pulp, and season with salt and black pepper. Cook for 6 minutes while stirring to break up

lumps until beef is no longer pink. Turn the heat off.
3. Spoon the beef into the boats and sprinkle with cheddar cheese.
4. Place on a greased baking sheet and cook to melt the cheese for 15 minutes until zucchini boats are tender.
5. Take out, cool for 2 minutes, and serve warm with a mixed green salad.

Nutrition: Calories: 335, Fats: 24 g, Carbohydrates: 7 g, Protein: 18 g

318. Avocado Shrimp Cucumber Bites

Preparation Time: 10 minutes
Cooking Time: 10 minutes
Servings: 6
Ingredients:

- 1 large cucumber, cut into thick circles
- 6 small shrimps
- 1/2 cup parmesan cheese, grated
- 1 teaspoon almond butter, cubed
- Salt and pepper to taste
- 1 teaspoon coriander, chopped

Directions:

1. Preheat the oven to 390°F.
2. Add wax paper on a baking sheet.
3. Arrange the cucumber pieces on the baking sheet.
4. Add one shrimp to each slice.
5. Add the butter cubes, cheese, salt, pepper, and coriander on top.
6. Bake for 10 minutes and then serve.

Nutrition: Fat: 2 g, Cholesterol: 51mg, Sodium: 240 mg, Potassium: 83 mg, Carbohydrates: 1 g, Protein: 4 g

319. Strawberry-Avocado Toast with Balsamic Glaze

Preparation Time: 5 minutes
Cooking Time: 30 minutes
Servings: 4
Ingredients:

- 1 avocado, peeled, pitted, and quartered
- 4 whole-wheat bread slices, toasted
- 4 ripe strawberries, cut into 1/4-inch slices
- 1 tablespoon balsamic glaze or reduction

Directions:
1. Mash one-quarter of the avocado on a slice of toast.
2. Layer one-quarter of the strawberry slices over the avocado, and finish with a drizzle of balsamic glaze.
3. Repeat with the remaining ingredients, and serve.
4. Tip: If you can't buy balsamic glaze, make your own! Put balsamic vinegar in a small saucepan and cook, uncovered, over low heat for roughly 45 minutes, or until it's reduced to nearly one-quarter of the original amount of liquid.

Nutrition: Fat: 8 g, Carbohydrates: 17 g, Fiber: 5 g, Protein: 5 g

320. Cinnamon Bun Blondies

Preparation Time: 10 minutes
Cooking Time: 30 minutes
Servings: 4
Ingredients:
- 4 sachets Lean & Green Cinnamon Cream Cheese Swirl Cake
- ½ teaspoon cinnamon
- ½ teaspoon baking powder
- 2/3 cup unsweetened almond milk
- 2 tablespoons unsalted butter, melted
- 3 tablespoons liquid egg whites, divided
- 1 1/3 ounces pecans, chopped
- ¼ cup light cream cheese, softened
- 1 packet sugar substitute
- ½ teaspoon vanilla extract

Directions:
1. Preheat the air fryer to 350°F for five minutes.
2. In a bowl, combine the first six ingredients and stir until well-combined. Fold in the pecans.
3. Pour into a greased mini loaf pan that will fit inside the air fryer basket.
4. Cover with foil and cook for 30 minutes. Cook in batches if necessary.
5. Meanwhile, mix the cream cheese, sugar substitute, and vanilla extract. Set aside.
6. Once the cinnamon buns are cooked, allow to cool.

7. Brush the top with the cream cheese mixture.

Nutrition: Calories: 179, Fat: 16 g, Protein: 5 g, Carbohydrates: 5 g

321. Egg and Vanilla Shake

Preparation Time: 5 minutes
Cooking Time: 5 minutes
Servings: 1
Ingredients:
- 2 sachets Lean & Green Essential Creamy Vanilla Shake
- 16 oz vanilla almond milk, unsweetened
- 2 eggs pasteurized; yolk separated
- ½ teaspoon rum extract
- ¼ teaspoon nutmeg

Directions:
1. In an air fryer-compatible cooking bowl, combine rum extract, vanilla shake, and vanilla almond milk.
2. Place the bowel in the air fryer and warm for 5 minutes at 205°C.
3. Take it out and transfer it into a blender.
4. Add egg yolk and blend until it becomes smoothy.
5. Put the egg white in a small bowl and beat it with a hand blender until it starts to foam.
6. Transfer the beaten egg into a large glass.
7. Pour the vanilla shake mixture over it and sprinkle a pinch of nutmeg.
8. Serve fresh

Nutrition: Calories: 404, Fat: 11 g, Protein: 11 g, Carbohydrates: 45 g

322. Peanut Butter Chocolate Donuts

Preparation Time: 10 minutes
Cooking Time: 15 minutes
Servings: 2
Ingredients:
- 3 oz Lean & Green Essential Golden Chocolate Chip Pancakes
- 3 oz Lean & Green Essential Decadent Double Chocolate Brownie
- 3 tablespoons liquid egg substitute

- 1/8 cup vanilla almond unsweetened milk
- ¼ teaspoon vanilla extract
- ¼ teaspoon baking powder
- Cooking spray, as required

For glaze:
- ¼ cup peanut butter, ground
- 2 tablespoons vanilla almond milk, unsweetened

Directions:
1. Preheat the air fryer to 175°C.
2. Place the chocolate pancake chips into a bowl and crumble.
3. Mix it brownies, milk, egg substitute, vanilla extract, and baking powder.
4. Spray some cooking oil onto the donut slots.
5. Transfer the mixture evenly into the 4 slots of the donut pan.
6. Place the pan in the air fryer and bake for 15 minutes until it turns well.
7. After that, take it out from the air fryer and allow it to cool for doing the glazing.
8. For the glazing, combine ground peanut butter and milk in a shallow bowl until it becomes smooth and thin.
9. Dip the donuts into the glaze and decorate with chocolate chips.

Nutrition: Calories: 397, Fat: 15 g, Protein: 7 g, Carbohydrates: 63 g

323. Sweet Potato Muffins

Preparation Time: 5 minutes
Cooking Time: 15 minutes
Servings: 2
Ingredients:
- 1 sachet Lean & Green Honey Sweet Potatoes
- 2 tablespoons egg beaters
- ¼ teaspoon baking powder
- ½ cup water
- 1/8 teaspoons cinnamon ground
- Cooking spray, as required
- 2 muffin cups

Directions:
1. Preheat the air fryer to 180°C.
2. In a medium bowl, combine well egg beaters, sweet potato, baking powder, and water.
3. Spray some cooking oil in the muffin cups.
4. Pour the mix into the muffin cups evenly.
5. Sprinkle cinnamon powder on top.
6. Place the muffin cups in the air fryer and bake for 15 minutes at 180°C.
7. After 15 minutes, remove and serve hot.

Nutrition: Calories: 24, Fat: 0 g, Carbohydrates: 4 g, Protein: 2 g

324. French Toast Sticks

Preparation Time: 5 minutes
Cooking Time: 4 minutes
Servings: 2
Ingredients:
- 2 sachets Lean & Green Essential Cinnamon Crunchy O's Cereal
- 2 tablespoons cream cheese, low fat, softened
- 6 tablespoons liquid egg substitute
- 2 tablespoons sugar-free syrup
- Cooking spray, as required

Directions:
1. In a blender, blitz Cinnamon Crunchy O's until its consistency turns to look like breadcrumbs.
2. Pour liquid egg substitute and cream cheese into the blender blend until it turns into a dough.
3. Make 6 French toast-like sticks out of the dough.
4. Slightly brush the air fryer grill with oil.
5. Place the French toast dough over the grill basket.
6. Set the temperature to 204°C and air fry for 4 minutes.

7. After air frying, serve by topping with sugar-free syrup.

Nutrition: Calories: 92, Fat: 3 g, Carbohydrates: 8 g, Protein: 7 g

325. Gingerbread with Cream Cheese Frosting

Preparation Time: 5 minutes
Cooking Time: 20 minutes
Servings: 2
Ingredients:
- 2 sachets Lean & Green Essential Spiced Gingerbread
- 4 tablespoons water
- 4 tablespoons whipped cream cheese with reduced-fat
- ½ teaspoon vanilla extract
- 8 drops liquid Stevia
- Cooking spray, as required

Directions:
1. Preheat the air fryer to 175°C.
2. Blend Lean & Green Essential Spiced Gingerbread and water in a bowl until it becomes a smooth paste.
3. Place a baking sheet on the air fryer basket and spray some cooking oil.
4. Using a cookie spoon, make 6 gingersnaps on the greased baking sheet.
5. Set the timer for 20 minutes and air fry it until it becomes crisp.
6. After baking, allow it cool.
7. For making the frosting, combine vanilla extract, cream cheese, and Stevia.
8. Serve the gingerbread topping with vanilla-cheese frost.

Nutrition: Calories: 182, Protein: 4 g, Carbohydrates: 28 g, Fats: 6 g

326. Peanut Butter Cookies

Preparation Time: 15 minutes
Cooking Time: 12 minutes
Servings: 2
Ingredients:
- 2 sachets Lean & Green Essential Silky Peanut Butter Shake
- ¼ teaspoon baking powder
- ¼ cup vanilla almond milk, unsweetened
- 1 teaspoon butter, melted
- ¼ teaspoon vanilla extract
- 1/8 teaspoons salt
- Cooking spray, as required

Directions:
1. Preheat the air fryer to 175°C.
2. Mix baking powder and peanut butter shake in a large bowl.
3. Add melted butter, vanilla almond milk, vanilla extract and combine well until it forms a dough. Pour an additional 1 tablespoon milk if required.
4. Now scoop out the cookie mixture using a cookie scooper and make 4 cookies.
5. Line the baking tray and spray some cooking oil.
6. Place the cookies onto it.
7. With a fork, make a crisscross mark by slightly pressing on the top of the cookies.
8. Drizzle some salt on top of the cookies.
9. Using the baking option and bake it at 175°C for 12 minutes.
10. Serve with unsweetened vanilla milk.

Nutrition: Calories: 207, Fats: 13 g, Carbohydrates: 16 g, Protein: 9 g

327. Sweet Potato Pecan Muffins

Preparation Time: 10 minutes
Cooking Time: 20 minutes
Servings: 2
Ingredients:
- 2 sachets Lean & Green Select Honey Sweet Potatoes
- 2 sachets Lean & Green Essential Spiced Gingerbread
- 1 cup water
- 6 tablespoons liquid egg substitute
- ¼ cup cashew milk, unsweetened
- ½ teaspoon pumpkin pie spice
- ½ teaspoon vanilla extract
- ½ teaspoon baking powder
- 1½ oz pecans, chopped
- Cooking spray, as required

Directions:
1. Preheat the air fryer to 180°C.
2. Follow the instructions on the packet to make the Honey Sweet Potatoes.

3. Allow it to cool for some time.
4. Mix the prepared honey sweet potatoes and all the other ingredients, except the pecans.
5. Lightly spray the muffin pan and transfer the mix to the slots evenly.
6. Top it with chopped pecans.
7. Place it in the air fryer tray and bake for 20 minutes.
8. Serve hot.

Nutrition: Calories: 383, Fat: 21 g, Carbohydrates: 47 g, Protein: 15 g

328. Mint Cookies

Preparation Time: 5 minutes
Cooking Time: 15 minutes
Servings: 2
Ingredients:
- 2 sachets Lean & Green Essentials Decadent Double Chocolate Brownie
- Lean & Green Essential Chocolate Mint Cookie Bars
- 2 tablespoons almond milk, unsweetened
- 2 egg white

Directions:
1. Preheat the air fryer to 180°C.
2. In a mixer blender, crush the chocolate mint bars.
3. Combine chocolate brownie, crushed chocolate mint bars, almond milk, and egg whites in a large bowl.
4. Evenly transfer the mix to 8 cookies ramekins.
5. Place it in the air fryer grill tray and bake for 15 minutes until the top becomes firm.
6. Allow it to settle down the heat and serve.

Nutrition: Calories: 187, Fat: 4 g, Carbohydrates: 32 g, Protein: 5 g

329. Parmesan Zucchini Rounds

Preparation Time: 25 minutes
Cooking Time: 20 minutes
Servings: 4
Ingredients:
- 4 zucchinis, sliced
- 1 ½ cups parmesan cheese, grated
- ¼ cup parsley, chopped

- 1 egg, whisked
- 1 egg white, whisked
- ½ teaspoon. garlic powder
- Cooking spray

Directions:
1. Take a bowl and mix the egg with egg whites, parmesan, parsley, and garlic powder, and whisk.
2. Dredge each zucchini slice in this mix, place them all in your air fryer's basket, grease them with cooking spray and cook at 370°F for 20 minutes.
3. Divide between plates and serve as a side dish.

Nutrition: Calories: 183, Fats: 6 g, Carbs: 3 g, Fiber: 2 g, Protein: 8 g

330. Green Bean Casserole

Preparation Time: 25 minutes
Cooking Time: 20 minutes
Servings: 4
Ingredients:
- 1 lb. fresh green beans, edges trimmed
- ½ oz. pork rinds, finely ground
- 1 oz. full-fat cream cheese
- ½ cup heavy whipping cream
- ¼ cup diced yellow onion
- ½ cup chopped white mushrooms
- ½ cup chicken broth
- 4 tablespoons unsalted butter
- ¼ teaspoon xanthan gum

Directions:
1. Over heat, melt the butter in a skillet.
2. Sauté the onion and mushrooms until soft and fragrant, about 3-5 minutes.
3. Add the heavy cream, cream cheese, and broth to the skillet. Lightly beat

until smooth. Boil and then simmer. Put the xanthan gum in the pan and remove it from heat.

4. Cut green beans into 2-inch pieces and place in 4-cup round pan. Pour sauce mixture over them and stir until covered. Fil the plate with ground pork rinds. Place in the fryer basket.

5. Set the temperature to 320°F and set the timer for 15 minutes. The top will be a golden and green bean fork when fully cooked. Serve hot.

Nutrition: Calories: 267, Fats: 23.4 g, Carbs: 9.7 g, Protein: 3.6 g

331. Zucchini Spaghetti
Preparation Time: 20 minutes
Cooking Time: 15 minutes
Servings: 4
Ingredients:
- 1 lb. zucchinis, cut with a spiralizer
- 1 cup parmesan, grated
- ¼ cup parsley, chopped
- ¼ cup olive oil
- 6 garlic cloves, minced
- ½ teaspoon red pepper flakes
- Salt and black pepper to taste

Directions:
1. In a pan that fits your air fryer, mix all the ingredients, toss, introduce in the fryer, and cook at 370°F
2. for 15 minutes.
3. Divide between plates and serve as a side dish.

Nutrition: Calories: 200, Fats: 6 g, Carbs: 4 g, Protein: 5 g

332. Delicious Brownie Bites
Preparation Time: 20 minutes
Cooking Time: 0 minutes
Servings: 13
Ingredients:
- ¼ cup unsweetened chocolate chips
- ¼ cup unsweetened cocoa powder
- 1 cup pecans, chopped
- ½ cup almond butter
- ½ teaspoon vanilla
- ½ cup monk fruit sweetener
- 1/8 teaspoons pink salt

Directions:
1. Add pecans, sweetener, vanilla a, almond butter, cocoa powder, and salt into the food processor and process until well combined.
2. Transfer brownie mixture into the large bowl. Add chocolate chips and fold well.
3. Make small round-shaped balls from the brownie mixture and place them onto a baking tray.
4. Place in the freezer for 20 minutes.
5. Serve and enjoy.

Nutrition: Calories: 108, Fats: 9 g, Carbs: 4 g, Protein: 2 g, Sugar: 1 g, Cholesterol: 0 mg

333. Cabbage and Radishes Mix
Preparation Time: 20 minutes
Cooking Time: 15 minutes
Servings: 4
Ingredients:
- 6 cups green cabbage, shredded
- ½ cup celery leaves, chopped
- ¼ cup green onions, chopped
- 6 radishes, sliced
- 3 tablespoons olive oil
- 2 tablespoons balsamic vinegar
- ½ teaspoon hot paprika
- 1 teaspoon lemon juice

Directions:
1. In your air fryer's pan, combine all the ingredients and toss well.
2. Place the pan in the fryer and cook at 380°F for 15 minutes.
3. Divide between plates and serve as a side dish.

Nutrition: Calories: 130, Fats: 4 g, Carbs: 4 g, Protein: 7 g

334. Coriander Artichokes
Preparation Time: 20 minutes
Cooking Time: 15 minutes
Servings: 4
Ingredients:
- 12 oz. artichoke hearts
- 1 tablespoon lemon juice
- 1 teaspoon coriander, ground
- ½ teaspoon cumin seeds
- ½ teaspoon olive oil
- Salt and black pepper to taste

Directions:
1. In a pan that fits your air fryer, mix all the ingredients, toss, introduce the pan in the fryer and cook at 370°F for 15 minutes.
2. Divide the mix between plates and serve as a side dish.

Nutrition: Calories: 200, Fats: 7 g, Carbs: 5 g, Protein: 8 g

335. Spinach and Artichokes Sauté

Preparation Time: 20 minutes
Cooking Time: 15 minutes
Servings: 4
Ingredients:
- 10 oz. artichoke hearts, halved
- 2 cups baby spinach
- 3 garlic cloves
- ¼ cup veggie stock
- 2 teaspoons lime juice
- Salt and black pepper to taste

Directions:
1. In a pan that fits your air fryer, mix all the ingredients, toss, introduce in the fryer, and cook at 370°F
2. for 15 minutes.
3. Divide between plates and serve as a side dish.

Nutrition: Calories: 209, Fats: 6 g, Carbs: 4 g, Protein: 8 g

336. Green Beans

Preparation Time: 5 minutes
Cooking Time: 20 minutes
Servings: 4
Ingredients:
- 6 cups green beans, trimmed
- 1 tablespoon hot paprika
- 2 tablespoons olive oil
- A pinch of salt and black pepper

Directions:
1. Take a bowl and mix the green beans with the other ingredients, toss, put them in the air fryer's basket and cook at 370°F for 20 minutes.
2. Divide between plates and serve as a side dish.

Nutrition: Calories: 120, Fats: 5 g, Carbs: 4 g, Protein: 2 g

337. Balsamic Cabbage

Preparation Time: 10 minutes
Cooking Time: 15 minutes
Servings: 4
Ingredients:
- 6 cups red cabbage, shredded
- 4 garlic cloves, minced
- 1 tablespoon olive oil
- 1 tablespoon balsamic vinegar
- Salt and black pepper to taste

Directions:
1. In a pan that fits the air fryer, combine all the ingredients, toss, introduce the pan in the oven, and cook at 380°F for 15 minutes.
2. Divide between plates and serve as a side dish.

Nutrition: Calories: 151, Fats: 2 g, Carbs: 5 g, Protein: 5 g

338. Smooth Peanut Butter Cream

Preparation Time: 10 minutes
Cooking Time: 0 minutes
Servings: 8
Ingredients:
- ¼ cup peanut butter
- 4 overripe bananas, chopped
- 1/3 cup cocoa powder
- 1/3 teaspoons vanilla extract
- 1/8 teaspoons salt

Directions:
1. In the blender, add all the listed ingredients and blend until smooth.
2. Serve immediately and enjoy.

Nutrition: Calories: 101, Fats: 5 g, Carbs: 14 g, Protein: 3 g, Sugar: 7 g, Cholesterol: 0 mg

339. Herbed Radish Sauté

Preparation Time: 5 minutes
Cooking Time: 15 minutes
Servings: 4
Ingredients:
- 2 bunches red radishes, halved
- 2 tablespoons parsley, chopped
- 2 tablespoons balsamic vinegar
- 1 tablespoon olive oil
- Salt and black pepper to taste

Directions:
1. Take a bowl and mix the radishes with the remaining ingredients, except the parsley; toss and put them in your air fryer's basket.
2. Cook at 400°F for 15 minutes, divide between plates, sprinkle the parsley on top, and serve as a side dish.

Nutrition: Calories: 180, Fats: 4 g, Carbs: 3 g, Protein: 5 g

340. Roasted Tomatoes
Preparation Time: 5 minutes
Cooking Time: 15 minutes
Servings: 4
Ingredients:
- 4 tomatoes, halved
- ½ cup parmesan, grated
- 1 tablespoon basil, chopped
- ½ teaspoon onion powder
- ½ teaspoon oregano, dried
- ½ teaspoon smoked paprika
- ½ teaspoon garlic powder
- Cooking spray

Directions:
1. Mix all the ingredients in a bowl except the cooking spray and the parmesan.
2. Arrange the tomatoes in your air fryer's pan, sprinkle the parmesan on top, and grease with cooking spray.
3. Cook at 370°F for 15 minutes, divide between plates, and serve.

Nutrition: Calories: 200, Fats: 7 g, Carbs: 4 g, Protein: 6 g

341. Kale and Walnuts
Preparation Time: 5 minutes
Cooking Time: 15 minutes
Servings: 4
Ingredients:
- 3 garlic cloves
- 10 cups kale, roughly chopped
- 1/3 cup parmesan, grated
- ½ cup almond milk
- ¼ cup walnuts, chopped
- 1 tablespoon butter, melted
- ¼ teaspoon. nutmeg, ground
- Salt and black pepper to taste

Directions:
1. In a pan that fits the air fryer, combine all the ingredients, toss, introduce the pan in the machine, and cook at 360°F for 15 minutes.
2. Divide between plates and serve.

Nutrition: Calories: 160, Fats: 7 g, Carbs: 4 g, Protein: 5 g

342. Bok Choy and Butter Sauce
Preparation Time: 5 minutes
Cooking Time: 15 minutes
Servings: 4
Ingredients:
- 2 bok choy heads, trimmed and cut into strips -1 tablespoon butter, melted
- 2 tablespoons chicken stock
- 1 teaspoon lemon juice
- 1 tablespoon olive oil
- A pinch of salt and black pepper

Directions:
1. In a pan that fits your air fryer, mix all the ingredients, toss, introduce the pan in the oven, and cook at 380°F for 15 minutes.
2. Divide between plates and serve as a side dish.

Nutrition: Calories: 141, Fats: 3 g, Carbs: 4 g, Protein: 3 g

343. Turmeric Mushroom
Preparation Time: 5 minutes
Cooking Time: 15 minutes
Servings: 4
Ingredients:
- 1 lb. brown mushrooms
- 4 garlic cloves, minced
- ¼ teaspoon cinnamon powder
- 1 teaspoon olive oil
- ½ teaspoon. turmeric powder
- Salt and black pepper to taste

Directions:
1. In a bowl, combine all the ingredients and toss.
2. Put the mushrooms in your air fryer's basket and cook at 370°F for 15 minutes. Divide the mix between plates and serve as a side dish.

Nutrition: Calories: 208, Fats: 7 g, Carbs: 5 g, Protein: 7 g

344. Chocolate Bars

Preparation Time: 10 minutes
Cooking Time: 20 minutes
Servings: 16
Ingredients:

- 15 oz. cream cheese, softened
- 15 oz. unsweetened dark chocolate
- 1 teaspoon vanilla
- 10 drops liquid stevia

Directions:

1. Grease 8-inch square dish and set aside.
2. In a saucepan, dissolve chocolate over low heat.
3. Add stevia and vanilla and stir well.
4. Remove pan from heat and set aside.
5. Add cream cheese into the blender and blend until smooth.
6. Add melted chocolate mixture into the cream cheese and blend until just combined.
7. Transfer mixture into the prepared dish and spread evenly, and place in the refrigerator until firm.
8. Slice and serve.

Nutrition: Calories: 230, Fats: 24 g, Carbs: 7.5 g, Sugar: 0.1 g, Protein: 6 g, Cholesterol: 29 mg

345. Blueberry Muffins

Preparation Time: 15 minutes
Cooking Time: 35 minutes
Servings: 12
Ingredients:

- 2 eggs
- ½ cup fresh blueberries
- 1 cup heavy cream
- 2 cups almond flour
- ¼ teaspoon lemon zest

- ½ teaspoon lemon extract
- 1 teaspoon baking powder
- 5 drops stevia - ¼ cup butter, melted

Directions:

1. Heat the cooker to 350°F. Line muffin tin with cupcake liners and set aside.
2. Add eggs into the bowl and whisk until mixed. Add remaining ingredients and mix to combine. Pour mixture into the prepared muffin tin and bake for 25 minutes.
3. Serve and enjoy.

Nutrition: Calories: 190, Fats: 17 g, Carbs: 5 g, Sugar: 1 g, Protein: 5 g, Cholesterol: 55 mg

346. Kale Chips

Preparation Time: 10 minutes
Cooking Time: 5 minutes
Servings: 4
Ingredients:

- 4 cups stemmed kale
- ½ teaspoon salt
- 2 teaspoons avocado oil

Directions:

1. Take a large bowl, sprinkle the cabbage in avocado oil, and sprinkle with salt. Place in the fryer basket.
2. Set the temperature to 400°F and set the timer for 5 minutes. The kale will be crispy when done. Serve immediately.

Nutrition: Calories: 25, Fat: 2.2 g, Carbs: 1.1 g, Protein: 0.5 g

347. Chia Pudding

Preparation Time: 20 minutes
Cooking Time: 0 minutes
Servings: 2
Ingredients:

- 4 tablespoons chia seeds

- 1 cup unsweetened coconut milk
- ½ cup raspberries

Directions:
1. Add raspberry and coconut milk into a blender and blend until smooth.
2. Pour the mixture into the glass jar.
3. Add chia seeds in a jar and stir well.
4. Seal the jar with a lid and shake well and place in the refrigerator for 3 hours.
5. Serve chilled and enjoy.

Nutrition: Calories: 360, Fats: 33 g, Carbs: 13 g, Protein: 6 g, Sugar: 5 g, Cholesterol: 0 mg

348. Avocado Pudding
Preparation Time: 20 minutes
Cooking Time: 0 minutes
Servings: 8
Ingredients:
- 2 ripe avocados, pitted and cut into pieces
- 1 tablespoon fresh lime juice
- 14 oz. can coconut milk
- 2 teaspoons liquid stevia
- 2 teaspoons vanilla

Directions:
1. Inside the blender, add all ingredients and blend until smooth.
2. Serve immediately and enjoy.

Nutrition: Calories: 317, Fats: 30 g, Carbs: 9 g, Protein: 3 g, Sugar: 0.5 g, Cholesterol: 0 mg

349. Peanut Butter Coconut Popsicle
Preparation Time: 15 minutes
Cooking Time: 0 minutes
Servings: 12
Ingredients:
- ½ cup peanut butter
- 1 teaspoon liquid stevia
- 2 cans unsweetened coconut milk

Directions:
1. In the blender, add all the listed ingredients and blend until smooth.
2. Pour mixture into the Popsicle molds and place in the freezer for 4 hours or until set.
3. Serve and enjoy.

Nutrition: Calories: 155, Fats: 15 g, Carbs: 4 g, Protein: 3 g, Sugar: 2 g, Cholesterol: 0 mg

350. Pumpkin Balls
Preparation Time: 15 minutes
Cooking Time: 0 minutes
Servings: 18
Ingredients:
- 1 cup almond butter
- 5 drops liquid stevia
- 2 tablespoons coconut flour
- 2 tablespoons pumpkin puree
- 1 teaspoon pumpkin pie spice

Directions:
1. Mix together pumpkin purée in a large bowl and almond butter until well combined.
2. Add liquid stevia, pumpkin pie spice, and coconut flour and mix well.
3. Make small balls from the mixture and place them onto a baking tray.
4. Place in the freezer for 1 hour.
5. Serve and enjoy.

Nutrition: Calories: 96, Fats: 8 g, Carbs: 4 g, Protein: 2 g, Sugar: 1 g, Cholesterol: 0 mg

5&1 Meal Plan

Day	Fueling Hacks	Breakfast	Lunch	Snacks	Dinner
1	Kale Chips	Alkaline Blueberry Spelt Pancakes	Greek Salad	Fluffy Bites	Zucchini Salmon Salad
2	Chia Pudding	Alkaline Blueberry Muffins	Asparagus and Smoked Salmon Salad	Coconut Fudge	Pan-Fried Salmon
3	Avocado Pudding	Crunchy Quinoa Meal	Shrimp Cobb Salad	Nutmeg Nougat	Grilled Salmon with Pineapple Salsa
4	Peanut Butter Coconut Popsicle	Coconut Pancakes	Toast with Smoked Salmon, Herbed Cream Cheese, and Greens	Sweet Almond Bites	Mediterranean Chickpea Salad
5	Pumpkin Balls	Quinoa Porridge	Crab Melt with Avocado and Egg	Strawberry Cheesecake Minis	Warm Chorizo Chickpea Salad
6	Vanilla Avocado Popsicles	Amaranth Porridge	Cranberry Salad	Cocoa Brownies	Greek Roasted Fish
7	Chocolate Popsicle	Banana Barley Porridge	Lemony Parmesan Salmon	Chocolate Orange Bites	Tomato Fish Bake

Day	Fueling Hacks	Breakfast	Lunch	Snacks	Dinner
1	Raspberry Ice Cream	Zucchini Muffins	Keto Cheesy Broccoli Soup	Caramel Cones	Garlicky Tomato Chicken Casserole
2	Chocolate Frosty	Millet Porridge	Creamy Low Carb Zucchini Alfredo	Cinnamon Bites	Chicken Cacciatore
3	Chocolate Almond Butter Brownie	Jackfruit Vegetable Fry	Amazing Low Carb Shrimp Lettuce Wraps	Sweet Chai Bites	Fennel Wild Rice Risotto
4	Peanut Butter Fudge	Zucchini Pancakes	Tasty Low Carb Cucumber Salad	Easy Vanilla Bombs	Wild Rice Prawn Salad
5	Almond Butter Fudge	Squash Hash	Classic Low Carb Cobb Salad	Marinated Eggs	Chicken Broccoli Salad with Avocado Dressing
6	Air Fryer Personal Mini Pizza	Pumpkin Spice Quinoa	Yummy Keto Mushroom Asparagus Frittata	Sausage and Cheese Dip	Seafood Paella
7	Air Fried Cheesy Chicken Omelet	Chocolate Cherry Crunch Granola	Yogurt Garlic Chicken	Tasty Onion and Cauliflower Dip	Herbed Roasted Chicken Breasts

Week 3

Day	Fueling Hacks	Breakfast	Lunch	Snacks	Dinner
1	Red Pepper & Kale Air Fried Egg Muffins	Mango Coconut Oatmeal	Flavorful Keto Taco Soup	Pesto Crackers	Mediterranean Chicken Salad
2	Asparagus Risotto with Chicken	Scrambled Eggs with Soy Sauce and Broccoli Slaw	Delicious Instant Pot Keto Buffalo Chicken Soup	Pumpkin Muffins	Jalapeno Lentil Burgers
3	Chicken Continental Salad	Tasty Breakfast Donuts	Creamy Low Carb Cream of Mushroom Soup	Bacon Cheeseburger	Grandma's Rice
4	Lemon Garlic Oregano Boneless Chicken	Cheesy Spicy Bacon Bowls	Easy Keto Chicken Soup	Cheeseburger Pie	Baked Beef Zucchini
5	Low Carb Air-Fried Calzones	Goat Cheese Zucchini Kale Quiche	Taco Casserole	Personal Pizza Biscuit	Baked Tuna with Asparagus
6	Air-Fried Tortilla Hawaiian Pizza	Ricotta Ramekins	Quick Keto Roasted Tomato Soup	Chicken and Mushrooms	Lamb Stuffed Avocado
7	Tasty Kale & Celery Crackers	Chicken Lo Mein	Delicious Low Carb Chicken Caesar Salad	Chicken Enchilada Bake	Mozzarella Sticks

Day	Fueling Hacks	Breakfast	Lunch	Snacks	Dinner
1	Herbed Radish Sauté	Pancakes with Berries	Honey Glazed Chicken Drumsticks	Greek Yogurt Muesli Parfaits	Avocado Taco Boats
2	Roasted Tomatoes	Omelet À La Margherita	Keto Zucchini Pizza	Lemon Cream	Cauliflower Rice
3	Kale and Walnuts	Omelet with Tomatoes and Spring Onions	Omega- Salad	Peanut Banana Yogurt Bowl	Jarlsberg Lunch Omelet
4	Bok Choy and Butter Sauce	Yogurt with Granola and Persimmon	Crab Cakes	Sweet Tropical Medley Smoothie	Jalapeno Cheese Balls
5	Turmeric Mushroom	Smoothie Bowl with Spinach, Mango and Muesli	Low Carb Black Beans Chili Chicken	Mediterranean Fruit Tart	Zucchini Omelet
6	Chocolate Bars	Fried Egg with Bacon	Quick Keto Blt Chicken Salad	Green Tea and Vanilla Cream	Courgettes Risotto
7	Blueberry Muffins	Smoothie Bowl with Berries, Poppy Seeds, Nuts and Seeds	Quick Healthy Avocado Tuna Salad	Warm Peach Compote	Cheesy Cauliflower Fritters

4&2&1 Meal Plan

Day	Fueling Hacks	Breakfast	Lunch	Snacks	Dinner
1	Delicious Brownie Bites	Whole Grain Bread and Avocado	Nut Granola & Smoothie Bowl	Honey Walnut Bars	Bell-Pepper Corn Wrapped in Tortilla
2	Cabbage and Radishes Mix	Porridge with Walnuts	Bacon and Egg Quesadillas	Lime Vanilla Fudge	Zucchini Parmesan Chips
3	Coriander Artichokes	Whole-Wheat Blueberry Muffins	Bacon and Cheese Frittata	Pear Sauce	Prosciutto Spinach Salad
4	Spinach and Artichokes Sauté	Hemp Seed Porridge	Bacon-Wrapped Asparagus	Honey Cream	Crispy Roasted Broccoli
5	Green Beans	Walnut Crunch Banana Bread	Spinach Chicken	Dragon Fruit, Pear and Spinach Salad	Grilled Ham & Cheese
6	Balsamic Cabbage	Plant-Powered Pancakes	Lemongrass Prawns	Kataifi	Mashed Garlic Turnips
7	Smooth Peanut Butter Cream	Mini Mac in a Bowl	Stuffed Mushrooms	Walnuts Kataifi	Air Fryer Asparagus

Day	Fueling Hacks	Breakfast	Lunch	Snacks	Dinner
1	Gingerbread with Cream Cheese Frosting	Shake Cake Fueling	Almond Porridge	Mediterranean Biscotti	Avocado Fries
2	Peanut Butter Cookies	Optavia Biscuit Pizza	Asparagus Frittata Recipe	Semolina Pie	Diced Cauliflower & Curry Chicken
3	Sweet Potato Pecan Muffins	Lean and Green Smoothie	Avocados Stuffed with Salmon	Vanilla Apple Compote	Jalapeno Coins
4	Mint Cookies	Lean and Green Chicken Pesto Pasta	Bacon and Brussels Sprout Breakfast	Cold Lemon Squares	Lasagna Spaghetti Squash
5	Parmesan Zucchini Rounds	Open-Face Egg Sandwiches with Cilantro-Jalapeño Spread	Bacon and Lemon Spiced Muffins	Minty Coconut Cream	Monkey Salad
6	Green Bean Casserole	Apple Kale Cucumber Smoothie	Hot Buffalo wings	Cherry Cream	Mu Shu Lunch Pork
7	Zucchini Spaghetti	Refreshing Cucumber Smoothie	Trout and Chili Nuts	Tiny Orange Cardamom Cookies	Fiery Jalapeno Poppers

Day	Fueling Hacks	Breakfast	Lunch	Snacks	Dinner
1	Avocado Shrimp Cucumber Bites	Cauliflower Veggie Smoothie	Family Fun Pizza	Sparkling Limoncello	Bacon & Chicken Patties
2	Strawberry-Avocado Toast with Balsamic Glaze	Soursop Smoothie	Mouth-Watering Pie	Mast-O Khiar (Persian Yogurt)	Garlic Chicken Balls
3	Cinnamon Bun Blondies	Cucumber-Ginger Water	Special Almond Cereal	Mediterranean Martini	Cheddar Bacon Burst
4	Egg and Vanilla Shake	Strawberry Milkshake	Awesome Avocado Muffins	Greek Mountain Tea	Blue Cheese Chicken Wedges
5	Peanut Butter Chocolate Donuts	Cactus Smoothie	WW Salad in A Jar	Santorini Sunrise	Healthy & Tasty Green Beans
6	Sweet Potato Muffins	Spinach and Cottage Cheese Sandwich	Yummy Smoked Salmon	Yogurt Mint	Cheesy Brussels Sprouts
7	French Toast Sticks	Feta and Pesto Wrap	Almond Coconut Cereal	Chocolate Fondue	Garlic Cauliflower Florets

Day	Fueling Hacks	Breakfast	Lunch	Snacks	Dinner
1	Rosemary	Cheese and Onion on Bagel	Easiest Tuna Cobbler Ever	Rice Pudding	Delicious Ratatouille
2	Baked Cheesy Eggplant	Bananas in Nut Cups	Deliciously Homemade Pork Buns	Braised Apples	Simple Green Beans
3	Tabasco Anzac	Apple Salad Sandwich	Mouthwatering Tuna Melts	Wine Figs	Air Fryer Tofu
4	Sweet Potato Casserole	Buttermilk Ice Cream Shake	Bacon Wings	Lemon Curd	Healthy Zucchini Patties
5	Easter Bunny	Buttermilk Shake	Pepper Pesto Lamb	Rhubarb Dessert	Healthy Asparagus Spears
6	High Protein Chipotle Cheddar Quesadilla	Cantaloupe Orange Milk Shakes	Tuna Spinach Casserole	Raspberry Compote	Spicy Brussels Sprouts
7	Zucchini Boats with Beef and Pimiento Rojo	Cheese on Rye Bread	Greek Style Mini Burger Pies	Poached Pears	Cheese Broccoli Fritters

We have shown you above some examples of weekly meal plans; now—by mixing the various recipes—you can get recipes for more than 1200 days. Enjoy!

Conclusion

Everyone eventually grows weary of eating the same thing. We crave new flavors, textures, and colors to stimulate our taste buds. This can be hard for those of us that are trying to lose weight. It's just too tempting to eat that piece of chocolate cake or drink that milkshake when we feel like we've been deprived of good food for too long — even if we know these foods will derail us from our goals. The Lean and Green Diet changes all that because it enhances the flavor of the foods you eat. No more bland, boring, tasteless meals anymore!

By following this plan, you will get all of your nutrients from a variety of natural foods. There are no supplements to take, just like in "regular" diets that restrict entire food groups. You won't find yourself in the doctor's office trying to treat nutrient deficiencies with pills and potions; you can get your necessary vitamins and minerals by eating delicious natural food instead. And the Lean and Green Diet is delicious!

The Lean and Green Diet is made up of two types of foods:

1. Lean foods such as lean meats, eggs, and fish; and
2. Green foods such as leafy greens like spinach and kale, cruciferous vegetables like broccoli and cauliflower, legumes like chickpeas and beans, brightly-colored fruits, herbs, spices, garlic, you name it! These two groups of whole-natural foods combine to provide a variety of flavors that you'll crave. There's no need to go hungry or consume boring meals anymore.

You will get all the nutrition you need from natural plant-based ingredients exclusively; no supplements are necessary. The Lean and Green Diet was created to offer a wide variety of flavors in just a few weeks. You'll be surprised at how simple **it is!**

The Lean and Green Diet consists of two phases:

Phase 1: The Cleanse all lasts for five days. It's essential to get your body adjusted, so you'll eliminate all the foods that have been clogging up your insides. Grease, heavy fats, processed carbs, chemicals all go out the door. After the cleanse, your body will become much more efficient at digesting lean proteins and natural plant-based foods, which means you won't need to eat as much to get enough nutrition.

Phase 2: The Main Course, the Main Course, lasts for the rest of the thirty-five days. You will continue to eat lean proteins and natural plant-based foods to get all your necessary vitamins and minerals.

If you get sick of eating these foods by day 5, you can always go back to phase 1 and start over again, that is if you feel **like it!**

Other benefits of the Lean and Green Diet:

1. It's easy to follow (and changes only need to be made once a month instead of every day).
2. It's not expensive.
3. You'll be healthy, happy, and fit!
4. Great for beginners and experienced dieters alike.
5. It's doable on a limited grocery budget.

The Lean and Green Diet will help you lose weight, feel better, run your body without toxins, have a healthier lifestyle, so what are you **waiting for?**

Made in United States
North Haven, CT
01 March 2022

16642609R00096